THE LIMITS OF
INTERPRETATION

Advances in Semiotics

Thomas A. Sebeok, General Editor

THE LIMITS OF INTERPRETATION

UMBERTO ECO

*Indiana
University
Press*

BLOOMINGTON AND INDIANAPOLIS

The paper used in this publication meets the minimum requirements of American National Standard for Information Sciences—Permanence of Paper for Printed Library Materials, ANSI Z39.48-1984.

™

MANUFACTURED IN THE UNITED STATES OF AMERICA

Library of Congress Cataloging-in-Publication Data

Eco, Umberto.
The limits of interpretation / Umberto Eco.
p.   cm. — (Advances in semiotics series)
Includes bibliographical references.
ISBN 0-253-31852-1
1. Criticism.   2. Semiotics and literature.
3. Reader-response criticism.
I. Title.   II. Series.
PN98.S46E26   1990
801'.95—dc20   89-45999
                                          CIP

2 3 4 5 94 93 92 91

CONTENTS

THE LIMITS OF
INTERPRETATION

Introduction

At the beginning of his *Mercury; or, The Secret and Swift Messenger* (1641), John Wilkins tells the following story:

> How strange a thing this Art of Writing did seem at its first Invention, we may guess by the late discovered Americans, who were amazed to see Men converse with Books, and could scarce make themselves to believe that a Paper could speak. . . .
>
> There is a pretty Relation to this Purpose, concerning an Indian Slave; who being sent by his Master with a Basket of Figs and a Letter, did by the Way eat up a great Part of his Carriage, conveying the Remainder unto the Person to whom he was directed; who when he had read the Letter, and not finding the Quantity of Figs answerable to what was spoken of, he accuses the Slave of eating them, telling him what the Letter said against him. But the Indian (notwithstanding this Proof) did confidently abjure the Fact, cursing the Paper, as being a false and lying Witness.
>
> After this, being sent again with the like Carriage, and a Letter expressing the just Number of Figs, that were to be delivered, he did again, according to his former Practice, devour a great Part of them by the Way; but before meddled with any, (to prevent all following Accusations) he first took the Letter, and hid that under a great Stone, assuring himself, that if it did not see him eating the Figs, it could never tell of him; but being now more strongly accused than before, he confesses the Fault, admiring the Divinity of the Paper, and for the future does promise his best Fidelity in every Employment. (3d ed. [London: Nicholson, 1707], pp. 3–4)

This page of Wilkins sounds certainly very different from many contemporary theories, where writing is taken as the paramount example of semiosis, and every written (or spoken) text is seen as a machine that produces an indefinite deferral. Those contemporary theories object indirectly to Wilkins that a text, once it is separated from its utterer (as well as from the utterer's intention) and from the concrete circumstances of its utterance (and by consequence from its intended referent) floats (so to speak) in the vacuum of a potentially infinite range of possible interpretations. As a consequence no text can be interpreted according to the utopia of a definite, original, and final authorized meaning. Language always says more than its unattainable literal meaning, which is lost from the very beginning of the textual utterance.

Bishop Wilkins—despite his adamant belief that the Moon is inhabited—was after all a man of remarkable intellectual stature, who said many things still important for the students of language and of semiosic processes in general. Look, for instance, at the drawing shown here, which appears in his *Essay towards a Real Character* (1668). Wilkins was so convinced that a theory of meaning was possible that he even tried (not first, but certainly in a pioneering way and by an extraordinary visual intuition) to provide a way to represent the meaning of syncategorematic terms. This picture shows that, provided we share some conventional rules concerning English language, when we say *upon* we surely mean something different from *under*. By the way, the picture shows also that such a difference in meaning is based on the structure of our body in a geo-astronomical space. One can be radically skeptical about the possibility of isolating universals of language, but one feels obliged to take Wilkins's picture seriously. It shows that in interpreting syncategorematic terms we must follow certain "directions." Even if the world were a labyrinth, we could pass through it by disregarding certain directional constraints.

How could Wilkins have objected to the counterobjections of many contemporary theories of reading as a deconstructive activity? Probably he would have said that in the case he was reporting (let us suppose that the letter was saying "Dear Friend, In this Basket brought by my Slave there are 30 Figs I send you as a Present. Looking forward . . . ") the Master was sure that the Basket mentioned in the Letter was the one carried by the Slave, that the carrying Slave was exactly the one to whom his Friend gave the Basket, and that there was a Relationship between the Expression *30* written in the Letter and the Number of Figs contained in the Basket.

Naturally, it would be easy to refute Wilkins's parabolic demonstration. It is sufficient to imagine that somebody really did send a slave with a basket, but along the way the original slave was killed and re-

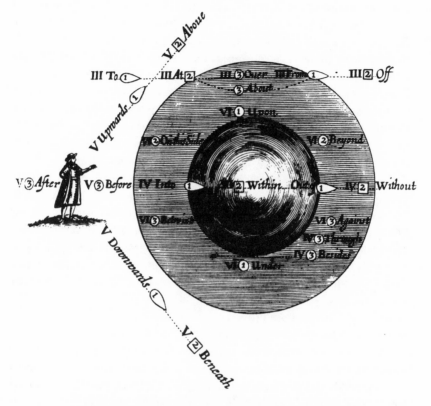

John Wilkins, *An Essay towards a Real Character, and a Philosophical Language* (London: Printed for S. Gellibrand, 1668), p. 311. Courtesy of the Lilly Library, Indiana University, Bloomington, Indiana

placed by another slave, belonging to a different person, and even the thirty figs, as individual entities, were replaced by twelve other figs. Moreover, let us imagine that the new slave brought the basket to a different addressee. We can also suppose that the new addressee did not know of any friend eager to cultivate him and to send him figs. Would it still be possible to decide what the letter was speaking about?

I think that we are still entitled to suppose that the reaction of the new addressee would have been, more or less, of this sort: "Somebody, God knows who, sent me a quantity of figs which is less than the one mentioned by the accompanying letter." (I also suppose that the new Addressee, being a Master, chastised the slave before trying to solve the Riddle: this, too, is a Semiotic Problem, but let us stick to our Main Question.)

What I wish to say is that, even when separated from its utterer, its arguable referent, and its circumstances of production, the message still spoke about some figs-in-a-basket. I wish also to suggest that, reading the letter, and before questioning the existence of the sender, the addressee was in the first instance convinced that a given Figs Sender was in question.

Let us suppose now (narrative imagination has no limits), not only that the original messenger was killed, but also that his killers ate all the figs, destroyed the basket, put the letter into a bottle and threw it into the ocean, so that it was found seventy years (or so) after Wilkins by Robinson Crusoe. No basket, no slave, no figs, only a letter. Notwithstanding this, I bet that the first reaction of Crusoe would have been: "Where are the figs?" Only after that first instinctive reaction could Crusoe have dreamed about all possible figs, all possible slaves, all possible senders, as well as about the possible nonexistence of any fig, slave, or sender, about the machineries of lying, and about his unfortunate destiny as an addressee definitely separated from any Transcendental Meaning.

Where are those figs? Provided Crusoe understands English, the letter says that there are, or were, somewhere, 30 fruits so and so, at least in the mind (or in the Possible Doxastic World) of a supposed sender or utterer of that message. And even if Crusoe decides that these scratches on a piece of paper are the accidental result of a chemical erosion, he faces only two possibilities: either to disregard them as an insignificant material event or to interpret them as if they were the words of an English text. Once having entertained the second hypothesis, Robinson is obliged to conclude that the letter speaks of figs—not of apples or of unicorns.

Now, let us suppose that the message in the bottle is found by a more sophisticated student in linguistics, hermeneutics, or semiotics. As smart as he or she is, such a new accidental addressee can make lots of more elaborate hypotheses, namely:

1. The message is a coded one, where *basket* stands for "army," *fig* for "1,000 soldiers," and *present* for "help," so that the intended meaning of the letter is that the sender is sending an army of 30,000 soldiers for helping the addressee. But even in this case the mentioned (and absent) soldiers should be 30,000, not, say, 180—unless in the private code of the sender one fig stands for six soldiers.

2. *Figs* can be intended (at least today) in a rhetorical sense (as in such expressions as *to be in good fig, to be in full fig, to be in poor fig*), and the message could support a different interpretation. But even in

this case the addressee should rely on certain preestablished conventional interpretations of *fig* which are not those foreseen by, say, *apple* or *cat*.

3. The addressee, being a critic used to interpreting medieval texts, supposes that the message in the bottle is an allegory, written by a poet: the addressee smells in that message a hidden, second sense based on a private poetic code, holding only for that text. *Figs* can be a synecdoche for "fruits," *fruits* can be a metaphor for "positive astral influences," *positive astral influences* can be an allegory for "Divine Grace," and so on and so forth. In this case the addressee could make various conflicting hypotheses, but I strongly believe that there are certain "economical" criteria on the grounds of which certain hypotheses will be more interesting than others. To validate his or her hypothesis, the addressee probably ought first to make certain conjectures about the possible sender and the possible historical period in which the text was produced. This has nothing to do with researching the intentions of the sender, but it certainly has to do with researching the cultural framework of the original message.

Probably our sophisticated interpreter should decide that the text found in the bottle referred on a given occasion to some existing figs and was indexically pointing to a given sender as well as to a given addressee and a given slave, but that afterward it lost all referential power. The addressee can dream of those lost actors, so ambiguously involved in exchanging things or symbols (perhaps to send figs meant, at a given historical moment, to make an uncanny innuendo), and could start from that anonymous message in order to try a variety of meanings and referents. . . . But the interpreter would not be entitled to say that the message can mean *everything*.

It can mean many things, but there are senses that would be preposterous to suggest. I do not think that there can be somebody eager to say that it means that Napoleon died in May 1821; but to challenge such a farfetched reading can be a reasonable starting point for concluding that there is at least something which that message cannot positively say. It says that once upon a time there was a basket full of figs.

I admit that in order to make such a statement one must first of all assume that sentences can have a "literal meaning," and I know that such a point is controversial. But I keep thinking that, within the boundaries of a given language, there is a literal meaning of lexical items and that it is the one listed first by dictionaries as well as the one that Everyman would first define when requested to say what a given word means. I thus assume that Everyman would first say that a fig is a kind of fruit. No reader-oriented theory can avoid such a constraint. Any act of freedom on the part of the reader can come *after*, not *before*, the acceptance of that constraint.

I understand that there is a difference between discussing the letter mentioned by Wilkins and discussing *Finnegans Wake*. I understand that the reading of *Finnegans Wake* can help us to cast doubt on even the supposed commonsensicality of Wilkins's example. But we cannot disregard the point of view of the Slave who witnessed for the first time the miracle of Texts and of their interpretation.

The essays collected here, except for three (the analysis of Pliny's letter and the essays on drama and Pirandello, written at the end of the 1970s), were published during the last five years. All of them deal, from different points of view, with the problem of interpretation and its limits, or constraints. It is merely accidental, but by no means irrelevant, that they appear a little after the English translation of an old book of mine, *Opera aperta,* written between 1957 and 1962 (now *The Open Work* [Cambridge: Harvard U.P., 1989]). In that book I advocated the active role of the interpreter in the reading of texts endowed with aesthetic value. When those pages were written, my readers focused mainly on the "open" side of the whole business, underestimating the fact that the open-ended reading I supported was an activity elicited by (and aiming at interpreting) a *work*. In other words, I was studying the dialectics between the rights of texts and the rights of their interpreters. I have the impression that, in the course of the last few decades, the rights of the interpreters have been overstressed. In the present essays I stress the limits of the act of interpretation.

It is neither accidental nor irrelevant that these essays follow my previous writings (*A Theory of Semiotics, The Role of the Reader, Semiotics and the Philosophy of Language,* all published by Indiana U.P.) in which I elaborated upon the Peircean idea of *unlimited semiosis.* I hope that the essays in this book (especially the one on Peirce) will make clear that the notion of unlimited semiosis does not lead to the conclusion that interpretation has no criteria. To say that interpretation (as the basic feature of semiosis) is potentially unlimited does not mean that interpretation has no object and that it "riverruns" for the mere sake of itself. To say that a text potentially has no end does not mean that *every* act of interpretation can have a happy ending.

Even the most radical deconstructionists accept the idea that there are interpretations which are blatantly unacceptable. This means that the interpreted text imposes some constraints upon its interpreters. The limits of interpretation coincide with the rights of the text (which does not mean with the rights of its author).

Even in the case of self-voiding texts (see the chapter "Small Worlds") we have semiosic objects which without any shade of doubt speak of their own impossibility. Let us be realistic: there is nothing more meaningful than a text which asserts that there is no meaning.

If there is something to be interpreted, the interpretation must speak of something which must be found somewhere, and in some way respected.

Returning to Wilkins, in a world dominated by Übermensch-Readers, let us first rank with the Slave. It is the only way to become, if not the Masters, at least the respectfully free Servants of Semiosis.

1

Two Models of Interpretation

1. Symbol and allegory

Some years ago I examined several senses of the word *symbol* (Eco 1984). Among them was the well-known distinction between symbol and allegory drawn by Goethe: "Symbolism transforms the experience into an idea and an idea into an image, so that the idea expressed through the image remains always active and unattainable and, even though expressed in all languages, remains inexpressible. Allegory transforms experience into a concept and a concept into an image, but so that the concept remains always defined and expressible by the image" (Goethe 1809:1112–1113). Goethe's definition seems perfectly in tune with the one advocated by idealistic philosophy, for which symbols are signifiers that convey imprecise clouds or nebulae of meaning that they leave continually unexploited or unexploitable.

But we know that there is another sense of the word *symbol.* If we take it in the sense of logicians and mathematicians, then a symbol is either a signifier correlated to its meaning by a law, that is, by a precise convention, and as such interpretable by other signifiers, or a variable that can be bound in many ways but that, once it has acquired a given value, cannot represent other values within the same context. If we take it in the sense of Hjelmslev (1943:113–114), we find as instances of symbol the Cross, the Hammer and Sickle, emblems, and heraldic images. In this sense symbols are allegories.

Early versions of this chapter were "At the Roots of the Modern Concept of Symbol," *Social Research* 52 (1985), no. 2; and "Welt als Text—Text als Welt," in *Streit der Interpretationen* (Konstanz: Universitätsverlag, 1987).

Such an ambivalence has its own roots in the Greek etymology. Originally a symbol was a token, the present half of a broken table or coin or medal, that performed its social and semiotic function by recalling the absent half to which it potentially could be reconnected. This potentiality was indeed crucial because, since the two halves could be reconnected, it was unnecessary to yearn for the reconnection. So, too, it happens today that, when we enter a theater with our ticket stub, nobody tries to check where its other half is; everyone trusts the semiotic nature of the token, which in this case works on the basis of an established and recognized convention.

But the present half of the broken medal, evoking the ghost of its absent companion and of the original wholeness, encouraged other senses of "symbol." The verb *symballein* thus meant to meet, to try an interpretation, to make a conjecture, to solve a riddle, to infer from something imprecise, because incomplete, something else that it suggested, evoked, revealed, but did not conventionally say. In this sense a symbol was an ominous sudden experience that announced vague consequences to be tentatively forecast. A symbol was a *semeion,* but one of an impalpable quality. It was a divine message, and when one speaks in tongues, everybody understands, but nobody can spell aloud what has been understood.

All the senses of "symbol" are thus equally archaic. When the supporters of the "romantic" sense try to trace its profoundly traditional origins, they look for an honorable pedigree but disregard the fact that the distinction between symbol and allegory is not archaic at all.

When in the Stoic milieu the first attempts were made to read the old poets allegorically, so as to find under the cloak of myth the evidence of natural truths, or when Philo of Alexandria started the allegorical reading of the Bible, there was no clear-cut distinction between symbol and allegory. Pépin (1970) and Auerbach (1944) say that the classical world took symbol and allegory as synonymous expressions and also called symbols certain coded images produced for educational purposes. Under such a linguistic usage was the idea that symbols too were rhetorical devices endowed with a precise meaning, obscurely outlined, but to be precisely found. And the same happened with the tradition of the Church Fathers and medieval culture.[1]

2. Pansemiotic metaphysics

There is, in the patristic and medieval tradition, an idea of symbolism as a way of speaking of something unknowable: in the Neoplatonic line of thought, as represented by Pseudo Dionysius, the divine source of all beings, the One, is defined as "the luminous dimness, a silence which teaches secretly, a flashing darkness which is neither body nor figure nor shape, which has no quantity, no quality, no weight, which is not in a place and does not see, has no sensitivity, is neither soul nor mind, has no imagination or opinion, is neither number nor order nor greatness, is not a substance, not eternity, not time, not obscurity, not error, not light, not truth . . . " (*Theol. myst.* passim).

How to speak of such nonentity and nonidentity if not by a language whose signs have no literal and univocal meaning but are "open" to contrasting interpretations? Dionysius speaks, for his negative theology, of symbols that are not translatable allegories. From a Neoplatonic perspective, we must say of the source of the cosmic emanation something which is true and false at the same time—since such a Source is beyond any rational knowledge and, from our point of view, appears as mere Nothingness. This contradictoriness of Neoplatonic symbols seems to share the ambiguity of the romantic symbol.

Nevertheless, the Neoplatonism of Dionysius—and, furthermore, that of his commentators such as Aquinas—is not a "strong" one: medieval Neoplatonist philosophers tried to translate the pantheistic idea of emanation into one of "participation." It is true that the One is absolutely transcendent and infinitely far from us, that we are made of a different "fabric" since we are the mere litter of His creative energy, but He is not contradictory in Himself. Contradictoriness belongs to our discourses about Him and arises from our imperfect knowledge of Him. But the knowledge He has of Himself is totally unambiguous. This is a very important point because, as we shall see, the Hermetic Platonism of the Renaissance maintains that the very core of every secret knowledge is the faith in the deep contradictoriness of reality. On the contrary, for medieval theology both contradictoriness and ambiguity are merely semiotic, not ontological.

Naturally, since we must speak of the Unspeakable, we name it Goodness, Truth, Beauty, Light, Jealousy, and so on, but these terms, says Dionysius, can be applied to Him only "supersubstantially." Moreover, since our divine names will always be inadequate, it is indispensable to choose them according to a criterion of dissimilarity. It is dangerous to name God Beauty or Light, because one can believe that such appellations convey some of His real qualities. We should rather call Him Lion, Panther, Bear, Monster. We should apply to Him the most provocative adjectives so that it be clear that the similarity we are looking for escapes us or can only be glimpsed at the cost of a disproportioned proportion (*De coel. hier.* 2).

Despite this, such a symbolic way of speaking has nothing to do with the sudden illumination, with the cognitive ecstasy, with the flashing vision of which modern theories of symbolism speak. The medieval metaphysical symbol is neither epiphany nor revelation of a truth concealed under the cloak of myth. Symbolism must make rationally conceivable the inadequacy of our reason and of our language. Challenged by this difficulty, Dionysius's commentators tried to translate his approach into rational terms: when Scotus Erigena (*De divisione naturae* 5.3) says that "nihil enim visibilium rerum, corporaliumque est, ut arbitror, quod non incorporale quid et intelligibile significet," he is no longer speaking of a network of ungraspable similitudes, but rather of that uninterrupted sequence of causes and effects that will later be called the Great Chain of Being.

Aquinas will definitely transform this approach into the doctrine of *analogia entis,* which aimed at being a proportional calculus. Thus at the very root of medieval pansemiotic metaphysics—which was sometimes defined as universal symbolism—is the Quest for a Code and the will to transform a poetic approximation into a philosophical statement.

3. Scriptural interpretation

Parallel to the Neoplatonic line of thought is the hermeneutic tradition of scriptural interpreters, interested in the symbolic language by which the Holy Scriptures speak to us.

The semiosic process involved in the reading of Scriptures was rather complicated: there was a first book speaking allegorically of the second one, and a second one speaking through parables of something else. Moreover, in this beautiful case of unlimited semiosis, there was a puzzling identification among the sender (the divine Logos), the signifying message (words, Logoi), the content (the divine message, Logos), the referent (Christ, the Logos)—a web of identities and differences, complicated by the fact that Christ, as Logos, insofar as he was the ensemble of all the divine archetypes, was fundamentally polysemous.

Thus both Testaments spoke at the same time of their sender, of their content, of their referent. Their meaning was the nebula of all possible archetypes. The Scriptures were in the position of saying everything, and everything was too much for interpreters interested in Truth (see Compagnon 1972 and the discussion in Eco 1984, ch. 4). The symbolic nature of the Holy Books thus had to be tamed; in order to do so, the symbolic mode had to be identified with the allegorical one.

This is a very delicate point, because without this profound need of a code, the scriptural interpretation would look very similar to our modern interpretive theories of deconstruction, pulsional interpretive drift, misprision, libidinal reading, free *jouissance*.

The Scriptures had potentially every possible meaning, but their reading had to be governed by a code, and that is why the Fathers proposed the theory of the allegorical senses. In the beginning the senses were three (literal, moral, mystic or pneumatic); then they became four (literal, allegorical, moral, and anagogical).

The theory of the four senses provided a sort of guarantee for the correct decoding of the Books. The patristic and Scholastic mind could never avoid the feeling of inexhaustible profundity of the Scriptures, frequently compared to an *infinita sensuum sylva* (Jerome *Ep.* 64.21), an *oceanum mysteriosum Dei, ut sic loquar, labyrinthum* (Jerome *In Gen.* 9.1), a *latissima sylva* (Origenes *In Ez.* 4), or of a sea where, if we enter with a small boat, our minds are caught by fear and we are submerged by its whirls (Origenes *In Gen.* 9.1).

Once again we feel here something which recalls the modern fascination of an open textual reading, and even the hermeneutic idea that a text magnetizes on it, so to speak, the whole of the readings it has elicited in the course of history (Gadamer 1960). But the patristic and medieval problem was how to reconcile the infinity of interpretation with the univocality of the message. The main question was how to read the Books by discovering in them, not new things, but the same everlasting truth rephrased in ever new ways: *non nova sed nove.*

Scriptural hermeneutics provided the modern sensitivity with a model of "open" reading, but in its own terms escaped such a temptation. This is why at that time symbol and allegory were indistinguishable from each other. In order to consider them as two different procedures, Western civilization had to elaborate a different notion of truth.

There is, however, a point where Christian tradition offered to modern symbolism an interpretive model. It was the way of deciding when, in a text, one can recognize an instance of symbolic mode. Augustine (*De Doctrina Christiana* 3) was the first to put forth a list of rules for ascertaining whether and when a fact told by the Scriptures had to be taken, not literally, but figuratively. Augustine knew that verbal tropes such as a metaphor can be easily detected because, if we take them literally, the text would look mendacious. But what to do with the report of events that makes sense literally but, notwithstanding, could be interpreted symbolically? Augustine says that one is entitled to smell a figurative sense every time the Scriptures say things that are literally understandable but contradict the principles of faith and morals. Jesus accepts being honored and anointed by a courtesan, but it is impossible that our Savior encouraged such a lascivious ritual. Therefore the story stands for something else. In the same way, one should smell a second sense when the Scriptures play upon inexplicable superfluities or use literal expressions such as proper names or series of numbers. This eagerness to conjecture the presence of a symbolic mode when facing trivial events or blatantly useless details cannot but recall modern poetic devices such as the Joycean epiphany or Eliot's objective correlative. We look for the symbolic mode, not at the level of rhetorical figures, but at the level of a more macroscopic textual strategy, when a text displays a sort of uncanny liberality, of otherwise inexplicable descriptive generosity.

It must be clear that Augustine looked for symbols, not in the case of rhetorical strategies, but in the case of reported events: since the beginning, scriptural symbolism aimed at privileging the *allegoria in factis* over the *allegoria in verbis*. The words of the Psalmist can certainly be read as endowed with a second sense—because the Holy Scriptures resort frequently to rhetorical devices; but what must necessarily be read beyond the letter are the series of "historical" events told by the Scriptures. God has predisposed the sacred history as a *liber scriptus digito suo,* and the characters of the Old Testament were pulled to act as they did in order to announce the characters and the events of the New.

According to Stoic teaching, signs were above all not words, *onomata,* but *semeia,* that is, natural events which can be taken as the symptoms of something else. Augustine received from the classical tradition the rhetorical rules allowing him to decode the allegories *in verbis,* but he did not have precise rules for the allegories *in factis*—and, as I have already said, the significant facts told by the Scriptures cannot be "open" to any interpretation.

Thus in order to understand the meaning of the facts told by the Bible, Augustine had to understand the meaning of the things the Bible mentions. This is the reason for which medieval civilization, extrapolating from the Hellenistic *Phisiologus* or Pliny's *Naturalis historia,* elaborated its own encyclopedic repertories, bestiaries, herbaries, lapidaries, *imagines mundi,* in order to assign a symbolic meaning to every piece of the furniture of the "real" world. In these encyclopedias the same object or creature can assume contrasting meanings, so that the lion is at the same time the figure of Christ and the figure of the devil. The work of the medieval commentators was to provide rules for a correct textual disambiguation. Symbols were ambiguous within the paradigm, never within the syntagm. An elephant, a unicorn, a jewel, a stone, a flower can assume many meanings, but when they show up in a given context they have to be decoded in the only possible right way.

Thus the rise of a scriptural hermeneutics encouraged the growth of a universal symbolism and the real world became as much "perfused with signs" as were the Holy Scriptures. But in both cases one should speak more rigorously of scriptural and universal allegorism. The Middle Ages could not have understood the antinomy outlined by Goethe.

However, the universal allegorism implemented a sort of hallucinatory experience of the world according to which mundane creatures and historical facts counted, not as "these" creatures and "these" facts, but insofar as they were standing for something else. Such an attitude could not be accepted by the Aristotelian naturalism of the thirteenth century.

4. Aquinas

Aquinas was pretty severe with profane poetry and allegorism *in verbis*. Poetry is an inferior doctrine: "poetica non capiuntur a ratione humana propter defectus veritatis qui est in his" (*Summa th.* I–II.101.2 ad 2). But since Aquinas was a poet himself, and a gifted one, he admitted that sometimes divine mysteries, insofar as they exceed our comprehension, must be revealed by rhetorical figures: "conveniens est sacrae scripturae divina et spiritualia sub similitudine corporalium tradere" (*Summa th.* I.1.9). However, apropos of the Holy Text, he recommends looking first of all for its literal or historical sense. When the Bible says that Hebrew people escaped from Egypt, it tells literally the truth. Only when one has grasped this literal sense can one try to catch, through it and beyond it, the spiritual sense, that is, those senses that the scriptural tradition assigned to the sacred books, namely, the allegorical, the moral, and the anagogical or mystical ones. Up to this point it does not seem that Aquinas is so original with respect to the previous tradition. But he makes two important statements:

1. The spiritual sense only holds for the facts told by the Scriptures. Only in the course of the sacred history has God acted on the mundane events to make them signify something else. There is no spiritual sense in the profane history, nor in the individuals and facts of the natural world. There is no mystical meaning in what happened after the Redemption. Human history is a story of facts, not of signs (see *Quodl.* VII.6.16). The universal allegorism is thus liquidated. Mundane events are restituted to their naturality. If they are meaningful, they are so only for the eyes of the philosopher who sees them as natural proofs of the existence of God, not

as symbolic messages. With Aquinas one witnesses a sort of secularization of postbiblical history and of the natural world.

2. If there is a spiritual sense in the Holy Scriptures, where facts mean something else, there is no spiritual sense in profane poetry. Poetry displays only its literal sense. The statement seems undoubtedly too crude and radical: Aquinas, as a poet, knew very well that poets use rhetorical figures and allegories. But the poetical second sense is a subspecies of the literal one, and Aquinas calls it "parabolic." This sense—the one of tropes and allegories—"non supergreditur modum litteralem" (*Quodl.* VII.6.16). It is simply a variety of the literal sense. When the Scriptures represent Christ by the image of a goat, one is not facing a case of *allegoria in factis* but of simple *allegoria in verbis*. This goat is not a fact that symbolizes future events but only a word that parabolically (literally) stands for the name "Christ" (*Summa th.* I.1.10 ad 3, and *Quodl.* VII.6.15).

In which way is the parabolic sense different from the spiritual senses of the Scriptures? To understand this highly controversial point, one must understand what Aquinas meant by "literal sense." He meant the sense "quem auctor intendit." The literal sense is not only the meaning of a sentence but also the meaning of its utterance. Modern pragmatics knows that a sentence such as "It is cold here" is, according to the dictionary, a simple statement about the temperature of a given place; but if the sentence is uttered in given circumstances, it can also convey the actual intentions, the intended meaning, of its utterer, for instance, "Please, let us go elsewhere." It must be clear that, for Aquinas, both sentence meaning and utterance meaning belong to the literal sense, since they represent what the utterer of the sentence had in his mind. From that point of view, one understands why the sense conveyed by tropes and allegories, insofar as it represents exactly what the author wanted to say, can be easily reduced to the literal sense. Why are the spiritual senses of the Scriptures not equally literal? Because the biblical authors were unaware of conveying, through their historical report, the senses that (in the mind of God) facts should have assumed for the future reader able to read, in the Old Testament, the forecast of the New. The authors of the Scriptures wrote under divine inspiration, ignoring what they were really saying (see Eco 1986a and 1956).

It does not seem, however, that Aquinas's proposal was so influential. A first disquieting instance of it is given by the theory of allegorical reading of the *Divine Comedy,* as put forth by Dante in the *Epistula* XIII.

5. Dante

Dante, presenting his poem to Cangrande della Scala, makes immediately clear that it has to be read as a polysemous (*polisemos*) message. One of the most celebrated examples of what Dante means by polysemy is given by his analysis of some verses of Psalm 113:

> In exitu Israel de Aegypto
> domus barbara de populo barbaro,
> facta est Judaea sanctificatio ejus etc.

Following medieval theory, Dante says apropos of the first verse of the Psalm:

> If we look at the letter it means the exodus of the sons of Israel from Egypt at the time of Moses; if we look at the allegory it means our redemption through Christ; if we look at the moral sense it means the conversion of the soul from the misery of sin to the state of grace; if we look at the mystical sense it means the departure of the sanctified spirit from the servitude of this corruption to the freedom of the eternal glory. (*Epistula* XIII)

Apparently there is nothing in this analysis which contradicts the main lines of the scriptural tradition. But many interpreters felt something uncanny. Here Dante is taking a case of biblical reading as an example of how to read his mundane poem! The most obvious solution, and it has been proposed by some interpreters, is that this letter is a forgery. It "should" be a forgery because Dante was supposed to be a faithful Thomist and this letter contradicts the Thomistic position according to which profane poetry has only a literal sense. Anyway, even given that the letter is a forgery, it has from the beginning been taken to be authentic, and this means that it did not sound repugnant to the ears of Dante's contemporaries. Moreover, the *Convivio* is certainly not a forgery, and in that treatise Dante provides clues for interpreting allegorically his own poems—even though still maintaining a distinction between allegory of poets and allegory of theologians, which the letter disregards.

In *Convivio* Dante explains what he intentionally meant in writing his poems. In this sense one could say that he does not detach himself from the Thomistic point of view: the allegorical sense of his poems still is a parabolic one because it represents what Dante intended to mean. On the contrary, in the letter the examples he gives make one think of blatant cases of *allegoria in factis*. And in other passages of the letter, as it has been remarked by others, he says that his *Divine Comedy* is inspired by a "modus tractandis" which is "poeticus, fictivus, descriptivus, digressivus, transumptivus" (all traditional features of the poetic discourse), but then he adds, "cum hoc diffinitivus, divisivus, probativus, improbativus, et exemplorum positivus," and these are features of the theological and philosophical discourse. Furthermore, we know that he had always read the facts told by mythology and classical poetry as if they were *allegoriae in factis.*

In such terms Dante speaks of the poets in *De vulgari eloquentia,* and in the *Comedy* Statius says of Virgil that he was to him "as the one who proceeds in the night and bears a light, not for himself but for those who follow him" (*Purgatory* XXII.67–69). This means that—according to Dante—Virgil was a seer: his poetry, and pagan poetry in general, conveyed spiritual senses of which the authors *were not aware.* Thus for Dante poets are continuing the work of the Holy Scriptures, and his poem is a new instance of prophetic writing. His poem is endowed with spiritual senses in the same way as the Scriptures were, and the poet is divinely inspired. If the poet is the one that writes what love inspires in him, his text can be submitted to the same allegorical reading as the Holy Scriptures, and the poet is right in inviting his reader to guess what is hidden "sotto il velame delli versi strani" (under the veil of the strange verses).

Thus, just at the moment in which Aquinas devaluates the poetic mode, poets, escaping from his intellectual influence, start a new mystical approach to the poetic text, opening a new way of reading that, through various avatars, will survive until our times.

What makes Dante still medieval is the fact that he believes that a poem has neither infinite nor indefinite meanings. Dante seems to maintain that the spiritual meanings are four and that they can be encoded and decoded according to encyclopedic conventions. Which means that not even Dante draws a precise line between symbol and allegory.

But if the scriptural interpreters were warranted about their "right" reading of the Scriptures because of a long tradition which provided the criteria for a correct interpretation, what will happen now that the profane world has been devoid of any mystic sense and it is uncertain under the inspiration of whom (God, Love, or other) the poet unconsciously speaks? In a way, the theological secularization of the natural world implemented by Aquinas has set free the mystical drives of the poetic activity.

6. The new paradigm

A relevant epistemological change was to take place in Italy during Humanism. The heraldic world of bestiaries and lapidaries had not fully lost its appeal. Natural sciences were on the verge of becoming more and more quantitatively and mathematically oriented, Aristotle seemed not to have anything more to say, and the new philosophers began exploring a new symbolic forest where living columns whispered, in Baudelarian terms, confused but fascinating words, coming from a Platonism revisited under the influence of the Kabbalah and the *Corpus Hermeticum*. In this new philosophical milieu the very idea of symbol underwent a profound change.

In order to conceive of a different idea of symbol, as something that sends one back to a mysterious and self-contradictory reality that cannot be conceptually expressed, one needs a "very strong" Neoplatonism. The medieval Neoplatonism was not strong enough because it was emasculated—or made more virile—by a strong idea of the divine transcendence. Let us instead call that of the origins "strong Neoplatonism," at least until Proclus, and its Gnostic versions, according to which at the top of the Great Fall of Beings there is a One who is not only unknowable and obscure but who, being independent of any determination, can contain all of them and is consequently the place of all contradictions.

In the framework of a strong Neoplatonism one should consider three basic assumptions, be they explicit or implicit: (i) There is a physical kinship, that is, an emanational continuity between every element of the world and the original One. (ii) The original One is self-contradictory, and in it one can find the *coincidentia oppositorum* (a Hermetic idea, indeed, but which at the dawn of modern times was reinforced by the philosophical views of Nicholas of Cues and Giordano Bruno). (iii) The One can be expressed only by negation and approximation, so that every possible representation of it cannot but refer to another representation, equally obscure and contradictory.

Then we meet the requirements for the development of a philosophy, of an aesthetics, and of a secret science of symbols as intuitive revelations that can be neither verbalized nor conceptualized.

The main features of the so-called Hermetic tradition that spread from the Renaissance and permeated romantic philosophy and many contemporary theories of artistic interpretation are the following:[2]

1. The refusal of the metric measure, the opposition of the qualitative to the quantitative, the belief that nothing is stable and that every element of the universe acts over any other through reciprocal action.

2. The refusal of causalism, so that the reciprocal action of the various elements of the universe does not follow the linear sequence of cause to effect but rather a sort of spiral-like logic of mutually sympathetic elements. If the universe is a network of similitudes and cosmic sympathies, then there are no privileged causal chains. The Hermetic tradition extends the refusal of causality even to history and philology, so that its logic seems to accept the principle *post hoc ergo ante hoc*. A typical example of such an attitude is the way in which every Hermetic thinker is able to demonstrate that the *Corpus Hermeticum* is not a late product of Hellenistic civilization—as Isaac Casaubon proved—but comes before Plato, before Pythagoras, before Egyptian civilization. The argument runs as follows: "That the *Corpus Hermeticum* contains ideas that evidently circulated at the times of Plato means that it appeared *before* Plato." To Western ears, educated on a causal epistemology, such an argument sounds offensive—and it is indeed logically disturbing—but it is enough to read some of the texts of the tradition to realize that, in its proper milieu, this argument is taken very seriously.

3. The refusal of dualism, so that the very identity principle collapses, as well as the one of the excluded middle; as a consequence, *tertium datur* (the idea of the coincidence of the opposites depends on this basic assumption).

4. The refusal of agnosticism. One should think that agnosticism is a very modern attitude and that from this point of view the Hermetic tradition cannot be opposed to the Scholastic one. But the Schoolmen, even though they were credulous, had, however, a very sharp sense of discrimination between opposites. They certainly did not use experimental methods for ascertaining what was and what was not the case, but they were profoundly interested in determining what was the case. Either a given idea reflected Aristotelian opinion or it did not: there was not a middle way or, if there was a possible reconciliation, as it happened with the typical arguments of Aquinas, the final reconciliation was the final truth. On the contrary, Hermetic thought, being nonagnostic, is Gnostic; it respects the whole of the traditional wisdom because even where there is contradiction between assumptions, each assumption can bear a part of truth, truth being the whole of a field of contrasting ideas.

5. The Hermetic tradition is based on the principle of similitude: *sicut superius sic inferius*. And once one has decided to fish for similitudes, one can find them everywhere: under certain descriptions, everything can be seen as similar to everything else.

Thus such a new symbolism grew up in the Hermetic atmosphere, from Pico della Mirandola and Ficino to Giordano Bruno, from Reuchlin and Robert Fludd to French Symbolism, Yeats, and many contemporary theories: speaking of the unshaped, symbols cannot have a definite meaning.

So it was that at the very moment in which theology, with Aquinas, was destroying the bases of the universal symbolism and allegorism, and the new science was beginning to speak of the world in quantitative terms, a new feeling was born among poets, Platonic philosophers, religious thinkers, Magi and Kabbalists. It was a new request for analogy and universal kinship, which influenced the new theories or the new practices of poetry and art, as well as new theories of myth, and definitely provided a new religion for many laymen who, in a secularized world, no longer believed in the God of theology but needed some other form of worship. Perhaps we should rewrite the traditional handbooks which tell the story of how, when, and why modern man escaped from the Dark Ages and entered the Age of Reason.

It is interesting that, being so radically different from Christian symbolism, modern symbolism obeys the same semiotic laws. In one case, one assumes that symbols do have a final meaning, but since it is the same everlasting message, there is an inexhaustible variety of signifiers for a unique signified. In the other case, symbols have any possible meaning because of the inner contradictoriness of reality, but since every symbol speaks about this fundamental contradictoriness, an inexhaustible quantity of signifiers always stand for their unique signified, the inexhaustibility of the senses of any text. One witnesses in both cases a form of "fundamentalism." In the former case, every text speaks of the rational and univocal discourse of God; in the latter, every text speaks of the irrational and ambiguous discourse of Hermes.

7. Myths and texts

Many modern theories have too strictly identified symbol with myth. If a myth is a tale, then it is a text, and this text—as Bachofen said—is the exegesis of a symbol. Let us take a myth as a text and, metaphorically, as the paramount instance of every possible text. A text is a place where the irreducible polysemy of symbols is in fact reduced because in a text symbols are anchored to their context. The medieval interpreters were right: one should look for the rules which allow a contextual disambiguation of the exaggerated fecundity of symbols. Modern sensitivity deals on the contrary with myths as if they were macro symbols and—while acknowledging the infinite polysemy of symbols—no longer recognizes the discipline that myths impose on the symbols they involve. Thus many modern theories are unable to recognize that symbols are paradigmatically open to infinite meanings but syntagmatically, that is, textually, open only to the indefinite, but by no means infinite, interpretations allowed by the context.

To recognize this principle does not mean to support the "repressive" idea that a text has a unique meaning, guaranteed by some interpretive authority. It means, on the contrary, that any act of interpretation is a dialectic between openness and form, initiative on the part of the interpreter and contextual pressure.

Medieval interpreters were wrong in taking the world as a univocal text; modern interpreters are wrong in taking every text as an unshaped world. Texts are the human way to reduce the world to a manageable format, open to an intersubjective interpretive discourse. Which means that, when symbols are inserted into a text, there is, perhaps, no way to decide which interpretation is the "good" one, but it is still possible to decide, on the basis of the context, which one is due, not to an effort of understanding "that" text, but rather to a hallucinatory response on the part of the addressee.

NOTES

1. Auerbach suggests that sometimes Dante, instead of designing complex allegories, sets forth characters such as Beatrice and Saint Bernard, who stand at the same time as real persons and as "types" representing higher truths. But even in this case one witnesses the presence of a rhetorical device, halfway between metonymy and antonomasia. There is nothing there that may recall the idea typical of romantic symbolism—of an obscure intuition that cannot be translated by a verbal paraphrase. Dantesque characters can be interpreted in the same way as those characters of the Old Testament who, as we shall see later, were intended as figures of the New. Since the times of Augustine this procedure was called *allegoria in factis,* as opposed to *allegoria in verbis,* and was later

called "typology." We shall see later that Dante simply applied to his profane poetry a procedure that was used for the sacred history.

2. I am following the suggestions of Durand (1979). I do not agree with his neo-Hermetic reinterpretation of the whole history of modern thought, but his "identikit" of the Hermetic tradition looks convincing.

2

Unlimited Semiosis and Drift: Pragmaticism vs. "Pragmatism"

1. Worlds and texts

The double metaphor of the world as a text and a text as a world has a venerable history. To interpret means to react to the text of the world or to the world of a text by producing other texts. To explain the way the solar system works by uttering Newton's laws or to utter a series of sentences to say that a given text means so and so are, at least in Peirce's sense, both forms of interpretations. The problem is not to challenge the old idea that the world is a text which can be interpreted, but rather to decide whether it has a fixed meaning, many possible meanings, or none at all.

Let me start with two quotations:

1. "What does the fish remind you of?"
   "Other fish."
   "And what do other fish remind you of?"
   "Other fish."

(Joseph Heller, *Catch 22,* New York,
Simon and Schuster, 1961, p. 290)

First presented as "Drift and Unlimited Semiosis" at the Indiana University Institute for Advanced Studies, July 19, 1983. A different version was presented at the C. S. Peirce Sesquicentennial Congress, Harvard University, September 1989.

2. *Hamlet:* Do you see yonder cloud that's almost in shape of a camel?
   Polonius: By th' mass, and 'tis like a camel indeed.
   Hamlet: Methinks it is like a weasel.
   Polonius: It is back'd like a weasel.
   Hamlet: Or like a whale?
   Polonius: Very like a whale.

(*Hamlet* III.2)

2. Two poles

The opposition between these two quotations reminds us that all along the course of history we are confronted with two ideas of interpretation. On one side it is assumed that to interpret a text means to find out the meaning intended by its original author or—in any case—its objective nature or essence, an essence which, as such, is independent of our interpretation. On the other side it is assumed that texts can be interpreted in infinite ways.

Taken as such, these two options are both instances of epistemological fanaticism. The first option is instantiated by various kinds of fundamentalism and of various forms of metaphysical realism (let us say, the one advocated by Aquinas or by Lenin in *Materialism and Empiriocriticism*). Knowledge is *adaequatio rei et intellectus*. The most outrageous example of the alternative option is certainly the one outlined above (ch. 1, section 6), that is, the paradigm of the *Hermetic semiosis*.

3. Hermetic drift

I shall call Hermetic drift the interpretive habit which dominated Renaissance Hermetism and which is based on the principles of universal analogy and sympathy, according to which every item of the furniture of the world is linked to every other element (or to many) of this sublunar world and to every element (or to many) of the superior world by means of similitudes or resemblances. It is through similitudes that the otherwise occult parenthood between things is manifested and every sublunar body bears the traces of that parenthood impressed on it as a *signature*.

The basic principle is not only that the similar can be known through the similar but also that from similarity to similarity everything can be connected with everything else, so that everything can be in turn either the expression or the content of any other thing. Since "any two things resemble one another just as strongly as any two others, if recondite resemblances are admitted" (Peirce, *C.P.* 1934:2.634), if the Renaissance Magus wanted to find an occult parenthood between the various items of the furniture of the world, he had to assume a very flexible notion of resemblance.

To show examples of flexible criteria of resemblance, let me quote, not the most radical occult and Hermetic theories, but rather some instances of a very reasonable semiotic technique, the one recommended by the authors of the arts of memory. Those authors were neither Kabbalists nor sorcerers summoning spirits. They simply wanted to build systems for remembering a series of ideas, objects, or names through another series of names, objects, or images of objects. Other authors (Rossi 1960; Yates 1966) have studied and described the complex constructions of *loci,* that is, of real architectural, sculptural, and pictorial structures that those theorists built in order to provide a systematic plane of expression for the contents to be memorized, signified, and recalled. It is clear, however, that these mnemotechnic apparatuses were something more than a practical device for remembering notions: it is not by chance or for decorative purposes that the systems of *loci* frequently assume the form of a Theater of the World or emulate cosmological models. They aim at representing an organic *imago mundi,* an image of a world which is the result of a divine textual strategy. Thus, to be semiotically efficient, they reproduce the presumed tangle of signatures on which the Universe as a significant Whole is based. As Ramus (1581) had remarked, memory is the shadow of the order (of the *dispositio*), and order is the syntax of the universe.

But even though an *ars memoriae* was conceived as a mere practical device, it had in any case to find recognizable links between a given image and the thing to be evoked. In order to establish such a relationship it was advisable to follow the same criteria that held for the interpretation of cosmic analogies. In this sense these *artes* tell us something about various socially and culturally established semiotic rules.

It suffices to leaf through the *Idea del Theatro* of the most audacious among the authors of memory treatises, Giulio Camillo Delminio (1567), to see how freely the most varied rhetorical practices come to be grouped together beneath the rubric of similarity. Even in a rapid reading of several chapters, one finds the following:

similarity of morphological traits: the centaur for horse racing, the sphere for astrology;

similarity of action: two fighting serpents for the military arts;

metonymy for historical or mythological contiguity: Vulcan for the arts of fire;

metonymy for cause: silkworms for clothing;

metonymy for effect: the flayed Marsias for the scene of a massacre;

metonymy for ruler and ruled: Neptune for the nautical arts;

metonymy for agent and action: Paris for the tribunal;

metonymy for agent and end: a maiden with a vial of fragrance for perfumery;

antonomasia: Prometheus, giver of fire, for the artisans;

vectorial iconism: Hercules drawing an arrow with three points and aiming toward the heavens for the sciences of heavenly things;

direct inference: Mercury with a cock for trade.

The most systematic of these works is perhaps Cosma Rosselli's *Thesaurus Artificiosae Memoriae* (1579). Rosselli lists the following correlations:

by a sample: a quantity of iron in order to recall iron;

by similarity, which in turn is subdivided into similarity of substance (the human being as the microcosmic image of the macrocosm) and of quantity (ten fingers for the Ten Commandments);

by metonymy and antonomasia: Atlas for the astronomers or for astronomy, a bear for the angry man, the lion for pride, Cicero for rhetoric;

by homonymy: the animal dog for the dog star;

by irony and contrast: the fool for the wise man;

by vestigial traces: the track for the wolf, the mirror in which Titus admired himself for Titus;

by a word of different pronunciation: *sanguine* for *sane*;

by similarity of name: Arista for Aristotle;

by genus and species: the leopard for the animal;

by pagan symbol: the eagle for Jove;

by peoples: the Parthians for arrows, the Phoenicians for the alphabet;

by zodiacal sign: the sign for the constellation;

by relation between an organ and its function;

by common attribute: the crow for Ethiopia;

by hieroglyphic: the ant for prudence;

and finally, totally idiosyncratic associations such as any monster of any sort for anything to be remembered.

The main feature of Hermetic drift seems to be the uncontrolled ability to shift from meaning to meaning, from similarity to similarity, from a connection to another. One is reminded of that game that consists in shifting from one term (say, *peg*) to another (say, *Plato*) in no more than six steps. If the game allows for every possible connection (be it metaphorical, metonimical, phonetic, or other) one can always win. Let us try: Peg—pig—bristle—brush—Mannerism—Idea—Plato.

Contrary to contemporary theories of drift (see below, section 5), Hermetic semiosis does not assert the absence of any univocal universal and transcendental meaning. It assumes that everything can recall everything else—provided we can isolate the right rhetorical connection—because there is a strong transcendent subject, the Neoplatonic One who (or which), being the principle of the universal contradiction, the place of the Coincidentia Oppositorum, and standing outside of every possible determination, being thus All and None and the Unspeakable Source of Everything at the same moment, permits everything to connect with everything else by a labyrinthine web of mutual referrals. It seems thus that Hermetic semiosis identifies in every text, as well as in the Great Text of the World, the Fullness of Meaning, not its absence.

Nevertheless, this world perfused with signatures, ruled, as it pretends, by the principle of universal significance, results in producing a perennial shift and deferral of any possible meaning. The meaning of a given word or of a given thing being another word or another thing, everything that has been said is in fact nothing else but an ambiguous allusion to something else.

In this sense the phantasmatic content of every expression is a secret, or an enigma that evokes a further enigma. The meaning of every symbol being another symbol, more mysterious than the previous one, the consequence is twofold: (i) there is no way to test the reliability of an interpretation, and (ii) the final content of every expression is a secret.

Since the process foresees the unlimited shifting from symbol to symbol, the meaning of a text is always postponed. The only meaning of a text is "I mean more." But since that "more" will be interpreted by a further "I mean more," the final meaning of a text is an empty secret.

Thus Hermetic semiosis transforms the whole world into a mere linguistic phenomenon but devoids language of any communicative power.

4. Hermetic drift and unlimited semiosis

The very idea of such a continuous shifting from meaning to meaning can evoke (at least for those who are hermetically eager to play with analogies) the Peircean idea of Unlimited Semiosis. At first glance certain quotations from Peirce seem to support the principle of an infinite interpretive drift. For instance:

> The meaning of a representation can be nothing but a representation. In fact it is nothing but the representation itself conceived as stripped of irrelevant clothing. But this clothing never can be completely stripped off: it is only changed for something more diaphanous. So there is an infinite regression here. Finally the interpretant is nothing but another representation to which the torch of truth is handed along; and as representation, it has its interpretant again. Lo, another infinite series. (C.P. 1.339)

Can we really speak of unlimited semiosis apropos of the Hermetic ability to shift from term to term, or from thing to thing? Can we speak of unlimited semiosis when we recognize the same technique implemented by contemporary readers who wander through texts in order to find in them secret puns, unheard-of etymologies, unconscious links, dances of "Slipping Beauties," ambiguous images that the clever reader can guess through the transparencies of the verbal texture even when no public agreement could support such an adventurous misreading? There is a fundamental principle in Peirce's semiotics: "A sign is something by knowing which we know something more" (8.332). On the contrary, the norm of Hermetic semiosis seems to be: "A sign is something by knowing which we know something *else*."

To know more (in Peirce's sense) means that, from interpretant to interpretant, the sign is more and more determined both in its breadth and in its depth. In the course of unlimited semiosis the interpretation approximates (even though asymptotically) the final logical interpretant, and at a certain stage of the process of interpretation we know more about the content of the representamen which started the interpretive chain. To know more does not mean to know everything, but it means that a sign entails all its remote illative consequences and the meaning of a proposition embraces "every obvious necessary deduction" (1934:5.165).

We can know more of a sign because we accept knowing its object according to a certain *ground,* that is, under a certain description, from the point of view of a given context, "in some respect or capacity" (2.228). In structuralistic terms, one could say that for Peirce semiosis is potentially unlimited from the point of view of the system but is not unlimited from the point of view of the process. In the course of a semiosic process we want to know only what is relevant according to a given *universe of discourse.*

Let me take an example of Hermetic semiosis defeated by a thinker who acted as Peirce would have acted. One of the most celebrated Hermetic arguments was this: the plant orchis has the same form of human testicles; therefore not only does orchis stand for testicles but also every operation accomplished on the plant can get a result on the human body. The Hermetic argument went further indeed: a relationship of resemblance was established not only between the plant and the testicles but also between both and other elements of the furniture of the macro- and microcosm, so that, by means of different rhetorical relationships (such as similarity, past or present contiguity, and so on), every one of these elements could stand for and act upon every other.

The objection raised by Francis Bacon (*Parasceve ad Historiam Naturalem et Experimentalem,* 1620) was the following: one must distinguish between a relationship of causality and a relationship of similarity. The roots of orchis are morphologically similar to male testicles, but the reason for which they have the same form is different. Being genetically different, the roots of the orchis are also functionally different from male testicles. Therefore these two phenomena can be interpreted as morphologically analogous, but their analogy stops within the universe of discourse of morphology and cannot be extended into other universes of discourse.

Peirce would have added that, if the interpretation of the roots of orchis as testicles does not produce a practical habit allowing the interpreters to operate successfully according to that interpretation, the process of semiosis has failed. In the same sense, one is entitled to try the most daring abductions, but if an abduction is not legitimated by further practical tests, the hypothesis cannot be entertained any longer.

Hermetic drift could be defined as an instance of connotative neoplasm. I do not wish to discuss at this moment whether connotation is a systematic phenomenon or a contextual effect (see Bonfantini 1987). In both cases, however, the phenomenon of connotation can still be represented by the diagram suggested by Hjelmslev and made popular by Barthes (figure 2.1). There is a phenomenon of connotation when a sign function (Expression plus Content) becomes in turn the expression of a further content.

However, in order to have connotation, that is, a second meaning of a sign, the whole underlying first sign is requested—Expression plus Content. *Pig* connotes "filthy person" because the first, literal meaning of this word contains negative semantic markers such as "stinky" and "dirty." The first sense of the word has to be kept in mind (or at least socially recorded by a dictionary) in order to make

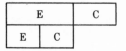

Figure 2.1

the second sense acceptable. If the meaning of *pig* were "gentle horse-like white animal with a horn in its front," the word could not connote "filthy person."[1]

A can connote B because of a strongly established metonymic relationship (for instance, cause for effect) or because some semantic markers characterize both contents of two sign functions (and in this sense metaphors are a subspecies of connotation), but not because of a mere phonetic similarity between expressions.

Moreover, even when a connotation becomes culturally recorded (like *pig* for "filthy person"), the connotative use must always be legitimated by the context. In a Walt Disney context the three little pigs are neither filthy nor unpleasant. In other cases it is the very contextual strategy that *posits* a connotation: see the example of Proust's *Recherche,* in which (both as a thing and as a word) a *madeleine* connotes the remembrance of one's own past. But outside Proustian contexts (comprehending also cases of intertextual citation), a madeleine is simply a sort of cake, as well as in Heller's text (see above, section 1) a fish was simply a fish (while in the context of early Christian iconography a fish, both as a word and as an image, connotes Jesus Christ).

Instead, in cases of neoplastic growth, as it happens in the most extreme cases of Hermetic drift, no contextual stricture holds any longer: not only is the interpreter entitled to shift from association to association, but also in doing so every connection becomes acceptable.

The diagram below (figure 2.2) aims at suggesting an idea of neoplastic connotative growth where at a certain point a mere phonetic association (Expression to Expression) opens a new pseudo-connotative chain where the content of the new sign no longer depends on the content of the first one.

Thus one faces a drift phenomenon which is analogous to what hap-

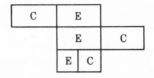

Figure 2.2

pens in a chain of family resemblances (see Bambrough 1961). Consider a series of things A, B, C, D, E, analyzable in terms of component properties a, b, c, d, e, f, g, h, so that each thing can possess some of the properties of the other, but not all of them. It is clear that, even with a short series, we can find a parenthood between two things that have nothing in common, provided they belong to a universal chain of uninterrupted relationships of similarity (figure 2.3).

At the end, no common property will unite A with E but one: they belong to the same network of family resemblances. Only this way can one know, according to the Paracelsian dictum, one thing within the other.[2] But in such a chain, at the moment we know E, any notion about A has vanished. Connotations proliferate like a cancer and at every step the previous sign is forgotten, obliterated, since the pleasure of the drift is given by the shifting from sign to sign and there is no purpose outside the enjoyment of travel through the labyrinth of signs or of things.

Provided one is able to go on playing such a game ad infinitum, one

A B C D E

a b c d   b c d e   c d e f   d e f g   e f g h

Figure 2.3

can shift from element to element of the universal furniture, but every element is cognitively characterized and determined only insofar as it refers to something else.

If we had to represent the ideal process of unlimited semiosis by a diagram similar to that used for connotation, we should probably outline something like that shown here (figure 2.4), where every content (or Immediate Object) of an expression (Representamen) is interpreted by another expression endowed with its own content, and so on potentially ad infinitum. But there is a sort of growth of the global content, an addition of determinations, since every new interpretant explains on a different ground the object of the previous one, and at the end one knows more about the origin of the chain as well as about the chain itself. A sign is indeed something by knowing which we know something more, but "that I could do something more does not mean that I have not finished it" (Boler 1964:394).

5. Unlimited semiosis and deconstruction

If unlimited semiosis has nothing to do with Hermetic drift, it has, however, been frequently quoted in order to characterize another form of drift, namely, that extolled by deconstruction.

According to Derrida, a written text is a machine that produces an indefinite deferral. Being by nature of a "testamentary essence," a text enjoys, or suffers, the absence of the subject of writing and of the designated thing or the referent (*Of Grammatology,* Eng. tr., 69). Any sign is "readable even if the moment of its production is irrevocably lost and even if I do not know what its alleged author-scriptor consciously in-

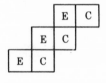

Figure 2.4

tended to say at the moment he wrote it, i.e. abandoned it to its essential drift" (1972, Eng. tr., 182).

To affirm that a sign suffers the absence of its author and of its referent does not necessarily mean that it has no objective or literal linguistic meaning. But Derrida wants to establish a practice (which is philosophical more than critical) for challenging those texts that look as though dominated by the idea of a definite, final, and authorized meaning. He wants to challenge, more than the sense of a text, that metaphysics of presence both of an interpretation based on the idea of a final meaning. He wants to show the power of language and its ability to say more than it literally pretends to say.

Once the text has been deprived of a subjective intention behind it, its readers no longer have the duty, or the possibility, to remain faithful to such an absent intention. It is thus possible to conclude that language is caught in a play of multiple signifying games; that a text cannot incorporate an absolute univocal meaning; that there is no transcendental signified; that the signifier is never co-present with a signified which is continually deferred and delayed; and that every signifier is related to another signifier so that there is nothing outside the significant chain, which goes on ad infinitum.

I have used on purpose the expression "ad infinitum" because it reminds us of a similar expression used by Peirce to define the process of unlimited semiosis. Can we say that the infinite drift of deconstruction is a form of unlimited semiosis in Peirce's sense? Such a suspicion can be encouraged by the fact that Rorty (1982), dealing with deconstruction and other forms of so-called textualism, has labeled them instances of "pragmatism":

> The intuitive realist thinks that there is such a thing as Philosophical Truth because he thinks that, deep down beneath all the texts, there is something which is not just one more text but that to which various texts are trying to be "adequate." The pragmatist does not think that there is anything like that. He does not even think that there is anything isolable as "the purposes which we construct vocabularies and cultures to fulfill" against which to test vocabularies and cultures. But he does think that in the process of playing vocabularies and cultures off against each other, we produce new and better ways of talking and acting—no better by reference to a previous known standard, but just better in the sense that they come to *seem* clearly better than their predecessors. (1982:xxxvii)

The pragmatism of which Rorty speaks is not the pragmaticism of Peirce. Rorty knows that Peirce only invented the word pragmatism but remained "the most Kantian of thinkers" (161). But even though Rorty prudently puts Peirce at the margins of such a kind of pragmatism, he puts deconstruction and Derrida within its boundaries. And it is exactly Derrida who summons Peirce.

6. Derrida on Peirce

In the second chapter of his *Grammatology,* Derrida looks for authorities able to legitimize his attempt to outline a semiosis of infinite play, of difference, of the infinite whirl of interpretation. Among the authors he quotes after Saussure and Jakobson, there is also Peirce. Derrida finds a series of fascinating passages according to which, for Peirce, symbols (here taken as equivalent to Saussurean signs) grow:

> In his project of semiotics, Peirce seems to have been more attentive than Saussure to the irreducibility of this becoming-unmotivated. In his terminology, one must speak of a becoming-unmotivated of the *symbol,* the notion of the symbol playing here a role analogous to that of the sign which Saussure opposes precisely to the symbol. . . .
> . . . Peirce complies with two apparently incompatible exigencies. The mistake here would be to sacrifice one for the other. It must be recognized that the symbolic (in Peirce's sense: of "the arbitrariness of the sign") is rooted in the nonsymbolic, in an anterior and related order of signification: "Symbols grow. They come into being by development out of other signs, particularly from icons, or from mixed signs." But these roots must not compromise the structural originality of the field of symbols, the autonomy of a domain, a production, and a play: "So it is only out of symbols that a new symbol can grow. Omne symbolum de symbolo." (*Of Grammatology*, Eng. tr., 48)

In another passage Derrida finds that pure rhetoric, the third branch of semiotics, "has the task to ascertain the laws by which in every scientific intelligence one sign gives birth to another" (49). Derrida can therefore conclude:

> Peirce goes very far in the direction that I have called the de-construction of the transcendental signified, which, at one time or another, would place a reassuring end to the reference from sign to sign. I have identified logocentrism and the metaphysics of presence as the exigent, powerful, systematic, and irrepressible desire for such a signified. Now Peirce considers the indefiniteness of reference as the criterion that allows us to recognize that we are indeed dealing with a system of signs. What broaches the movement of signification is what makes its interruption impossible. The thing itself is a sign. An unacceptable proposition for Husserl, whose phenomenology remains therefore—in its "principle of principles"—the most radi-

cal and most critical restoration of the metaphysics of presence. The difference between Husserl's and Peirce's phenomenologies is fundamental since it concerns the concept of the sign and of the manifestation of presence, the relationship between the re-presentation and the originary presentation of the thing itself (truth). On this point Peirce is undoubtedly closer to the inventor of the word *phenomenology*: Lambert proposed in fact to "reduce the theory of things to the theory of signs." According to the "phanaeroscopy" or "phenomenology" of Peirce, *manifestation* itself does not reveal a presence, it makes a sign. One may read in the *Principle of Phenomenology* that "the idea of *manifestation* is the idea of a sign." There is thus no phenomenality reducing the sign or the representer so that the thing signified may be allowed to glow finally in the luminosity of its presence. The so-called "thing itself" is always already a *representamen* shielded from the simplicity of intuitive evidence. The *representamen* functions only by giving rise to an *interpretant* that itself becomes a sign and so on to infinity. The self-identity of the signified conceals itself unceasingly and is always on the move. The property of the *representamen* is to be itself and another, to be produced as a structure of reference, to be separated from itself. The property of the *representamen* is not to be proper (propre), that is to say absolutely proximate to itself (prope, proprius). The *represented* is always already a *representamen*. . . . From the moment that there is meaning there are nothing but signs. We think only in signs. (49–50)

Thus it seems that the whole Peircean theory of unlimited semiosis supports the position of Derrida by which

> if reading must not be content with doubling the text, it cannot legitimately transgress the text toward something other than it, toward a referent (a reality that is metaphysical, historical, psychobiographical, etc.) or toward a signified object outside the text whose content could take place, could have taken place, outside language. . . . There is nothing outside the text (il n'y a pas de hors-texte). (158)

Is this interpretation of Peirce philologically, and philosophically, correct? I understand how ironic my question can sound. If Derrida assumed that his interpretation is the good one, he should also assume that Peirce's text had a *privileged meaning* to be isolated, recognized as such and spelled out unambiguously. Derrida would be the first to say that his reading makes Peirce's text move forward, beyond the alleged intentions of its author. But if we are not entitled, from the Derridian point of view, to ask if Derrida read Peirce well, we are fully entitled to ask, from the point of view of Peirce, if he would have been satisfied with Derrida's interpretation.

Certainly Peirce supports the idea of unlimited semiosis: a sign is "anything which determines something else (its interpretant) to refer to an object to which itself refers (its object) in the same way, this interpretant becoming in turn a sign, and so on ad infinitum. . . . If the series of successive interpretants comes to an end, the sign is thereby rendered imperfect, at least" (2.300).

Peirce could not do differently, since he was assuming (as he did in "Questions concerning certain faculties claimed for man") that (i) we have no power of introspection, and all knowledge of the internal world is derived by hypothetical reasoning; (ii) we have no power of intuition, and every cognition is determined by previous cognitions; (iii) we have no power of thinking without signs; and (iv) we have no conception of the absolutely incognizable. But in spite of this, deconstructive drift and unlimited semiosis cannot be equivalent concepts.

I do not agree with Searle when he says that "Derrida has a distressing penchant for saying things that are obviously false" (1977:203). On the contrary, Derrida has a fascinating penchant for saying things that are nonobviously true, or true in a nonobvious way. When he says that the concept of communication cannot be reduced to the idea of transport of a unified meaning, that the notion of literal meaning is problematic, that the current concept of context risks being inadequated; when he stresses, in a text, the absence of the sender, of the addressee, and of the referent and explores all the possibilities of a nonunivocal interpretability of it; when he reminds us that every sign can be *cited* and in so doing can break with every given context, engendering an infinity of new contexts in a manner which is absolutely illimitable—in these and in many other cases he says things that no semiotician can disregard. But frequently Derrida—in order to stress nonobvious truths—disregards very obvious truths that nobody can reasonably pass over in silence. Rorty would say that "he has no interest in bringing 'his philosophy' into accord with common sense" (1982:87). I think rather that Derrida takes many of these obvious truths for granted—while frequently some of his followers do not.

If it is true that a notion of literal meaning is highly problematic, it cannot be denied that in order to explore all the possibilities of a text, even those that its author did not conceive of, the interpreter must first of all take for granted a zero-degree meaning, the one authorized by the dullest and the simplest of the existing dictionaries, the one authorized by the state of a given language in a given historical moment, the one that every member of a community of healthy native speakers cannot deny. Every sentence can be interpreted metaphorically: even the assertion *John eats an apple every morning* can be interpreted as "John repeats Adam's sin every day." But in order to support such an interpretation, everybody must take for granted that *apple* means a given fruit, that

Adam is intended as the first man, and that, according to our biblical competence, Adam ate a forbidden fruit.

Derrida would be—and indeed he was—the first to deny that we can always use language as an instance of drift and the first to refuse the objection that there are no criteria for verifying the reasonableness of a textual interpretation. In *Grammatology* he reminds his readers that without all the instruments of traditional criticism "critical production will risk developing in any direction at all and authorize itself to say almost anything. But this indispensable guard-rail has always only *protected*, it has never *opened* a reading" (Eng. tr., 158).

Let us for a while protect the reading of Peirce, rather than open it too much.

7. Peirce alone

It is true that Peirce speaks of a possible infinite interpretation. This is possible because reality appears to us in the form of a continuum where there are no absolute individuals, and this is the principle of synechism: "A true continuum is something whose possibilities of determination no multitude of individuals can exhaust" (1934:6.170). Reality is a continuum which swims in indeterminacy (1.171–172), and just because of this the principle of continuity is "fallibilism objectified" (1.171). In a continuum where one can isolate infinite undetermined individuals, the possibility of error is always present, and therefore semiosis is potentially unlimited. "The absolute individuals can not only not be realized in sense or thought, but can not exist, properly speaking. . . . All, therefore, that we perceive or think, or that exists, is general. . . . That which exists is the object of a true conception. This conception may be made more determinate than any assignable conception: and therefore it is never so determinate that it is capable of no further determination" (3.93).

This indeterminacy of our knowledge involves vagueness: "A subject is determinate in respect to any character which inheres in it or is (universally and affirmatively) predicted of it. . . . In all other respects it is indeterminated" (5.447). In this sense Peirce is affirming a principle of contextuality: something can be truly asserted within a given universe of discourse and under a given description, but this assertion does not exhaust all the other, and potentially infinite, determinations of that object. Every judgment is conjectural in nature, and common sense, even when true, is always vague (5.181, 7.646–647). "A sign is objectively vague insofar as leaving its interpretation more or less indeterminate it reserves for some other possible sign or experience the function of completing the determination" (4.505).[3]

But there are other ideas in Peirce that seem to undermine Derrida's reading. If the theory of unlimited semiosis can appear, in Rorty's terms, as an instance of textualism, that is to say, of idealism, we cannot disregard the realistic overtones of Peirce's idealism.[4] Besides, I have already quoted the assertion of Rorty, who considers Peirce still Kantian and in this sense opposed to the current pragmatistic textualism.

Despite fallibilism, synechism, vagueness, for Peirce "the idea of meaning is such as to involve some reference to a purpose" (5.166). The idea of a purpose, pretty natural for a pragmaticist, is pretty embarrassing for a "pragmatist" (in Rorty's sense). A purpose is, without any shade of doubt, and at least in the Peircean framework, connected with something which lies outside language. Maybe it has nothing to do with a transcendental subject, but it has to do with referents, with the external world, and links the idea of interpretation to the idea of interpreting according to a given meaning. When Peirce provides his famous definition of *lithium* as a packet of instructions aimed at permitting not only the identification but also the production of a specimen of lithium, he remarks: "The peculiarity of this definition is that it tells you what the word *lithium* denotes by prescribing what you are to *do* in order to gain a perceptive acquaintance with the object of the word" (2.330).

Semiosis is unlimited and, through the series of interpretants, explains itself by itself, but there are at least two cases in which semiosis is confronted with something external to it.

The first case is that of indices. I am eager to challenge Peirce's idea that indices, in order to be understood as signs, must be connected to the object they designate. (I think it is possible to define the meaning of an indexical sign without making recourse to its actual referent; see Eco 1976:2.11.5.) But it is irrefutable that in the act of indication (when one says *this* and points his fingers toward a given object of the world), indices are in some way linked to an item of the extralinguistic or extrasemiosic world.[5]

The second case is due to the fact that every semiosic act is determined by a Dynamic Object which "is the Reality which by some means contrives to determine the sign to its Representamen" (4.536). We produce representamens because we are compelled by something external to the circle of semiosis. The Dynamic Object cannot be a piece of the furniture of the physical world but it can be a thought, an emotion, a motion, a feeling, a belief. We can say that a text can be interpreted independently of the intention of its utterer, but we cannot deny that any text is uttered by somebody according to his/her actual intention, and this original intention was motivated by a Dynamic Object (or was itself the Dynamic Object).

It is true that for Peirce the Dynamic Object can never be attained in its actual individual identity but is known only through the Immediate Object, and it is as an Immediate Object that the representamen offers it to further interpretations. Peircean semiotics could even be compatible with a radical Berkeleyan hypothesis: the alleged Dynamic Object can even be a mere figment produced by God and projected by Him upon our mind. If perception is—as it is for Peirce—semiosis, then even at the original moment of our perceptive acquaintance with the external world the external world becomes understandable to us only under the form of an Immediate Object. For Peirce, when the sign is produced the Dynamic Object is no more *there* (and before the sign was produced it was not an object at all). What is present to our mind and to the semiosic discourse is only the Immediate Object to be interpreted by other signs. But the presence of the representamen as well as the presence (in the mind or elsewhere) of the Immediate Object means that in some way the Dynamic Object, which is not there, *was* somewhere. Being not present, or not-being-there, the object of an act of interpretation *has been.*

Moreover, the Dynamic Object that *was,* and which is absent in the ghost of the Immediate One, to be translated into the potentially infinite chain of its interpretants, *will be* or *ought to be.* The quasi-Heideggerian sound of this statement should not mislead us: I am simply repeating with Peirce that "an endless series of representations, each representing the one behind it [and until this point Derrida could not but agree with this formula], may be conceived to have an absolute object as its limit" (1.339). Here it appears something that cannot find a place within the deconstructive framework: outside the immediate interpretant, the emotional, the energetic, and the logical one—all internal to the course of semiosis—there is the final logical interpretant, that is, the Habit.

The Habit is a disposition to act upon the world, and this possibility to act, as well as the recognition of this possibility as a Law, requires something which is very close to a transcendental instance: a community as an intersubjective guarantee of a nonintuitive, nonnaively realistic, but rather conjectural, notion of truth. Otherwise we could not understand why, given an infinite series of representations, the interpretant is "another representation to which the torch of truth is handed along" (1.339).[6]

"The ultimate meaning of a proposition is the law expressed in the conditionals" (5.491). The meaning of a descriptive proposition is the condition of its verification (2.511., 2.639., 2.640., 2.511., 5.203., 5.198., 5.402., 5.423). There is a real perfection of knowledge by which "reality is constituted" (5.356).

If for the pragmatic maxim (5.462) the meaning of any proposition is nothing more than the conceivable practical effects which the assertion would imply if the proposition were true, then the process of interpretation must stop—at least for some time—outside language—at least in the sense in which not every practical effect is a semiosic one. It is true that even the practical effect must then be spelled out by and through language, and that the very agreement among the members of the community cannot but take the form of a new chain of signs. Nevertheless, the agreement concerns something—be it a practical effect or the possibility of a practical effect—that is produced outside semiosis.

There is something for Peirce that transcends the individual intention of the interpreter, and it is the transcendental idea of a community, or the idea of a community as a transcendental principle. This principle is not transcendental in the Kantian sense, because it does not come before but *after* the semiosic process; it is not the structure of the human mind that produces the interpretation but the reality that the semiosis builds up. Anyway, from the moment in which the community is pulled to agree with a given interpretation, there is, if not an objective, at least an *intersubjective* meaning which acquires a privilege over any other possible interpretation spelled out without the agreement of the community. Peirce makes clear that the community of researchers is independent of what we think (5.405). The result of the universal inquiry points toward a common core of ideas (5.407). There is an activity of communitarian thought that works as the Destiny (5.408). There is a true conclusion of semiosis and it is Reality (5.384). "The fact that diverse thinkers agree in a common result is not to be taken simply as a brute fact" (Smith 1983:39). There is an ideal perfection of knowledge (5.356).

The thought or opinion that defines reality must therefore belong to a community of knowers, and this community must be structured and disciplined in accordance with supra-individual principles. The real is "the idea in which the community ultimately settles down" (6.610). "The opinion which is fated to be ultimately agreed to by all who investigate is what we mean by the truth, and the object represented in this opinion is the real" (5.407).

"The real, then, is what, sooner or later, information and reasoning would finally result in, and which is therefore independent of the vagaries of me and you. . . . The very origin of the conception of reality shows that this conception essentially involves the notion of a community" (5.311).

The process of knowledge is not an individual affair: "In storming the stronghold of truth one mounts upon the shoulders of another who has in the ordinary apprehension failed, but has in truth succeeded by virtue of the lesson of his failure" (7.51, 4.547). The truth can at least be reached in the long run (2.758).

There is community because there is no intuition in the Cartesian sense. The transcendental meaning is not there and cannot be grasped by an eidetic intuition: Derrida was correct in saying that the phenomenology of Peirce does not—like Husserl's—reveal a presence. But if the sign does not reveal the thing itself, the process of semiosis produces in the long run a socially shared notion of the thing that the community is engaged to take as if it were in itself true. The transcendental meaning is not at the origins of the process but must be postulated as a possible and transitory end of every process.

8. Conclusions

In section 1 above, it has been accepted that the notion of interpretation holds for worlds seen as texts as well as for texts seen as worlds. Consequently, all the remarks above can be applied to the critical activity of text interpretation.

In the Peircean line of thought it can be asserted that any community of interpreters, in the course of their common inquiry about what kind of object the text they are reading is, can frequently reach (even though nondefinitively and in a fallible way) an agreement about it.

In the next chapter it will be clear that to reach an agreement about the nature of a given text does not mean either (a) that the interpreters must trace back to the original intention of its author or (b) that such a text must have a unique and final meaning. There are (see Eco 1962a) "open" texts that support multiple interpretations, and any common agreement about them ought to concern just their open nature and the textual strategies that make them work that way.

But, even though the interpreters cannot decide which interpretation is the privileged one, they can agree on the fact that certain interpretations are not contextually legitimated. Thus, even though using a text as a playground for implementing unlimited semiosis, they can agree that at certain moments the "play of musement" can transitorily stop by producing a consensual judgment. Indeed, symbols grow but do not remain empty.

The reason for which I have insisted so much on the differences between Peirce's positions and various forms of drift is that in many recent studies I have remarked a general tendency to take unlimited semiosis in the sense of a free reading in which the will of the interpreters, to use Rorty's metaphor, "beats the texts into a shape which will serve their own purposes." My own purpose in beating (respectfully) Peirce was simply to stress that things are not that simple. Since in the following chapter it will be stressed that, if it is very difficult to decide whether a given interpretation is a good one, it is, however, always possible to decide whether it is a bad one, my purpose was to say, not so much what unlimited semiosis is, but at least what it *is not* and *cannot* be.

NOTES

1. To speak of connotation one needs a clear-cut distinction between literal and figurative meaning, and such a distinction is today more and more challenged. (For a survey of the most recent debates, see Dascal 1987:259–269.) However, it is still possible to assume a statistical notion of literal meaning as zero-degree relative to contexts (Cohen 1966:22; Ricoeur 1975:180ff) artificially constructed (Genette 1966:211; Groupe μ 1970:30ff). This zero degree would be that meaning accepted in technical and scientific contexts. If one asks an electrician what he means by *dark*, he would probably answer "without light, obscure." Webster (at the item *dark* as adjective) provides first the same technical definition and records "sinister" and "evil" as secondary definitions. Only this way one can understand why, at the beginning of Dante's *Divine Comedy*, *dark wood* signifies, by connotation and as a metaphor, the sinister and evil life of a sinner. In every connotative relationship the first sense does not disappear in order to produce the second one; on the contrary, the second sense must be understood on the grounds of the first one. To say that figurative meanings presuppose the literal does not mean that the actual addressee of a connotative expression ought to realize its literal meaning in order to understand the figurative one. An actual speaker can use the ready-made expression *what a mess* to designate a confused situation without thinking of the original culinary meaning of *mess* (a portion of food that, when composed of different pieces of meat and vegetables, can be a hodgepodge). But in order to explain why the empirical speaker was entitled to intend what he actually intended to mean by his utterance, a theory of connotation presupposes a complex semantic representation of *mess* which, first of all, takes into account the properties that compose its literal meaning. Only so is it possible to justify that *mess* can also connote a confused collection or mass of things and events, a muddle, a jumble.

2. I disregard the fact that in the magic perspective not only one thing be-

comes the signifier of the other, but, because of a sort of identification between things and words, one can act upon the other, so that the principle of universal resemblance becomes at the same time the principle of universal sympathy and of mutual interaction.

3. Vagueness depends on synechism: "Since no object in the universe can ever be fully determinate with respect to its having or not having every known property, it follows that any proposition about the universe is vague in the sense that it cannot hope to fully specify a determinate set of properties" (Almeder 1983:331). See also Nadin (1983:163): "Vagueness hence represents a sort of relationship between absolute, final determination, which in fact is not attained (the condition of an ideal, therefore) and actual determination of meaning (again as sense, meaning, signification) in concrete semioses."

4. "The current attempts at a theory of reality are to a great extent characterized by the insight that the problem of reality is now freed from the controversy between idealism and realism which had long been unfruitful, and must be treated on another level. The first and decisive step in the new direction was taken by Peirce. . . . This misleading phenomenon explains why, in his writings, he sometimes calls his own position 'idealistic' and sometimes 'realistic,' without essentially changing it" (Oehler 1979:70).

5. As for a discussion of Derrida's critique of "presence," only after having written this paper did I read the important remarks of Scholes (1989) about "pragmatic presence": see pp. 71–74 on "occasional" expressions such as *this* and *now*.

6. The problem of the Habit involves the pragmatic maxim: "Consider what effects, that might conceivably have practical bearings, we conceive the object of our conception to have. Thus our conception of these effects is the whole of our conceptions of the object" (5.402). "The meaning of any proposition is itself given in another proposition which is simply a general description of all the conceivable experimental phenomena which the assertion of the original proposition predicts" (Almeder 1983:329; *C.P.,* 5.427).

3

Intentio Lectoris:
The State of the Art

During the last decades we have witnessed a change of paradigm in the theories of textual interpretation. In a structuralistic framework, to take into account the role of the addressee looked like a disturbing intrusion since the current dogma was that a textual structure should be analyzed in itself and for the sake of itself, to try to isolate its formal structures. In contrast, during the 1970s literary theorists, as well as linguists and semioticians, have focused on the pragmatic aspect of reading. The dialectics between Author and Reader, Sender and Addressee, Narrator and Narratee has generated a crowd, indeed impressive, of semiotic or extrafictional narrators, subjects of the uttered utterance (*énonciation énoncée*), focalizers, voices, metanarrators, as well as an equally impressive crowd of virtual, ideal, implied or implicit, model, projected, presumed, informed readers, metareaders, archireaders, and so on.

Many different theoretical approaches (hermeneutics, the aesthetics of reception, reader-response criticism, semiotic theories of interpretative cooperation, until the scarcely homogeneous archipelago of deconstruction) have in common an interest in *the textual roots of the interpretative phenomenon.* This means that they are not focusing on the empirical results of given personal or collective acts of reading (studied by a sociology of reception) but rather on the very function of construc-

Early versions of this chapter were "Theorien Interpretativer Kooperation," a lecture given at Konstanz University, May 1986 (now in Eco 1987); and "Intentio Lectoris," a lecture for the Queens College Visiting Humanist Series, New York, Fall 1987 (see *Differentia* 2 [Spring 1988]).

tion—or deconstruction—of a text performed by its interpreter—insofar as such a function is implemented, encouraged, prescribed, or permitted by the textual linear manifestation.

The basic assumption underlying each of these theories is that the functioning of a text can be explained by taking into account not only its generative process but also (or, for the most radical theories, exclusively) the role performed by the addressee and the way in which the text foresees and directs this kind of interpretive cooperation. It must also be stressed that such an addressee-oriented approach concerns not only literary and artistic texts but also every sort of semiosic phenomenon, including everyday linguistic utterances, visual signals, and so on.

In other words, the addressee-oriented theories assume that the meaning of every message depends on the interpretive choices of its receptor: even the meaning of the most univocal message uttered in the course of the most normal communicative intercourse depends on the response of its addressee, and this response is in some way context-sensitive. Naturally such an allegedly open-ended nature of the message is more evident in those texts that have been conceived in order to magnify such a semiosic possibility, that is, by so-called artistic texts.

During earlier decades only works of art (specifically those produced according to the criteria of a "modernistic" tradition) were taken as texts able to intentionally display, provocatively, their open-ended nature. On the contrary, in the last decades such a nature has been theoretically rooted into the very nature of any kind of text. In other words, before such a change of paradigm, artistic texts were seen as the only cases in which a semiosic system, be it verbal or other, magnified the role of the addressee—the basic and normal function of any semiosic system being instead that of allowing an ideal condition of univocality, independent of the idiosyncrasies of the receptor. With the new paradigm semiotic theories have insisted on the fact that—even though in everyday life we are obliged to exchange many univocal messages, working (hardly) in order to reduce their ambiguity—the dialectis between sender, addressee and context is at the very core of semiosis.

This paper will, however, focus on the change of paradigm *in literary theories.* Facing the new paradigm, I shall take a "moderate" standpoint, arguing against some intemperance of so-called reader-response criticism. I shall claim that a theory of interpretation—even when it assumes that texts are open to multiple readings—must also assume that it is possible to reach an agreement, if not about the meanings that a text encourages, at least about those that a text discourages. Since literary texts are today viewed as the most blatant case of unlimited semiosis, it will be worthwhile to debate the problem of textuality where the very notion of text seems to dissolve into a whirl of individual readings.

1. Archaeology

Undoubtedly the universe of literary studies has been haunted during the last years by the ghost of the reader. To prove this assumption it will be interesting to ascertain how and to what extent such a ghost has been conjured up by different theorists, coming from different theoretical traditions. The first who explicitly spoke of an "implied author" ("carrying the reader with him") was certainly Wayne Booth (1961). After him we can isolate two independent lines of research, which until a certain moment ignored each other, namely, the semiotico-structural and the hermeneutic.

The first line stems from *Communications* 8. In this now "historical" issue, Barthes (1966) spoke of a material author that cannot be identified with the narrator; Todorov (1966) evoked the opposition "image of the narrator—image of the author" and recovered the previous theories of the point of view (from H. James, Percy Lubbock, and Forster until Pouillon); Genette (1966) started to elaborate the categories (definitely dealt with in 1972) of *voice* and *focalization*. Then, through some observations of Kristeva (1970) on "textual productivity," certain lucid pages of Lotman (1970), the still empirical concept of "archilecteur" by Riffaterre (1971), and the discussions about the conservative standpoint of Hirsch (1967), the debate developed through the most elaborated notions of *implied reader* in Corti (1976) and Chatman (1978).

It is interesting that the last two authors drew their definition directly from Booth, ignoring the similar definition proposed by Iser in 1972. Likewise, I elaborated my notion of Model Reader along the mainstream of the semiotic-structuralistic line (Eco 1979a), matching these results with some suggestions borrowed from various discussions on the modal logic of narrativity (mainly van Djik and Schmidt) as well as from some hints furnished by Weinrich—not to speak of the idea of an "ideal reader" designed by Joyce in *Finnegans Wake*. It is also interesting that Corti (1976) traces the discussion on the nonempirical author back to Foucault (1969), where, in a poststructuralistic atmosphere, the problem of the author is posited as a "way of being within the discourse," as a field of conceptual coherence, as a stylistic unity, which as such could not but elicit the corresponding idea of a reader as a way of recognizing such a being-within-the-discourse.

The second lineage is represented by Iser, who starts from the proposal of Booth but elaborates his suggestion on the basis of a different tradition (Ingarden, Gadamer, Jauss). Iser was also largely influenced (as it is demonstrated by the bibliographical references of *Der implizite Leser* (1972) by the Anglo-Saxon theorists of narrativity (well known by Todorov and Genette) and by Joycean criticism. One finds in Iser's first book few references to the structuralistic lineage (the only important source is Mukarovsky). It is only in *Der Akt des Lesens* (1976) that Iser brilliantly (and better informed than his structuralistic colleagues) tries to reconnect the two lineages, with references to Jakobson, Lotman, Hirsch, Riffaterre, as well as to some of my remarks of the early 1960s (see Eco 1962a). Such an insistence on the moment of reading, coming from different directions, seems to reveal a felicitous plot of the *Zeitgeist.* And, speaking of the *Zeitgeist,* it is curious that at the beginning of the 1980s Charles Fillmore, coming from the autonomous and different tradition of generative semantics (critically reviewed), wrote the essay "Ideal Readers and Real Readers" (1981)—without any conscious reference to the aforementioned debates.

Certainly all these author-reader oppositions do not have the same theoretical status (for a brilliant map of their mutual differences and identities, see Pugliatti 1985). However, the most important problem is to ascertain whether such a reader-oriented atmosphere really represented a new trend in aesthetic and semiotic studies or not.

As a matter of fact, the whole history of aesthetics can be traced to a history of theories of interpretation and of the effect that a work of art has on its addressee. One can consider as response-oriented the Aristotelian *Poetics,* the pseudo-Longinian aesthetics of the Sublime, the medieval theories of beauty as the final result of a "vision," the new reading of Aristotle performed by the Renaissance theorists of drama, many eighteenth-century theories of art and beauty, most of Kantian aesthetics, not to speak of many contemporary critical and philosophical approaches.

In his *Reception Theory* (1984), Robert Holub ranks among the precursors of the German reception theory (a) Russian Formalists, with their notion of "device" as the way in which the work of art elicits a particular type of perception; (b) Ingarden's attention to the reading process, his notion of the literary work as a skeleton, or "schematized structure," to be completed by the reader, and his idea, clearly due to Husserl's influence, of the dialectics between the work as an invariant and the plurality of *profiles* through which it can be concretized by the interpreter; (c) the aesthetics of Mukarovsky; (d) Gadamer's hermeneutics; and (e) the early German sociology of literature.

As for contemporary semiotic theories, from the beginning they took into account the pragmatic moment. Even without speaking of the central role played by interpretation and "unlimited semiosis" in Peirce's thought, it would be enough to remark that Charles Morris in *Foundations of a Theory of Signs* (1938) reminded that a reference to the role of the interpreter was always present in Greek and Latin rhetoric, in the communication theory of the Sophists, in Aristotle, not to mention Augustine, for whom signs were characterized by the fact that they produce an idea in the mind of their receiver.

During the 1960s, many Italian semiotic approaches were influenced by sociological studies on the reception of mass media. In 1965, at the convention held in Perugia on the relationship between television and its audience, I, Paolo Fabbri, and others insisted that it is not enough to study what a message says according to the code of its senders but is also necessary to study what it says according to the codes of its addressees (the idea of "aberrant decoding," proposed at that time, was further elaborated in Eco 1968 and 1976).

Thus in the 1960s the problem of reception was posited (or re-posited) by semiotics as a reaction against (i) the structuralistic idea that a textual object was something independent of its interpretations and (ii) the stiffness of many formal semantics flourishing in the Anglo-Saxon area, where the meaning of terms and sentences was studied independently of their context. Only later were the dictionary-like semantics challenged by encyclopedia-like models that tried to introduce into the core of the semantic representation pragmatic elements also—and only recently have cognitive sciences and Artificial Intelligence decided that an encyclopedic model seems to be the most convenient way to represent meaning and to process texts (on this debate, see Eco, 1976, 1984, as well as Eco et al., eds., 1988). In order to reach such an awareness it has been necessary that linguistics move toward pragmatic phenomena, and in this sense the role of the speech-act theory should not be underestimated.[1]

In the literary domain, Wolfgang Iser (1972) was probably the first to acknowledge the convergence between the new linguistic perspectives and the literary theory of reception, devoting as he did a whole chapter of *Der Akt des Lesens* to the problems raised by Austin and Searle (five years before the first organic attempt, by Pratt [1977], to elaborate a theory of literary discourse based on the speech-act theory).

Thus what Jauss (1969) was announcing as a profound change in the paradigm of literary scholarship was in fact a general change taking place in the semiotic paradigm in general—even though this change was not a brand-new discovery but rather the complex concoction of different venerable approaches that had characterized at many times the whole history of aesthetics and a great part of the history of semiotics.

Nevertheless, it is not true that *nihil sub sole novum.* Old (theoretical) objects can reflect a different light in the sun, according to the season. I remember how outrageous-sounding to many was my *Opera aperta* (1962), in which I stated that artistic and literary works, by foreseeing a system of psychological, cultural, and historical expectations on the part of their addressees, try to produce what Joyce called "an ideal reader."[2] Obviously at that time, speaking of works of art, I was interested in the fact that such an ideal reader was obliged to suffer an ideal insomnia in order to question the book ad infinitum. If there is a consistent difference between *Opera aperta* (1962a) and *The Role of the Reader* (1979), it is that in the second book I try to find the roots of artistic "openness" in the very nature of any communicative process as well as in the very nature of any system of signification (as already advocated by my *A Theory of Semiotics,* 1976). In any case, in 1962 my problem was how and to what extent a text should foresee the reactions of its addressee.

In *Opera aperta*—at least at the time of the first Italian edition, written between 1957 and 1962—I was still moving in a pre-semiotic area, inspired as I was by Information Theory, the semantics of Richards, the epistemology of Piaget, Merleau-Ponty's phenomenology of perception, transactional psychology, and the aesthetic theory of interpretation of Luigi Pareyson. In that book, and with a jargon I feel ashamed of today, I was writing:

> Now we must shift our attention from the message, as a source of possible information, to the communicative relationship between message and addressee, where the interpretative decision of the receptor contributes in establishing the value of the possible information. . . . If one wants to analyze the possibilities of a communicative structure one must take into account the receptor pole. To consider this psychological pole means to acknowledge the formal possibility—as such indispensable in order to explain both the structure and the effect of the message—by which a message signifies only insofar as it is interpreted from the point of view of a given situation—a psychological as well as a historical, social and anthropological one. (Eco 1962, 2d ed., 131ff)

In 1967, speaking in the course of an interview about my book, just translated into French, Claude Lévi-Strauss said that he was reluctant to accept my perspective because a work of art

is an object endowed with precise properties, that must be analytically isolated, and this work can be entirely defined on the grounds of such properties. When Jakobson and myself tried to make a structural analysis of a
Baudelaire sonnet, we did not approach it as an "open work" in which we
could find everything that has been filled in by the following epochs; we
approached it as an object which, once created, had the stiffness—so to
speak—of a crystal; we confined ourselves to bring into evidence these
properties. (Caruso 1967:81–82)

I have already discussed this opinion in the introductory chapter of *The
Role of the Reader,* making clear that, by stressing the role of the interpreter, I was not assuming that in an "open work" one can find that
"everything" has been filled in by its different empirical readers, irrespective of or despite the properties of the textual objects. I was, on the
contrary, assuming that an artistic text contained, among its major analyzable properties, certain structural devices that encourage and elicit
interpretive choices. However, I am quoting that old discussion in order to show how daring it was during the 1960s to introduce the "act of
reading" into the description and evaluation of the text to be read.

In *Opera aperta,* even though stressing the role of the interpreter
ready to risk an ideal insomnia in order to pursue infinite interpretations, I was insisting that to interpret a text means to interpret *that* text,
not one's own personal drives. Depending as I was on the aesthetics of
interpretation of Luigi Pareyson, I was still speaking of a dialectics between fidelity and freedom. I am stressing this point because, if during
the "structural sixties" my addressee-oriented position (neither so provocative nor so unbearably original) appeared so "radical," today it
would sound pretty conservative, at least from the point of view of the
most radical reader-response theories.[3]

2. A web of critical options

The opposition between a generative approach (according to which the
theory isolates the rules for the production of a textual object that can
be understood independently of its effects) and an interpretive approach is not homogeneous with triangular contrast, widely discussed
in the course of a secular critical debate, among interpretation as research of the *intentio auctoris,* interpretation as the research of the *intentio operis,* and interpretation as imposition of the *intentio lectoris.*

The classical debate aimed at finding in a text either (a) what its
author intended to say or (b) what the text says independently of the
intentions of its author. Only after accepting the second horn of the

dilemma can one ask whether what is found is (i) what the text says by virtue of its textual coherence and of an original underlying signification system or (ii) what the addressees found in it by virtue of their own systems of expectations.

Such a debate is of paramount importance, but its terms only partially overlap the opposition generation/interpretation. One can describe a text as generated according to certain rules without assuming that its author followed them intentionally and consciously. One can adopt a hermeneutic viewpoint leaving unprejudiced whether the interpretation must find what the author meant or what Being says through language— in the second case, leaving unprejudiced whether the voice of Being is influenced by the drives of the addressee or not. If one crosses the opposition generation/interpretation with the trichotomy of intentions, one can get six different potential theories and critical methods.

Facing the possibility, displayed by a text, of eliciting infinite or indefinite interpretations, the Middle Ages and the Renaissance reacted with two different hermeneutic options. Medieval interpreters looked for a plurality of senses without refusing a sort of identity principle (a text cannot support contradictory interpretations), whereas the symbolists of the Renaissance, following the idea of the *coincidentia oppositorum,* defined the ideal text as that which allows the most contradictory readings.

Moreover, the adoption of the Renaissance model generates a secondary contradiction, since a hermetico-symbolic reading can search for in the text either (i) the infinity of senses planned by the author or (ii) the infinity of senses that the author ignored. Naturally the option (ii) generates a further choice, namely, whether these unforeseen senses are discovered because of the *intentio operis* or despite it, forced into the text by an arbitrary decision of the reader. Even if one says, as Valery did, that "il n'y a pas de vrai sens d'un texte," one has not yet decided on which of the three intentions the infinity of interpretations depends.

Medieval and Renaissance Kabbalists maintained that the Torah was open to infinite interpretations because it could be rewritten in infinite ways by combining its letters, but such an infinity of readings (as well as of writings)—certainly dependent on the initiative of the reader—was nonetheless planned by the divine Author.

To privilege the initiative of the reader does not necessarily mean to guarantee the infinity of readings. If one privileges the initiative of the reader, one must also consider the possibility of an active reader who decides to read a text univocally: it is a privilege of fundamentalists to read the Bible according to a single literal sense.

We can conceive of an aesthetics claiming that poetic texts can be infinitely interpreted because their author wanted them to be read this way; or an aesthetics which claims that texts must be read univocally despite the intentions of their authors, who were compelled by the laws of language, and, once they wrote something, were bound to read it in the only authorized and possible sense.

One can read a text conceived as absolutely univocal as if it were infinitely interpretable: see, for instance, the reading performed by Derrida (1977) upon a text of Searle in "Limited Inc." One can perform psychedelic trips upon a text that cannot be but univocal according to the *intentio operis* (for instance, when one muses oneirically upon the railway timetable). Alternatively, one can read as univocal a text whose author wanted it to be infinitely interpretable (as would be the case of fundamentalists if by chance the Kabbalists were right) or read univocally a text that from the point of view of linguistic rules should be considered rather ambiguous (for instance, reading *Oedipus Rex* as a plain mystery story where what counts is only to find out the guilty one).

It is in light of this embarrassingly vast typology that we should reconsider many contemporary critical currents that can superficially be ranked, all together, under the headings of response-oriented theories. For instance, from the point of view of the classical sociology of literature, one is interested in recording what different readers do with a text, but one does not have to be worried by the problem of the *intentio*. The sociology of literature describes social usages, socialized interpretations, and the actual public effect of a text, not the formal devices or the hermeneutic mechanism that has produced those usages and those interpretations. In contrast, the aesthetics of reception maintains that a literary work is enriched by the various interpretations it underwent along the centuries and, while considering the dialectics between textual devices and the horizon of expectations of the readers, does not deny that every interpretation can and must be compared with the textual object and with the *intentio operis*.

Likewise, the semiotic theories of interpretive cooperation, such as my theory of the Model Reader (Eco 1979), look at the textual strategy as a system of instructions aiming at producing a possible reader whose profile is designed by and within the text, can be extrapolated from it and described independently of and even before any empirical reading.

In a totally different way, the most radical practices of deconstruction privilege the initiative of the reader and reduce the text to an ambiguous bunch of still unshaped possibilities, thus transforming texts into mere stimuli for the interpretive drift.

3. An apology of the literal sense

Every discourse on the freedom of interpretation must start from a defense of literal sense. In 1985 Ronald Reagan, during a microphone test before a public speech, said p (namely, "In a few minutes I'll push the red button and I'll start bombing the Soviet Union," or something similar). P was—as Linear Text Manifestation—an English sentence that according to common codes means exactly what it intuitively means. Once provided an intelligent machine with paraphrase rules, p could be translated as "the person uttering the pronoun "I" will in the next approximately two hundred seconds send American missiles toward the Soviet territory." If texts have intentions, p had the intention to say so.

The newsmen who heard p wondered whether its utterer too had the intention to say so. Asked about that, Reagan said that he was joking. He said so—as far as the *intentio operis* was concerned—but according to the *intentio auctoris* he only *pretended* to say so. According to common sense, those who believed that the sentence-meaning coincided with the intended authorial meaning were wrong.

In severely criticizing Reagan's joke, some newsmen, however, tried to make an innuendo (*intentio lectoris*) and inferred that the real intention of Reagan was to suggest nonchalantly that he was such a tough guy that, if he wanted, he could have done what he only pretended to do (also because he had the performative power of doing things with words).

This story is scarcely suitable for my purposes because it is a report about a fact, that is, about a "real" communicative intercourse during which senders and addressees had the chance of checking the discrepancies between sentence-meaning and authorial meaning. Let us suppose, then, that this was not a piece of news but a piece of fiction (told in the form "Once a man said so and so, and people believed so and so, and then that man added so and so . . . "). In this case we have lost any guarantee about the authorial intention, this author having simply become one of the characters of the narration. How to interpret this story? It can be the story of a man making a joke, the story of a man who jokes but shouldn't, the story of a man who pretends to joke but as a matter of fact is uttering a menace, the story of a tragic world where even innocent jokes can be taken seriously, the story of how the same jocular sentence can change its meaning according to the status and the role of its utterer. . . . Would we say that this story has a single sense, that it has all the senses listed above, or that only some of them can be considered as the "correct" ones?

Some years ago Derrida wrote me a letter to inform me that he and other people were establishing in Paris the Collège International de Philosophie and to ask me for a letter of support. I bet Derrida was assuming that (i) I had to assume that he was telling the truth; (ii) I had to read his program as a univocal discourse as far as both the actual situation and his project were concerned; (iii) my signature requested at the end of my letter would have been taken more seriously than Derrida's at the end of "Signature, évenement, contexte." Naturally, according to my *Erwartungshorizon*, Derrida's letter could have assumed for me many other additional meanings, even the most contradictory ones, and could have elicited many additional inferences about its "intended meaning"; nevertheless, any additional inference ought to be based on its first layer of allegedly literal meaning.

In *Grammatology* Derrida reminds his readers of the necessary function of all the instruments of traditional criticism: "Without this recognition and this respect, critical production will risk developing in any direction at all—and authorize itself to say almost anything. But this indispensable guard-rail has always only *protected,* it has never *opened* a reading" (Eng. tr., 158). I feel sympathetic with the project of opening readings, but I also feel the fundamental duty of protecting them in order to open them, since I consider it risky to open a text before having duly protected it.

Thus, returning to Reagan's story, my conclusion is that, in order to extrapolate from it any possible sense, one is first of all obliged to recognize that it had a literal sense, namely, that on a given day a man said *p* and that *p,* according to the English code, means what it intuitively means.

4. Two levels of interpretation

Before going ahead with the problem of interpretation we must first settle a terminological question. We must distinguish between *semantic* and *critical* interpretation (or, if one prefers, between *semiosic* and *semiotic* interpretation).

Semantic interpretation is the result of the process by which an addressee, facing a Linear Text Manifestation, fills it up with a given meaning. Every response-oriented approach deals first of all with this type of interpretation, which is a natural semiosic phenomenon.

Critical interpretation is, on the contrary, a metalinguistic activity—a semiotic approach—which aims at describing and explaining for which formal reasons a given text produces a given response (and in this sense it can also assume the form of an aesthetic analysis).

In this sense every text is susceptible to being both semantically and critically interpreted, but only a few texts consciously foresee both kinds of response. Ordinary sentences (such as *give me that bottle* or *the cat is on the mat* uttered by a layman), only expect a semantic response. On the contrary, aesthetic texts or the sentence *the cat is on the mat* uttered by a linguist as an example of possible semantic ambiguity also foresee a critical interpreter. Likewise, when I say that every text designs its own Model Reader, I am in fact implying that many texts aim at producing *two* Model Readers, a first level, or a naive one, supposed to understand semantically what the text says, and a second level, or critical one, supposed to appreciate the way in which the text says so. A sentence such as *they are flying planes* foresees a naive reader who keeps wondering which meaning to choose—and who supposedly looks at the textual environment or at the circumstance of utterance in order to support the best choice—and a critical reader able univocally and formally to explain the syntactic reasons that make the sentence ambiguous. Similarly, a mystery tale displays an astute narrative strategy in order to produce a naive Model Reader eager to fall into the traps of the narrator (to feel fear or to suspect the innocent one) but usually wants to produce also a critical Model Reader able to enjoy, at a second reading, the brilliant narrative strategy by which the first-level, naive reader was designed.

One could say that, while the semantic reader is planned or instructed by the verbal strategy, the critical one is such on the grounds of a mere interpretive decision—nothing in the text appearing as an explicit appeal to a second-level reading. But it must be noticed that many artistic devices, for instance, stylistic violation of the norm, or defamiliarization, seem to work exactly as self-focusing appeals: the text is made in such a way as to attract the attention of a critical reader. Moreover, there are texts that explicitly require a second-level reading. Take, for instance, Agatha Christie's *The Murder of Roger Ackroyd,* which is narrated by a character who, at the end, will be discovered by Poirot to be the murderer. After his confession, the narrator informs the readers that, if they had paid due attention, they could have understood at which precise moment he committed his crime because in some reticent way he did say it. See also my analysis of Allais's "Un drame bien parisien" (Eco 1979), where it is shown how much the text, while step by step deceiving naive readers, at the same time provides them with a lot of clues that could have prevented them from falling into the textual trap. Obviously these clues can be detected only in the course of a second reading.

Richard Rorty ("Idealism and Textualism," 1982) says that in the present century "there are people who write as if there were nothing but texts" and makes a distinction between two kinds of textualism. The first is instantiated by those who disregard the intention of the author and look in the text for a principle of internal coherence and/or for a sufficient cause for certain very precise effects it has on a presumed ideal reader. The second is instantiated by those critics who consider every reading as a misreading (the "misreaders"). For them "the critic asks neither the author nor the text about their intentions but simply beats the text into a shape which will serve his own purpose. He makes the text refer to whatever is relevant to that purpose." In this sense their model "is not the curious collector of clever gadgets taking them apart to see what makes them work and carefully ignoring any extrinsic end they may have, but the psychoanalyst blithely interpreting a dream or a joke as a symptom of homicidal mania" (151).

Rorty thinks that both positions are a form of pragmatism (pragmatism being for him the refusal to think of truth as correspondence to reality—and reality being, I assume, both the external referent of the text and the intention of its author) and suggests that the first type of theorist is a weak pragmatist because "he thinks that there really is a secret and that once it's discovered we shall have gotten the text right," so that for him "criticism is discovery rather than creation" (152). On the contrary, the strong pragmatist does not make any difference between finding and making. I agree with such a characterization, but with two qualifications.

First, in which sense does a weak pragmatist, when trying to find the secret of a text, aim at getting this text right? One has to decide whether by "getting the text right" one means a right semantic or a right critical interpretation. Those readers who, according to the Jamesian metaphor proposed by Iser (1976, ch. 1), look into a text in order to find in it "the figure in the carpet," a single unrevealed secret meaning, are—I think—looking for a sort of "concealed" semantic interpretation. But the critic looking for the "secret code" probably looks *critically* for the describable strategy that produces infinite ways to get a text semantically right. To analyze and describe the textual devices of *Ulysses* means to show how Joyce acted in order to create many alternative figures in his carpet, without deciding how many they can be and which of them are the best ones. Moreover, since—as I shall discuss later—even a critical reading is always conjectural, there can be many ways of finding out and describing the "secret code" that allows many ways of reading a text. Thus I do not think that the textualists of the first type are necessarily "weak" pragmatists, because they do not try to reduce a text to any univocal semantic reading.

Second, I suspect that many "strong" pragmatists are not pragmatists at all—at least in Rorty's sense—because the "misreader" employs a text in order to know something which stands outside the text and that is in some way more "real" than the text itself, namely, the unconscious mechanism of *la chaine significante.* In any case, even though a pragmatist, certainly the misreader is not a "textualist." Probably misreaders think, as Rorty assumes, that there is nothing but texts; however, they are interested in every possible text except the one they are reading. As a matter of fact, "strong" pragmatists are concerned only with the infinite semantic readings of the text they are beating, but I suspect that they are scarcely interested in the way it works.

5. Interpretation and use

I can accept the distinction proposed by Rorty as a convenient opposition between *interpreting* (critically) and merely *using* a text. To critically interpret a text means to read it in order to discover, along with our reactions to it, something about its nature. To use a text means to start from it in order to get something else, even accepting the risk of misinterpreting it from the semantic point of view. If I tear out the pages of my Bible to wrap my pipe tobacco in them, I am using this Bible, but it would be daring to call me a textualist—even though I am, if not a strong pragmatist, certainly a very pragmatic person. If I get sexual enjoyment from a pornographic book, I am not using it, because in order to elaborate my sexual fantasies I had to semantically interpret its sentences. On the contrary, if—let us suppose—I look into the *Elements* of Euclid to infer that their author was a scotophiliac, obsessed with abstract images, then I am using it because I renounce interpreting its definitions and theorems semantically.

The quasi-psychoanalytic reading that Derrida makes of Poe's *The Purloined Letter* in "Le facteur de la verité" (1980) represents a good critical interpretation of that story. Derrida insists that he is not analyzing the unconscious of the author but rather the unconscious of the text. He is interpreting because he respects the *intentio operis.*

When he draws an interpretation from the fact that the letter is found in a paper holder hanging from a nail under the center of a fireplace, Derrida first takes "literally" the possible world designed by the narration as well as the sense of the words used by Poe to stage this world. Then he tries to isolate a second, "symbolic" meaning that this text is conveying, probably beyond the intentions of the author. Right or wrong, Derrida supports his second-level semantic interpretation with textual evidences. In doing so he also performs a critical interpretation, because he shows how the text can produce that second-level meaning.

For contrast, let us consider the reading of Poe by Maria Bonaparte (1952). Part of her reading represents a good example of interpretation. For instance, she reads *Morella, Ligeia,* and *Eleonora* and shows that all three texts have the same underlying "fabula": a man in love with an exceptional woman who dies of consumption, so that the man swears eternal grief; but he does not keep his promise and loves another woman; finally, the dead one reappears and wraps the new one in the mantle of her funereal power. In a nontechnical way Bonaparte identifies in these three texts the same *actantial* structures, speaks of the structure of an obsession, but reads that obsession as a textual one, and in so doing reveals the *intentio operis.*

Unfortunately, such a beautiful textual analysis is interwoven with biographical remarks that connect textual evidences with aspects (known by extratextual sources) of Poe's private life. When Bonaparte says that Poe was dominated by the impression he felt as a child when he saw his mother, dead of consumption, lying on the catafalque, when she says that in his adult life and in his work he was so morbidly attracted by women with funereal features, when she reads his stories populated by living corpses in order to explain his personal necrophilia—then she is using, not interpreting, texts.

6. Interpretation and conjecture

It is clear that I am trying to keep a dialectical link between *intentio operis* and *intentio lectoris.* The problem is that, if one perhaps knows what is meant by "intention of the reader," it seems more difficult to define abstractly what is meant by "intention of the text."

The text intention is not displayed by the Linear Text Manifestation. Or, if it is displayed, it is so in the sense of the purloined letter. One has to decide to "see" it. Thus it is possible to speak of text intention only as the result of a *conjecture* on the part of the reader. The initiative of the reader basically consists in making a conjecture about the text intention.

A text is a device conceived in order to produce its Model Reader. I repeat that this reader is not the one who makes the "only right" conjecture. A text can foresee a Model Reader entitled to try infinite conjectures. The empirical reader is only an actor who makes conjectures about the kind of Model Reader postulated by the text. Since the intention of the text is basically to produce a Model Reader able to make conjectures about it, the initiative of the Model Reader consists in figuring out a Model Author that is not the empirical one and that, at the end, coincides with the intention of the text.

Thus, more than a parameter to use in order to validate the interpretation, the text is an object that the interpretation builds up in the course of the circular effort of validating itself on the basis of what it makes up as its result. I am not ashamed to admit that I am so defining the old and still valid "hermeneutic circle."

The logic of interpretation is the Peircean logic of abduction. To make a conjecture means to figure out a Law that can explain a Result. The "secret code" of a text is such a Law. One could say that in the natural sciences the conjecture has to try only the Law, since the Result is under the eyes of everybody, while in textual interpretation only the discovery of a "good" Law makes the Result acceptable. But I do not think that the difference is so clear-cut. Even in the natural sciences no fact can be taken as a significant Result without having first and vaguely decided that this fact among innumerable others can be selected as a curious Result to be explained.

To isolate a fact as a curious Result means to have already obscurely thought of a Law of which that fact could be the Result. When I start reading a text I never know, from the beginning, whether I am approaching it from the point of view of a suitable intention. My initiative starts to become exciting when I discover that my intention could meet the intention of that text.

How to prove a conjecture about the *intentio operis*? The only way is to check it against the text as a coherent whole. This idea, too, is an old one and comes from Augustine (*De doctrina christiana* 2–3): any interpretation given of a certain portion of a text can be accepted if it is confirmed and must be rejected if it is challenged by another portion of the same text. In this sense the internal textual coherence controls the otherwise uncontrollable drives of the reader.

Once Borges suggested that it would be exciting to read the *Imitation of Christ* as if it were written by Celine. The game is amusing and could be intellectually fruitful. I tried: I discovered sentences that could have been written by Celine ("Grace loves low things and is not disgusted by thorny ones, and likes filthy clothes . . . "). But this kind of reading offers a suitable "grid" for very few sentences of the *Imitatio*.

All the rest, most of the book, resists this reading. If, on the contrary I read the book according to the Christian medieval encyclopedia, it appears textually coherent in each of its parts.

Besides, no responsible deconstructionist has ever challenged such a position. J. Hillis Miller (1980:611) says that "the readings of deconstructive criticism are not the willful imposition by a subjectivity of a theory on the texts, but are coerced by the texts themselves." Elsewhere (1970:ix) he writes that "it is not true that . . . all readings are equally valid. Some readings are certainly wrong. . . . To reveal one aspect of a work of an author often means ignoring or shading other aspects. . . . Some approaches reach more deeply into the structure of the text than others."

7. The falsifiability of misinterpretations

We can thus accept a sort of Popper-like principle according to which if there are not rules that help to ascertain which interpretations are the "best ones," there is at least a rule for ascertaining which ones are "bad." This rule says that the internal coherence of a text must be taken as the parameter for its interpretations. But in order to do so, one needs, at least for a short time, a metalanguage which permits the comparison between a given text and its semantic or critical interpretations. Since any new interpretation enriches the text and the text consists in its objective Linear Text Manifestation plus the interpretations it received in the course of history, this metalanguage should also allow the comparison between a new interpretation and the old ones.

I understand that from the point of view of a radical deconstruction theory such an assumption can sound unpleasantly neopositivistic, and that every notion of deconstruction and drift challenges the very possibility of a metalanguage. But a metalanguage does not have to be different from (and more powerful than) ordinary language. The idea of interpretation requires that a "piece" of ordinary language be used as the "interpretant" (in the Peircean sense) of another "piece" of ordinary language. When one says that /man/ means "human male adult," one is interpreting ordinary language through ordinary language, and the second sign is the interpretant of the first one, as well as the first can become the interpretant of the second. The metalanguage of interpretation is not different from its object language. It is a portion of the same language, and in this sense to interpret is a function that every language performs when it speaks of itself.

It is not the case of asking if this can be done. We are doing it, every day. The provocative self-evidence of my last argument suggests that we can prove it only by showing that any of its alternatives is self-contradictory.

Let us suppose that there is a theory that *literally* (not metaphorically) asserts that every interpretation is a misinterpretation. Let us suppose that there are two texts, Alpha and Beta, and that Alpha has been proposed to a reader in order to elicit the textually recorded misinterpretation Sigma. Take a literate subject X, previously informed that any interpretation must be a misinterpretation, and give him or her the three texts Alpha, Beta, and Sigma. Ask X if Sigma misinterprets Alpha or Beta. Supposing that X says that Sigma is a misinterpretation of Alpha, would we say that X is right? Supposing, on the contrary, that X says that Sigma is a misinterpretation of Beta, would we say that X is wrong?

In both cases, to approve or to disprove X's answer means to believe not only that a text controls and selects its own interpretations but also that it controls and selects its own misinterpretations. The one approving or disproving X's answers would then act as one who does not really believe that every interpretation is a misinterpretation, since he or she would use the original text as a parameter for discriminating between texts that misinterpret it and texts that misinterpret something else. Any approval or disproval of X's answer would presuppose (i) a previous interpretation of Alpha, which should be considered the only correct one, and (ii) a metalanguage which describes and shows on which grounds Sigma is or is not a misinterpretation of it. It would be embarrassing to maintain that a text elicits only misinterpretation except when it is correctly interpreted by the warrant of other readers' misinterpretations. But it is exactly what happens with a radical theory of misinterpretation.

There is another way to escape the contradiction. One should assume that every answer of X is the good one. Sigma can be indifferently the misinterpretation of Alpha, of Beta, and of any other possible text. But at this point, why define Sigma (which is undoubtedly a text in its own right) as the misinterpretation of something else? If it is the misinterpretation of everything, it then is the misinterpretation of nothing. It exists for its own sake and does not need to be compared with any other text.

The solution is elegant, but it produces a small inconvenience. It destroys definitely the very category of textual interpretation. There are texts, but of these nobody can speak. Or, if one speaks, nobody can say what one says. Texts, at most, are used as stimuli to produce other texts, but once a new text is produced, it cannot be referred to its stimulus.

8. Conclusions

To defend the rights of interpretation against the mere use of a text does not mean that texts must never be used. We are using texts every day and we need to do so, for many respectable reasons. It is only important to distinguish use from interpretation. A critical reader could also say why certain texts have been used in a certain way, finding in their structure the reasons for their use or misuse. In this sense a sociological analysis of the free uses of texts can support a further interpretation of them.

In any case, use and interpretation are abstract theoretical possibilities. Every empirical reading is always an unpredictable mixture of both. It can happen that a play started as use ends by producing a fruitful new interpretation—or vice versa. Sometimes to use texts means to free them from previous interpretations, to discover new aspects of them, to realize that before they had been illicitly interpreted, to find out a new and more explicative *intentio operis,* that too many uncontrolled intentions of the readers (perhaps disguised as a faithful quest for the intention of the author) had polluted and obscured.

There is also a *pretextual* reading, performed not in order to interpret the text but to show how much language can produce unlimited semiosis. Such a pretextual reading has a philosophical function: "Deconstruction does not consist in moving from one concept to another, but in reversing and displacing a conceptual order as well as the non-conceptual order with which it is articulated" (Derrida 1972: Eng. tr., 195).

I think that there is a difference between such a philosophical practice and the decision to take it as a model for literary criticism and for a new trend in textual interpretation. In some of these cases texts are *used* rather than *interpreted.* But I confess that it is frequently very hard to distinguish between use and interpretation. Some of the chapters of this book deal with such a problem, trying to check with concrete examples whether there are, and to what extent, limits of interpretation.

NOTES

1. In the framework of analytic philosophy, the first and still fundamental appeal for an encyclopedia-oriented approach came from Quine 1951 ("Two Dogmas of Empiricism").

2. I realize now that my idea of a system of expectations, even though built on the grounds of other theoretical influences, was not so dissimilar from Jauss's notion of *Erwartungshorizon*.

3. English-language readers can now see the essays of *Opera aperta,* recently translated as *The Open Work* (Cambridge: Harvard University Press, 1989). In the English edition there is also an essay in which I revisit the theory of interpretation of Luigi Pareyson.

4

Small Worlds

1. Fictional worlds

It seems a matter of common sense to say that in the fictional world conceived by Shakespeare it is true that Hamlet was a bachelor and it is false that he was married. Philosophers ready to object that fictional sentences lack reference and are thereby false—or that both the statements about Hamlet would have the same truth value (Russell 1919:169)—do not take into account the fact that there are persons gambling away their future on the grounds of the recognized falsity or truth of similar statements. Any student asserting that Hamlet was married to Ophelia would fail in English, and nobody could reasonably criticize his/her teacher for having relied on such a reasonable notion of truth.

In order to reconcile common sense with the rights of alethic logic, many theories of fiction have borrowed the notion of Possible World from modal logic. It sounds correct to say that in the fictional world invented by Robert Louis Stevenson, Long John Silver (i) entertains a series of hopes and strong beliefs and thus outlines a doxastic world where he succeeds in putting his hands (or his only foot) on the coveted treasure of the eponymous Island and (ii) performs many deeds in order to make the future course of events in the real world match the state of his doxastic one.

This chapter is a reelaboration of my Report 3 at the Nobel Symposium 65 on Possible Worlds in Humanities, Arts and Sciences, Lidings, August 1986.

Nevertheless, one might suspect that

(i) the notion of Possible World extolled by a Possible Worlds Semantics or Model Theory of Possible Worlds has nothing in common with the homonymous notion extolled by the various theories of fiction and narrativity;

(ii) independent of the above question, the notion of Possible World does not add anything interesting to the understanding of fictional phenomena.[1]

2. Empty vs. furnished worlds

In a Model Theory, Possible Worlds concern sets, not individuals, and a Possible Worlds Semantics cannot be a psycholinguistically realistic theory of language understanding: "It is the structure provided by the possible worlds theory that does the work, not the choice of a particular possible world, if the latter makes sense at all" (Partee 1988:118). "A semantical game is not played on a single model, but on a space of models on which suitable alternativeness relations are defined" (Hintikka 1988:58). The possible worlds of a Model Theory must be *empty*. They are simply advocated for the sake of a formal calculus considering intensions as functions from possible worlds to extensions.

On the contrary, it seems evident that in the framework of a narrative analysis, either one considers given *furnished* and nonempty worlds or there will be no difference between a fiction theory and a logic of counterfactuals.[2]

However, there is something in common between the worlds of Possible Worlds Semantics and the worlds of a fiction theory. From its very beginning, the notion of possible world as dealt with by Model Theory is a metaphor coming from literature (in the sense that every world dreamed of, or resulting from a counterfactual, is a fictional world). A possible world is what a complete novel describes (Hintikka 1967 and 1969). Moreover, every time the Model Theory furnishes an example of possible world it gives it under the form of an individual furnished world or of a portion of it (if Caesar did not cross the Rubicon . . .).

According to Hintikka (1988:54ff), in a Model Theory possible worlds are instruments of a *language of calculus,* which is independent of the object language it describes, while they could not be used within the framework of a *language as universal medium,* which can only speak about itself. On the contrary, in a theory of fiction possible worlds are states of affairs which are described in terms of the same language as their narrative object. However (as proposed in Eco 1979), these descriptions can be analogically translated into world-matrices that, without permitting any calculus, provide the possibility of comparing different states of affairs *under a certain description* and making clear whether they can be mutually accessible or not and in which way they differ. Doležel (1988:228ff) has persuasively demonstrated that a theory of fictional objects can become more fruitful if it abandons a one-world model in order to adopt a possible worlds frame.

Thus, even though a theory of fiction will not emerge from a mechanical appropriation of the conceptual system of a Possible Worlds Semantics, such a theory has some right to exist. Let us say that the notion of possible world in a theory of fiction must concern furnished worlds in terms of the following features:

A fictional possible world is a series of linguistic descriptions that readers are supposed to interpret as referring to a possible state of affairs where if p is true then non-p is false (such a requirement being flexible since there also are, as we shall see, impossible possible worlds).

This state of affairs is made up of individuals endowed with properties.

These properties are ruled by certain laws, so that certain properties can be mutually contradictory and a given property x can entail the property y.

Since individuals can have the property of doing so, they undergo changes, lose or acquire new properties (in this sense a possible world is also a course of events and can be described as a temporally ordered succession of states).

Possible worlds can be viewed either as "real" states of affairs (see, for instance, the realistic approach in Lewis 1980) or as cultural constructs, matter of stipulation or semiotic products. I shall follow the second hypothesis, according to the perspective outlined in Eco 1979. Being a cultural construct, a possible world cannot be identified with the Linear Text Manifestation that describes it. The text describing such a state or course of events is a linguistic strategy which is supposed to trigger an interpretation on the part of the Model Reader. This interpretation (however expressed) represents the possible world outlined in the course of the cooperative interaction between the text and the Model Reader.

In order to compare worlds, one must take even the real or actual world as a cultural construct. The so-called actual world is the world to which we refer—rightly or wrongly—as the world described by the *Encyclopedia Britannica* or *Time* magazine (a world in which Napoleon died on St. Helena, two plus two equals four, it is impossible to be the father of oneself, and Sherlock Holmes never existed—if not as a fictional character). The actual world is the one we know through a multitude of world pictures or stated descriptions, and these pictures are epistemic worlds that are frequently mutually exclusive. The whole of the pictures of the actual world is the potentially maximal and complete encyclopedia of it (on the purely regulative nature of such a potential encyclopedia, see Eco 1979 and 1984). "Possible worlds are not discovered in some remote, invisible or transcendent depositories, they are *constructed* by human minds and hands. This explanation has been explicitly given by Kripke: 'One stipulates possible worlds, one does not discover them by powerful microscopes' " (Doležel 1988:236).

Even though the real world is considered a cultural construct, one might still wonder about the ontological status of the described universe. Such a problem does not exist for narrative possible worlds. Being outlined by a text, they exist outside the text only as the result of an interpretation and have the same ontological status of any other doxastic world (on the cultural nature of any world, see the recent remarks of Goodman and Elgin 1988, ch. 3).

Hintikka (1988:55), speaking of possible worlds as considered in a Model Theory, said that in describing a possible world we are free to choose the universe of discourse it is designed to apply to. Thus possible worlds are always *small worlds,* "that is, a relatively short course of local events in some nook or corner of the actual world." The same holds for fictional worlds: in order to lead its readers to conceive of a possible fictional world, a text must invite them to a relatively easy "cosmological" task—as we shall see in the following sections, mainly in sections 5 and 6.

3. Technical vs. metaphorical approach

The notion of furnished possible worlds proves to be useful in dealing with many phenomena concerning artistic creation. Nevertheless, it should not be misused. There are cases in which to speak of possible worlds is mere metaphor.

When Keats says that Beauty is Truth and Truth is Beauty, he only expresses his personal view of the actual world. We can simply say that he is right or wrong, but we need to deal with his world view in terms of possible worlds only if we must compare it with the ideas of Saint Bernard, who believed that in this world Divine Beauty was True while the Artistic one was mendacious.

Even in this case, however, I would speak of two theoretical models set up in order to explain the actual world. The *entia rationis* and the cultural constructs used in science and philosophy are not possible worlds. One can say that square roots, *universalia,* or *modus ponens* belong to a Third World à la Popper, but a Third World (if any), even if one takes it as a Platonic Ideal Realm, is not a "possible" one. It is as real and perhaps more real than the empirical one.

Euclidean geometry does not portray a possible world. It is an abstract portrait of the actual one. It can become the portrait of a possible world only if we take it as the portrait of Abbott's Flatland.

Possible worlds are cultural constructs but not every cultural construct is a possible world. For instance, in trying out a scientific hypothesis—in the sense of Peirce's abductions—we figure out possible Laws that, if they held, could explain many inexplicable phenomena. But these adventures of our mind have as their sole aim to prove that the "imagined" Law also holds in the "real" world—or in the world we construct as the real one. Possibility is a means, not an end in itself. We explore the plurality of *possibilia* to find a suitable model for *realia*.

Likewise, I do not think that metaphors outline possible worlds (as is assumed, for instance, by Levin 1979:124ff). In its simplest form, a metaphor is a shortened simile: "Tom is a lion" means that Tom, under a certain description, has some of the properties of a lion (say, force and courage). Naturally, if one takes this metaphor literally there is a case of infelicitous communication or at least of semantic inconsistency, since it is impossible—in the actual world—to be at the same time human and beast. But if we take it as a figure of speech and interpret it consequently, then it tells something that cannot be challenged from the point of view of our world knowledge: it tells that *in the actual world* Tom has (allegedly) these properties. This metaphor, once disambiguated, can appear as a false statement about the actual world (someone can deny that Tom is truly courageous) but not as a true statement about a possible world. If, on the contrary, I say that in Homer's world Achilles is a lion, I tell something true in Homer's world, while leaving unprejudiced whether this is true or not in the world of historical, if any, experience. Even the most obscure metaphor does not outline an alternative world: it simply obscurely suggests that one should see certain individuals of the reference world as characterized by unheard-of properties.

It is useful to use the notion of possible world when one refers to a state of affairs, but only if one needs to compare at least two alternative states of affairs. If one says that Donald Duck is an invention by Disney and that we have few chances to meet him on Sunset Boulevard, one certainly says that Donald Duck belongs to a world of fantasy, but no specific Possible Worlds Theory is requested in order to discover or to prove such a triviality. If, on the contrary, one analyzes a very peculiar movie as *Who Framed Roger Rabbit?* in which cartoons interact with allegedly "real" characters, then problems of mutual accessibility between different worlds can be legitimately debated.

If Tom says that he hopes to buy a big boat, his sentence expresses a propositional attitude that, as such, outlines the possible world of

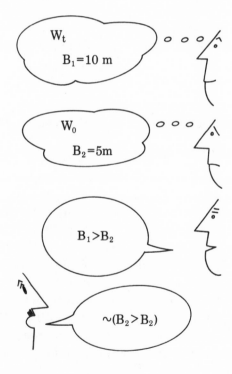

Figure 4.1

Tom's fancies; but we need a notion of possible world only if we must compare at least two propositional attitudes. Let me quote a famous silly dialogue (mentioned in Russell 1905):

Tom (looking for the first time at John's boat): I believed that your boat was bigger than that.
John: No, my boat is not bigger than that.

The whole modal conundrum can be easily explained as shown here (figure 4.1). Tom, in the world Wt of his imagination, thinks that John's boat B1 is, let us say, ten meters long. Then Tom, in the actual world Wo of his experience, sees the real boat B2 and remarks that it is five meters long. Subsequently, he compares the B1 of his doxastic world to the B2 of his real world and remarks that B1 was bigger than B2.

John, who has never studied modal logic, mixes the worlds up and deals with B1 and B2 as if both belonged to the same Wo. In this case a notion of possible world proves to be useful to explain a conversational ambiguity that depends on a cognitive difficulty.

4. Why possible worlds are useful for a theory of fiction

If the exchange between Tom and John were recounted as a funny piece of fiction, its treatment in terms of possible worlds would explain why the story sounds amusing: it stages the interaction between two individuals one of which is unable to discriminate between incompatible worlds.

Suppose that John and Tom live in a very simple world endowed only with a couple of properties, namely, Boat (scored as M, or Marine Vehicle) and Big. We can decide that, under a certain description, certain properties are essential and others accidental. In order to define a property as textually essential, Hintikka (1969) said that if I speak of a man I saw without being sure whether he was Tom or John, this man will be the same in every possible world since it is essentially the man I saw.

From this point of view (and freely using suggestions from Rescher 1973), our story of John's boat can be represented as follows (where Wt is the world of Tom's beliefs and Wj the world in which both Tom and John live and perceive the actual John's boat):

Wt	M	B
x	(+)	+

Wj	M	B
y	(+)	−

Given two worlds Wt and Wj where the same properties hold, we can say that x in Wt is a possible counterpart of y in Wj because both share the same essential properties (scored within parentheses). The two worlds are mutually accessible.

Suppose now that John and Tom interact this way:

> *Tom:* I thought that the big thing you
>   dreamed of was your boat.
> *John:* No, it was not a boat.

In this case the world matrices will be the following (where D = the object of a dream):

Wt	D	M	B
x1	(+)	(+)	+

Wj	D	M	B
x2	(+)	(−)	+
y	−	(+)	−

In Tom's doxastic world Wt there is an xl, which is the supposed subject matter of John's dreams and which is a big boat. In John's doxastic world there are two things, namely, a small boat y, which never obsessed his dreams, and a big thing x2, which was the subject of his dream and which unfortunately is not a boat. X1, x2 and y will be reciprocally supernumeraries (different individuals); there would not be cross-identity, but these two worlds would equally be mutually accessible. By manipulating the Wt matrix, it is possible to design both x2 and y, and by manipulating Wj matrix it is possible to design x1. We can say that either world is "conceivable" from the point of view of the alternative one.

Suppose now that in Wt the property Red holds (while John is a Daltonist and cannot discriminate colors), and suppose that the dialogue sounds like this:

> *Tom:* I have seen your boats. I want to
>   buy the red one.
> *John:* Which one?

For Tom, Red is—in that context—an essential property of x1. Tom wants to buy only red boats. John cannot conceive of Tom's world in the same way as the inhabitants of Flatland cannot conceive of a sphere. John distinguishes his boats only according to their size, not to their color:

Wt	M	B	R
x1	(+)	+	(+)
x2	(+)	−	(−)

Wj	M	B
y1	(+)	+
y2	(+)	−

John cannot conceive of Tom's world, but Tom can conceive of John's Wj as a world in which—in terms of Wt matrix—colors remain undecided. Both y1 and y2 can be designed in Wt as

Wt	M	B	R
y1	(+)	+	?
y2	(+)	−	?

In analyzing fiction one must frequently decide in which sense—on the grounds of our knowledge of the actual world—we can evaluate individuals and events of imaginary worlds (differences between romance and novel, realism and fantasy, whether the Napoleon of Tolstoy is identical with or different from the historical one, and so on).

Since in every state of a story things can go on in different ways, the pragmatics of reading is based on our ability to make forecasts at every narrative disjunction. Take the paramount case of criminal stories where the author wants to elicit false forecasts on the part of the readers in order to frustrate them.

We are also interested in validating true statements about fictions. To say that it is true that—in the world designed by Conan Doyle—Sherlock Holmes was a bachelor is not only interesting for trivia games: it can become important and relevant when one is challenging irresponsible cases of so-called deconstruction or free misreading. A fictional text has an ontology of its own which must be respected.

There is another reason why the comparison between worlds can become important in fiction. Many fictional texts are systems of embedded doxastic worlds. Suppose that in a novel the author says that p, then adds that Tom believes that non-p and that John believes that Tom erroneously believes that p. The reader must decide to what extent these various propositional attitudes are mutually compatible and accessible.

In order to clarify this point, we must understand that fictional necessity differs from logical necessity. Fictional necessity is an individuation principle. If John is fictionally the son of Tom, John must always be isolated as the son of Tom, and Tom as the father of John. In Eco 1979 I called this kind of necessity an S-property, that is, a property which is necessary inside a given possible world by virtue of the mutual definition of the individuals in play. In German the meaning of *Holz* is determined by its structural borderlines with the meaning of *Wald;* in the narrative world Wn of *Madame Bovary* there is no other way to identify Emma than as the wife of Charles, who in turn has been identified as the boy seen by the Narrator at the beginning of the novel. Any other world in which Madame Bovary were the wife of the baldest King of France would be another (non-Flaubertian) world, furnished with different individuals. Therefore, the S-property characterizing Emma is the relation eMc (where e = Emma, c = Charles and M = to be married with).

To see all the consequences we can draw from this approach, let us consider the two worlds dominating Sophocles's *Oedipus Rex;* the Wo of the beliefs of Oedipus and the Wf of the knowledge of Tyresias, who knew the *fabula*—the *fabula* being taken by Sophocles as the report on the real course of events. Let us consider the following relations K = killer of; S = son of; M = husband of. For the sake of economy the minus sign scores the inverse relation (victim of, parent of, wife of):

Wo	oKx	yKl	zSj	zSl	oMj		Wf	oKl	oSl	oSj	oMj
o	+				+		o	+	+	+	+
l		−		−			l	−	−		
j			−		−		j			−	−
x	−										
y		+									
z			+	+							

In Wo there is Oedipus, who killed an unknown wayfarer x and who married Jocasta; Laius, who was killed by an unknown wayfarer y and who was the father of a lost z; Jocasta, who was the mother of a lost z and who is presently the wife of Oedipus. In Wf x, z, and y have disappeared. The actual world described by the *fabula* (validated by Sophocles) displays—alas—fewer individuals than the illusory world of Oedipus's beliefs. But since in both fictional worlds individuals are characterized by different relational (S-necessary) properties, there is no possible identity between the merely homonymous individuals of the two worlds.

Oedipus Rex is the story of a tragic inaccessibility. Oedipus blinds himself because he was unable to see that he was living a world that was not accessible to and from the real one. In order to understand his tragedy, the Model Reader is supposed to reconstruct the *fabula* (the story, what really happened) as a temporally ordered course of events and—at the same time—to outline the different worlds represented by the diagrams above.

The notion of possible world is useful for a theory of fiction because it helps to decide in which sense a fictional character cannot communicate with his or her counterparts in the actual world. Such a problem is not as whimsical as it seems. Oedipus cannot conceive of the world of Sophocles—otherwise he would have not married his mother. Fictional characters live in a *handicapped* world. When we really understand their fate, then we start to suspect that we too, as citizens of the actual world, frequently undergo our destiny just because we think of our world in the same way as the fictional characters think of their own. Fiction suggests that perhaps our view of the actual world is as imperfect as that of fictional characters. This is the way successful fictional characters become paramount examples of the "real" human condition.

5. Small worlds

According to Doležel (1988:233ff), fictional worlds are *incomplete* and *semantically unhomogeneous:* they are handicapped and *small* worlds.

Insofar as it is handicapped, a fictional world is not a maximal and complete state of affairs. In the real world if "John lives in Paris" is true, it is also true that John lives in the capital of France, that he lives north of Milan and south of Stockholm, and that he lives in the city whose first bishop was Saint Denis. Such a series of requirements do not hold for doxastic worlds. If it is true that John believes that Tom lives in Paris, this does not mean that John believes that Tom lives north of Milan.

Fictional worlds are as incomplete as the doxastic ones. At the beginning of Pohl and Kornbluth's *The Space Merchants* (see Delaney 1980), we read:

"I rubbed the depilatory soap over my face and rinsed it with the trickle from the fresh-water tap."

In a sentence referring to the real world, one would feel *fresh* as a redundancy since usually faucets are freshwater faucets. So far as one suspects that this sentence is describing a fictional world, one understands that it is providing indirect information about a certain world where in the normal wash bowls the tap of fresh water is opposed to the tap of salt water (while in our world the opposition is cold-hot). Even though the story did not continue providing further information, the readers would be eager to infer that the story in question deals with an SF world where there is a shortage of fresh water.

However, until the novel gives further information, we are bound to think that both fresh and salt water are H_2O. In this sense it seems that fictional worlds are parasitical worlds because, if alternative properties are not spelled out, we take for granted the properties holding in the real world.

6. Requirements for setting up small worlds

In order to outline a fictional world in which many things must be taken for granted and many others must be accepted even though scarcely credible, a text seems to tell its Model Reader: "Trust me. Do not be too subtle and take what I tell you as if it were true." In this sense a fictional text has a performative nature: "A non-actualized possible state of affairs becomes a fictional existent by being authenticated in a felicitously uttered literary speech act" (Doležel 1988:237). Such an authentication assumes usually the form of an invitation to cooperate in setting up a *conceivable* world at the cost of a certain flexibility or superficiality.

There are differences between possible, credible, verisimilar, and conceivable worlds. Barbara Hall Partee (1988:118) suggests that conceivable worlds are not the same as possible worlds: some conceivable states of affairs may in fact be impossible, and some possible worlds may be beyond our powers of conception. Let us consider a series of cases:

(i) There are possible worlds that look *verisimilar* and credible, and we can conceive of them. For instance, I can conceive of a future world where this paper can be translated into Finnish, and I can conceive of a past world where Lord Trelawney and Doctor Livesey really sailed with Captain Smollett to find Treasure Island.

(ii) There are possible worlds that sound *nonverisimilar* and scarcely credible from the point of view of our actual experience, for instance, worlds in which animals speak. However, I can conceive of such worlds by flexibly readjusting the experience of the world I live in: it is sufficient to imagine that animals can have humanlike phonatory organs and a more complex brain structure. This kind of cooperation requests flexibility and superficiality: in order scientifically to conceive of animals with different physiological features I should reconsider the whole course of evolution, thus conceiving of a vast quantity of different biological laws—what I certainly do not do when reading *Little Red Riding Hood*. In order to accept the fact that a wolf speaks to a girl, I conceive of a local, nonhomogeneous small world. I act as a nearsighted observer able to isolate big shapes but unable to analyze their background. I can do so because I am used to doing the same in the world of my actual experience: I speak and I accept as conceivable the fact that I can speak but—due to the social division of semantic labor—I take for granted that there are evolutionary reasons of this phenomenon without knowing them. In the same way I can conceive of worlds which—under a more severe inquiry—should appear as incredible and nonverisimilar.

(iii) There are *inconceivable worlds* that—however possible or impossible they may be—are in any case beyond our powers of conception, because their alleged individuals or properties violate our logical or epistemological habits. We cannot conceive of worlds furnished with square circles that can be bought for an amount of dollars corresponding to the highest even number. However, as evident in the lines above, such a world can be *mentioned* (the reason why it can be mentioned, that is, the reason why language can name nonexistent and inconceivable entities, cannot be discussed here). In similar cases the Model Reader is requested to display exaggeratedly generous flexibility and superficiality, since he or she is supposed to take for granted something he or she cannot even conceive of. The difference between taking for mentioned and taking for conceivable can probably help to trace borderlines between romance and novel, fantasy and realism.

(iv) Inconceivable worlds are probably an extreme instance of *impossible possible worlds,* that is, worlds that the Model Reader is led to conceive of just to understand that it is impossible to do so. Doležel (1988:238ff) speaks to this apropos of *self-voiding texts* and *self-disclosing metafiction.*

   In such cases "on the one hand, possible entities seem to be brought into fictional existence since conventional authentication procedures are applied; on the other hand, the status of this existence is made dubious because the very foundation of the authenticating mechanism is undermined." These impossible fictional worlds include inner contradictions. Doležel makes the example of Robbe-Grillet's *La maison de rendez-vous,* where one and the same event is introduced in several conflicting versions, one and the same place is and is not the setting of the novel, events are ordered in contradictory temporal sequences, one and the same fictional entity recurs in several existential modes, and so on.

To understand better how self-disclosing metafiction works, one should consider the distinction between *semantic* and *critical* interpretation (see above, ch. 3, "*Intentio lectoris*"). Semantic interpretation is the result of the process by which the reader, facing a Linear Text Manifestation, fills it up with a given meaning. Critical interpretation is, on the contrary, a metalinguistic activity which aims at describing and explaining for which formal reasons a given text produces a given response.

In this sense every text is susceptible to being both semantically and critically interpreted, but only few texts consciously foresee both kinds of Model Reader. Many pieces of fiction (for instance, novels of detection) display an astute narrative strategy in order to produce a naive Model Reader eager to fall into the traps of the narrator (to feel fear or to suspect the innocent one) but usually also foresee a critical Model Reader able to enjoy, at a second reading, the brilliant narrative strategy by which the first-level naive reader has been designed (see above, ch. 3, section 4).

The same happens with self-voiding fiction. At a first interpretive level, it gives at the same time both the illusion of a coherent world and the feeling of some inexplicable impossibility. At a second interpretive level (the critical one), the text can be understood in its self-voiding nature.

A visual instance of an impossible possible world is the famous drawing by Penrose (an archetype for many pictorial *impossibilia* such as Escher's engravings). At a very superficial glance this figure looks "possible," but, if we follow its lines according to their spatially oriented course, we realize that it cannot work: a world where such an object could exist is perhaps possible but surely beyond our powers of conception, however flexible and superficial we can decide to be. The pleasure we draw from impossible possible worlds is the pleasure of our logical and perceptual defeat—or the pleasure of a "self-disclosing" text which speaks of its own inability to describe *impossibilia* (on this matter, see also Danto 1988; and Régnier 1988).

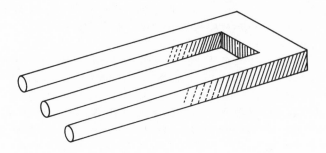

Figure 4.2

An impossible world is presented by a discourse which shows why a story is impossible. An impossible possible world does not merely mention something inconceivable. It builds up the very conditions of its own inconceivability. Both Penrose's figure and Robbe-Grillet's novel are materially possible *qua* visual or verbal texts, but they seem to refer to something that cannot be.

There is a difference between visual and verbal impossible possible worlds, due to different strategies in the cooperative appeal implemented by the Linear Text Manifestation. A visual illusion is a short-term process, since visual signs are spatially displayed all together— while with verbal language the temporal (or spatial) linearity of the signifiers makes the recognition of inconsistency more difficult. Being immediately perceived as a whole, Penrose's figure encourages an immediate, more analytical scanning, so that its inconsistency can be suddenly detected. On the contrary, in a verbal text, the linear and temporally ordered (step by step) scanning makes more difficult a global analysis of the whole text—that requires an interplay of long- and short-term memory. Thus in verbal texts the representation of impossible possible worlds can be taken superficially as conceivable for pages and pages before the contradiction they display is realized. To render more and more puzzling such a feeling of imbalance, these texts can use several syntactic strategies.

As an example of long-term illusion (and of the linguistic strategy that makes it possible), let me quote a typical SF situation, instantiated by many novels—and recently borrowed by a movie, *Back to the Future.*

Suppose a story where a narrative character (let us call him Tom1) travels into the future, where he arrives as Tom2, and then travels backward in time, coming back to the present as Tom3, ten minutes before his former departure. Here Tom3 can meet Tom1, who is on the verge of leaving. At this point Tom3 travels again to the future, arrives there as Tom4 a few minutes after the former arrival of Tom2, and meets him.

If we transform the story into a visual diagram (figure 4.3), it will be similar to a Penrose drawing. It is impossible to accept a situation where the same character splits into four different Toms. But in the course of the narrative discourse the contradiction disappears because of a simple linguistic trick: the Tom who says "I" is always the one with the higher exponent. When this story becomes a movie—temporally organized like the verbal tale—we always see the situation from the point of view of the "higher" Tom. Only through such linguistic and cinematic machinery does a text partially conceal the conditions of its referential impossibility.

Figure 4.3

Self-disclosing metafiction shows how impossible worlds are impossible. SF, on the contrary, sets up impossible worlds that give the illusion of being conceivable.

7. Cooperative good will

Up to now, flexibility and superficiality looked like cooperative qualities required for setting up scarcely credible states of affairs. However, in light of the remarks above, we should say that a certain flexibility is always requested also for verisimilar and credible states of affairs.

As a matter of fact, even when invited to outline a very small world, the Model Reader is never provided with satisfactory information. Even when invited to extrapolate from an alleged experience of our actual world, such an experience is frequently simply postulated.[3]

Let us start reading a novel (by a mere chance I have chosen Ann Radcliffe's *The Mysteries of Udolpho,* 1794):

> On the pleasant banks of the Garonne, in the province of Gascony, stood, in the year 1584, the chateau of Monsieur St. Aubert. From its windows were seen the pastoral landscapes of Guienne and Gascony stretching along the river, gay with luxuriant woods and vine, and plantations of olives.

It is doubtful whether an English reader of the late eighteenth century knew enough about Garonne, Gascony, and the corresponding landscape. However, even an uninformed reader was able to infer from the lexeme *banks* that Garonne is a river. Probably the Model Reader was supposed to figure out a typical southern European environment with vines and olives, but it is uncertain whether a reader living in London, who had never left Great Britain, was able to conceive of such a pale-green and blue landscape. It does not matter. The Model Reader of Radcliffe was invited to pretend to know all this. The Model Reader was and is invited to behave as if he or she were familiar with French hills. Probably the world he or she outlines is different from the one Ann Radcliffe had in mind when writing, but this does not matter. For the purposes of the story, every cliché-like conception of a French landscape can work.

Fictional worlds are the only ones in which sometimes a theory of rigid designation holds completely. If the narrator says that there was a place called Treasure Island, the Model Reader is invited to trust a mysterious baptismal chain by virtue of which someone christened a given individual island by that name. For the rest, the Reader is invited to assign to that Island all the standard properties he or she would be eager to assign to any South Seas island, and for the purposes of the narration this would be sufficient.

I have said above that in a narrative text Emma Bovary can be identified only by S-necessary properties, that is, by the fact that she was the wife of the only individual mentioned by the narrator at the beginning of the novel. But these S-properties are very feeble.

Let us analyze the following passage from Hugo's *Quatrevingt-treize.* The Marquis de Lantenac is sending his sailor Halmalo to alert all the followers of the antirevolutionary uprising. He is giving Halmalo the following instructions:

> "Now listen. Do you know the woods?"
> "All of them."
> "Of the whole district?"
> "From Noirmoutier to Laval."
> "Do you know their names too?"
> "I know the woods; I know their names, I know about everything."
>   . . . .
> "Listen well to this. This is the order: Up! Revolt! No quarter! On the edge of this wood of Saint-Aubin you will give the call. You will repeat it thrice. The third time you will see a man spring out of the ground."
> "Out of a hole under the trees. I know."
> "This man will be Planchenault, who is also called the King's Heart. You will show him this knot. He will understand. Then, by routes you must find out, you will go to the wood of Astillé: there you will find a cripple, who is surnamed Mousqueton, and who shows pity to none. You will tell him I love him, and that he is to set the parishes in motion. From there you will go to the wood of Couesbon, which is a league from Ploërmel. You will give the owl-cry; a man will come out of a hole; he will be Thuault, seneschal of Ploërmel, who has belonged to what is called the Constituent Assembly, but on the good side. You will tell him to arm the castle of Couesbon, which belongs to the Marquis de Guer, a refugee. Ravines, little woods, ground uneven—a good place. Thuault is a clever, straightforward man. Thence you will go to Saint-Guen-les-Toits, and you will talk with Jean Chouan, who is, in my mind, the real chief. From there you will go to the wood of Ville-Anglose, where you will see Guitter, whom they call Saint-Martin: you will bid him have his eye on a certain Courmesnil, who is the son-in-law of old Goupil de Préfelu. . . . "

The list continues for several pages. Obviously, Hugo was not interested in describing definite places and persons but only in suggesting the size and complexity of the antirevolutionary network. The Reader is not supposed to know anything about the location of the forest of Saint-Aubin or about the life of Planchenault; otherwise the whole *Encyclopedie Larousse* would not be sufficient to understand what happens in Hugo's novel. The Reader is supposed to take all these names as mere rigid designators referring to imprecise baptismal ceremonies. The reader willing to replace each of them with a description could only use such expressions as "a place in Northern France" or "an individual known by Lantenac".

The Model Reader does not have to figure out each place and individual mentioned by the novel. It is sufficient he or she *pretends to believe to know them.* The Model Reader is not only required to display an enormous flexibility and superficiality, he or she is also required to display a consistent *good will*.

If the Model Reader behaves so, he/she will enjoy the story. Otherwise he/she will be condemned to an everlasting encyclopedic research. It can happen that there exist readers wondering how many inhabitants Saint-Guen-les-Toits could have had, or what the name of Charles Bovary's grandfather was. But such fussy readers would not be the Model ones. They are craving for maximal worlds, while fiction can survive only by playing on Small Worlds.

NOTES

1. Such were the topics of the Nobel Symposium on Possible Worlds in Humanities, Arts and Sciences held in Lidingo, on the outskirts of Stockholm, in August 1986 (Allen 1989), where epistemologists, historians of science, logicians, analytic philosophers, semioticians, linguists, narratologists, critics, artists, and scientists met to discuss such a point. My present reflections depend on many of the papers presented at the symposium and on the following discussion.

2. The best solution would be to consider the possible worlds of a fiction theory simply as linguistic objects, that is, descriptions of states and events that are the case in a given narrative context. In this sense, however, one should accept the objection raised by Partee (1988:94, 158) apropos of Carnap's state descriptions: being sets of sentences they are not possible worlds because possible worlds "are part of the model structures in terms of which languages are interpreted"; possible worlds are alternative ways things might have been and not descriptions of these ways. Otherwise, to say that a narrative text outlines one or more possible worlds would be only a more sophisticated way of saying that every narrative text tells stories about unreal events.

3. I owe this suggestion to Bas van Fraassen, personal communication on *The Role of the Reader*.

5

Interpreting Serials

1. Introduction

Modern aesthetics and modern theories of art (and by "modern" I mean those born with Mannerism, developed through Romanticism, and provocatively restated by the early-twentieth-century avant-gardes) have frequently identified the artistic value with novelty and high information. The pleasurable repetition of an already known pattern was considered typical of Crafts—not Art—and industry.

A good craftsman, as well as an industrial factory, produces many tokens, or occurrences of the same type or model. One appreciates the type, and appreciates the way the token meets the requirements of the type; but the modern aesthetics did not recognize such a procedure as an artistic one. That is why the Romantic aesthetics made such a careful distinction between "major" and "minor" arts, arts and crafts. To draw a parallel with sciences, crafts and industry were similar to the correct application of an already known law to a new case. Art (and by art I mean also literature, poetry, movies, and so on) corresponded rather to a "scientific revolution": every work of modern art figures out a new law, imposes a new paradigm, a new way of looking at the world.

Modern aesthetics frequently forgot that the classical theory of art, from ancient Greece to the Middle Ages, was not so eager to stress a distinction between arts and crafts. The same term *(techne, ars)* was used

A different version of this chapter was published as "Innovation and Repetition: Between Modern and Post-Modern Aesthetics," *Daedalus* 114 (1985).

to designate both the performance of a barber, or shipbuilder, and the work of a painter or poet. The classical aesthetics was not so anxious for innovation at any cost: on the contrary, it frequently appreciated as "beautiful" the good tokens of an everlasting type. Even in those cases in which modern sensitivity enjoys the "revolution" performed by a classical artist, his contemporaries enjoyed the opposite aspect of his work, that is, his respect for previous models.

This is the reason for which modern aesthetics was so severe apropos of the industrial-like products of the mass media. A popular song, a TV commercial, a comic strip, a detective novel, a western movie were seen as more or less successful tokens of a given model or type. As such, they were judged as pleasurable but nonartistic. Furthermore, this excess of pleasurability and repetition, and this lack of innovation, were felt to be a commercial trick (the product had to meet the expectations of its audience), not the provocative proposal of a new (and difficult to accept) world vision. The products of mass media were equated with the products of industry, insofar as they were produced in series, and the "serial" production was considered alien to the artistic invention.

2. The era of repetition

I would like to consider now the case of a historical period (our own) when iteration and repetition seem to dominate the whole world of artistic creativity, and in which it is difficult to distinguish between the repetition of the media and the repetition of the so-called major arts. In this period one is facing the postmodern aesthetics, which is revisiting the very concepts of repetition and iteration with a different profile. Recently in Italy such a debate has flourished under the standard of a "new aesthetics of seriality" (see Costa 1983; Russo 1984; Casetti 1984; and Calabrese 1987). I recommend that readers take, in this case, "seriality" as a very wide category or, if one wishes, as another term for repetitive art.

Seriality and repetition are largely inflated concepts. Both philosophy and art have accustomed us to some technical meanings of these terms that would do well to be eliminated. I shall not speak of repetition in the sense of Kierkegaard, nor of "répétition différente" in the sense of Deleuze. In the history of contemporary music, series and seriality have been understood in a sense more or less opposite to what we are discussing here. The dodecaphonic "series" is the opposite of the repetitive seriality typical of all the media, because there a given succession of twelve sounds is used once and only once, within a single composition.

If you open a current dictionary, you will find that *to repeat* means "to say something or do something the second time or again and again; iteration of the same word, act or idea." *Series* means "a continued succession of similar things." It is a matter of establishing what it means to say "again" or "the same or similar things".

To serialize means, in some way, to repeat. Therefore, we shall have to define a first meaning of *to repeat* by which the term means to make a replica of the same abstract type. Two sheets of typing paper are both replicas of the same commercial type. In this sense one thing is the same as another when the former exhibits the same properties as the latter, at least under a certain description: two sheets of typing paper are the same from the point of view of our functional needs, even though they are not the same for a physicist interested in the molecular structure of the objects. From the point of view of industrial mass production, two tokens can be considered replicas of the same type when for a normal person with normal requirements, in the absence of evident imperfection, it is irrelevant whether one chooses one instead of the other. Two copies of a film or of a book are replicas of the same type (see below, ch. 12, "Fakes and Forgeries"). The repetitiveness and the seriality that interest us here look instead at something that at first glance does not appear as the same (equal) to something else.

Let us now consider the universe of mass media and see the case in which (i) something is offered as original and different (according to the requirements of modern aesthetics), (ii) we are aware that this something is repeating something else that we already know, and (iii) notwithstanding this—better, just because of it—we like it (and we buy it).

2.1. THE RETAKE

The first type of repetition is the retake. In this case one recycles the characters of a previous successful story in order to exploit them, by telling what happened to them after the end of their first adventure. The most famous example of retake is Dumas's *Twenty Years Later;* the most recent ones are the "to be continued" versions of *Star Wars* or *Superman.* The retake depends on a commercial decision.

2.2. THE REMAKE

The remake consists in telling again a previous successful story. See the innumerable editions of *Dr. Jekyll* or of *Mutiny on the Bounty*.

2.3. THE SERIES

The series works upon a fixed situation and a restricted number of fixed pivotal characters, around whom the secondary and changing ones turn. The secondary characters must give the impression that the new story is different from the preceding ones while in fact the narrative scheme does not change (see, for example, my analysis of the seriality of Rex Stout's and Superman stories in Eco 1979).

To the same type belong the TV serials such as *All in the Family* or *Columbo* (the same feature concerns different TV genres that range from soap opera to situation comedy to detective serial). With a series one believes one is enjoying the novelty of the story (which is always the same) while in fact one is enjoying it because of the recurrence of a narrative scheme that remains constant. The series in this sense responds to the infantile need of always hearing the same story, of being consoled by the "return of the Identical," superficially disguised.

The series consoles us (the consumers) because it rewards our ability to foresee: we are happy because we discover our own ability to guess what will happen. We are satisfied because we find again what we had expected. We do not attribute this happy result to the obviousness of the narrative structure but to our own presumed capacities to make forecasts. We do not think, "The author has constructed the story in a way that I could guess the end," but rather, "I was so smart to guess the end in spite of the efforts the author made to deceive me."

We find a variation of the series in the structure of the flashback: we see, for example, some comic-strip stories (such as *Superman*) in which the character is not followed along in a straight line during the course of his life, but is continually rediscovered at different moments of his life, obsessively revisited in order to find there new opportunities for new narratives. It seems as if these moments of his life have fled from the narrator out of absentmindedness, but their rediscovery does not change the psychological profile of the character, which has already been fixed, once and for all. In topological terms, this subtype of the series may be defined as a *loop*.

Usually the loop series comes to be devised for commercial reasons: it is a matter of considering how to keep the series alive, of obviating the natural problem of the aging of the character. Instead of having characters put up with new adventures (that would imply their inexorable march toward death), they are made continually to relive their past. The loop solution produces paradoxes that were already the target of innumerable parodies. Characters have a little future but an enormous past, and in any case, nothing of their past will ever have to change the mythological present in which they have been presented to the reader from the beginning. Ten different lives would not suffice to make Little Orphan Annie undergo what she underwent in the first (and only) ten years of her life.

The spiral is another variation of the series. In the stories of Charlie Brown, apparently nothing happens; each character is obsessively repeating his/her standard performance. And yet in every strip the character of Charlie Brown or Snoopy is enriched and deepened. This does not happen either with Nero Wolfe, or with Starsky and Hutch: we are always interested in their new adventures, but we already know all we need to know about their psychologies, their habits, their capacities, their ethical standpoints.

I would add finally that form of seriality which in cinema and television is motivated less by the narrative structure than by the nature of the actor himself: the mere presence of John Wayne or Jerry Lewis (when either is not directed by a great director, and even in that case) succeeds in making, always, the same film. The author tries to invent different stories, but the public recognizes (with satisfaction) always and ever the same story, under superficial disguises.

2.4. THE SAGA

The saga is different from the series insofar as it concerns the story of a family and is interested in the "historical" lapse of time. It is genealogical. In the saga, the actors do age; the saga is a history of aging of individuals, families, people, groups. The saga can have a continuous lineage (the character is followed from birth to death; the same is then done for his son, his grandson, and so on and on, potentially forever), or it can be treelike (there is a patriarch, then the various narrative branches that concern not only his direct descendants but also the collateral lines and the kin, all branching out infinitely. The most familiar (and recent) instance of saga is certainly *Dallas*.

The saga is a series in disguise. It differs from the series in that the characters change (they change also because the actors age); but in reality the saga repeats, despite its historicized form, celebrating in appearance the passage of time, the same story. As with ancient sagas, the deeds of the gallant ancestors are the same as the deeds of their descendants. In *Dallas,* grandfathers and grandsons undergo more or less the same ordeals: struggle for wealth and for power, life, death, defeat, victory, adultery, love, hate, envy, illusion, and delusion.

2.5. INTERTEXTUAL DIALOGUE

By intertextual dialogue I mean the phenomenon by which a given text echoes previous texts. Many forms of intertextuality are outside my present concerns. I am not interested, for example, in stylistic quotation, in those cases in which a text quotes, in a more or less explicit way, a stylistic feature, a way of narrating typical of another author—either as a form of parody or in order to pay homage to a great and acknowledged master. There are imperceptible quotations, of which not even the author is aware, that are the normal effect of the game of artistic influence. There are also quotations of which the author is aware but which should remain ungraspable by the consumer. In these cases we are usually in the presence of a banal case of plagiarism.

What is more interesting is when the quotation is explicit and recognizable, as happens in postmodern literature and art, which blatantly and ironically play on the intertextuality (novel on the techniques of the narrative, poetry on poetry, art on art). There is a procedure typical of the postmodern narrative that has been much used recently in the field of mass communications: it concerns the ironic quotation of the commonplace (topos). Let us remember the killing of the Arab giant in *Raiders of the Lost Ark* and the staircase of Odessa in Woody Allen's *Bananas*. What joins these two quotations? In both cases, the spectator, in order to enjoy the allusion, must know the original topoi. In the case of the giant, it is a situation typical of the genre; in the case of *Bananas*—on the contrary—the topos appears for the first and only time in a single work, and only after that quotation the topos becomes a shibboleth for movie critics and moviegoers.

In both cases the topoi are recorded by the encyclopedia of the spectator; they make up a part of the treasury of the collective imagination and as such they come to be called on. What differentiates the two quotations is the fact that the topos in *Raiders* is quoted in order to contradict it (what we expect to happen in similar cases will not), whereas in *Bananas* the topos is introduced only because of its incongruity (the staircase has nothing to do with the rest of the story).

The first case recalls the series of cartoons published years ago by *Mad* ("A Film Which We Would Like To See"). For example, the heroine, in the West, tied by bandits to the railroad tracks: the alternating shots show on one side the approaching train and on the other the furious cavalcade of rescuers trying to arrive ahead of the locomotive. In the end, the girl (contrary to all the expectations suggested by the topos evoked) is crushed by the train. Here we are faced with a comic ploy which exploits the presupposition (correct) that the public will recognize the original topos, will apply to the quotation the normal system of expectations (I mean the expectations that this piece of encyclopedic information is supposed to elicit), and will then enjoy the way in which its expectations are frustrated. At this point the ingenuous spectator, at first frustrated, overcomes his frustration and transforms himself into a critical spectator, who appreciates the way in which he was tricked. (For these two types of Model Reader, see above, ch. 3, *Intentio Lectoris*.)

In the case of *Bananas,* we are at a different level: the spectator with whom the text establishes an implicit agreement (tongue-in-cheek) is not the ingenuous one (who can be struck at most by the apparition of an incongruous event) but the critical one who appreciates the ironic ploy of the quotation and enjoys its desired incongruity. In both cases, however, we have a critical side effect: aware of the quotation, the spectator is brought to elaborate ironically on the nature of such a device and to acknowledge the fact that one has been invited to play upon one's encyclopedic competence.

The game becomes complicated in the "retake" of *Raiders,* that is, in *Indiana Jones and the Temple of Doom.* Here the hero encounters not one but two giant enemies. In the first case, we are expecting that, according to the classical schemes of the adventure film, the hero will be unarmed, and we laugh when we discover that instead the hero has a pistol and easily kills his adversary. In the second case, the director knows that the spectators (having already seen the preceding film) will expect the hero to be armed, and indeed Indiana Jones quickly looks for his pistol. He does not find it, and the spectators laugh because the expectation created by the first film is this time frustrated.

The cases cited put into play an intertextual encyclopedia. We have texts that are quoted from other texts, and the knowledge of the preceding ones—taken for granted—is supposed to be necessary to the enjoyment of the new one. More interesting for the analysis of the new intertextuality in the media is the example of *ET,* in the scene where the creature from outer space (an invention of Spielberg) is led into a city during Halloween and he encounters another personage, disguised as the gnome in *The Empire Strikes Back* (an invention of Lucas). ET is jolted and seeks to hurl himself upon the gnome in order to embrace him, as if he had met an old friend. Here the spectators must know many things: they must certainly know of the existence of another film (intertextual knowledge), but they must also know that both monsters were created by Rambaldi and that the directors of the two films are linked together for various reasons (not least because they are the two most successful directors of the decade); they must, in short, have not only a knowledge of the texts but also a knowledge of the world, of circumstances external to the texts. One notices, naturally, that the knowledge of the texts and of the world are only two chapters of the encyclopedic knowledge possible and that, therefore, in a certain measure, the text always makes reference to the same cultural patrimony.

Such phenomena of "intertextual dialogue" were once typical of experimental art and presupposed a very sophisticated Model Reader. The fact that similar devices have now become more common in the media world leads us to see that the media are carrying on—and presupposing—the possession of pieces of information already conveyed by other media. The text of *ET* "knows" that the public has learned from newspapers or television everything about Rambaldi, Lucas, and Spielberg. The media seem, in this play of extratextual quotation, to make reference to the world, but in effect they are referring to the contents of other messages sent by other media. The game is played, so to speak, on a "broadened" intertextuality. Any difference between knowledge of the world (understood naively as a knowledge derived from an extratextual experience) and intertextual knowledge has practically vanished. Our reflections to come, then, must question not only the phenomenon of repetition within a single work or a series of works but also all the phenomena that make various strategies of repetition producible, understandable, and commercially possible. In other words, repetition and seriality in the media bring up new problems for the sociology of culture.

Another form of intertextuality is the genre embedding that today is very common in the mass media. For example, every Broadway musical (in the theater or on film) is, as a rule, nothing other than the story of how a Broadway musical is put on. The Broadway genre seems to require (postulate) a vast intertextual knowledge: in fact, it creates and institutes the required competence and the presuppositions indispensable to its understanding. Every one of these films or plays tells how a Broadway musical is put on and furnishes us in effect all the information about the genre it belongs to. The spectacle gives the public the sensation of knowing ahead of time that which it does not yet know and will know only at the moment. We stand facing the case of a colossal preterition (or "passing over"). In this sense the musical is a didactic work that takes account of the idealized rules of its own production.

Finally, we have the work that speaks of itself: not the work that speaks of a genre to which it belongs, but a work that speaks of its own structure and of the way in which it was made. Critics and aestheticians were inclined to think that this device was an exclusive feature of the works of the avant-garde and was alien to mass communications. Aesthetics knows this problem and indeed gave it a name long ago: it is the Hegelian problem of the Death of Art. But in these later times there have been cases of productions in the mass media capable of self-irony, and some of the examples mentioned above seem to me of great inter-

est. Even here the line between "highbrow" arts and "lowbrow" arts
seems to have become very thin.

3. A moderated or "modern" aesthetic solution

Let us now try to review the phenomena listed above from the point
of view of a "modern" conception of aesthetic value, according to
which every work aesthetically "well done" is endowed with two
characteristics:

It must achieve a dialectic between order and novelty, in other words,
between scheme and innovation.

This dialectic must be perceived by the consumer, who must grasp not
only the contents of the message but also the way in which the message
transmits those contents.

This being the case, nothing prevents the types of repetition listed
above from achieving the conditions necessary to the realization of the
aesthetic value, and the history of the arts is ready to furnish us with
satisfactory examples for each of the types in our classification.

3.1. THE RETAKE

The retake is not strictly condemned to repetition. An illustrious
example of retake is the many different stories of the Arthurian cycle,
telling again and again the vicissitudes of Lancelot or Perceval. Ariosto's *Orlando Furioso* is nothing else but a retake of Boiardo's *Orlando
Innamorato,* and precisely because of the success of the first, which was
in its turn a retake of the themes of the Breton cycle. Boiardo and Ariosto added a goodly amount of irony to material that was very "serious" and "taken seriously" by previous readers. But even the third
Superman is ironical in regard to the first (mystical and very, very serious). It appears as the retake of an archetype inspired by the gospel,
made by winking at the films of Frank Tashlin.

3.2. THE REMAKE

The history of arts and literature is full of pseudo-remakes that were
able to tell something different every time. The whole of Shakespeare is
a remake of preceding stories. Therefore, "interesting" remakes can escape repetition.

3.3. THE SERIES

Once again we must remember that every text presupposes and constructs always a double Model Reader—a naive and a "smart" one, a semantic reader and a semiotic or critical reader. The former uses the work as semantic machinery and is the victim of the strategies of the author who will lead him little by little along a series of previsions and expectations. The latter evaluates the work as an aesthetic product and enjoys the strategies implemented in order to produce a Model Reader of the first level. This second-level reader is the one who enjoys the seriality of the series, not so much for the return of the same thing (which the naive reader believed was different), but for the strategy of the variations. In other words, the second-level reader enjoys the way in which the same story is worked over to appear to be different.

This enjoyment of variations is obviously encouraged by the more sophisticated series. Indeed, we can classify the products of serial narratives along a continuum that takes into account the different gradations of the reading agreement between the text and the "smart" reader (as opposed to the naive one). It is evident that even the most banal narrative product allows the reader to become by an autonomous decision a critical reader, able to recognize the innovative strategies (if any). But there are serial works that establish an explicit agreement with the critical reader and thus, so to speak, challenge him to acknowledge the innovative aspects of the text.

Belonging to this category are the television films of Lieutenant Columbo. It is worth noticing that in this series the authors spell out from the beginning who the murderer is. The spectator is not so much invited to play the naive game of guessing (whodunit?) as much as (i) to enjoy Columbo's detection technique, appreciated as an encore to a well-known piece of bravura, and (ii) to discover in what way the author will succeed in winning his bet, which consists in having Columbo do what he always does, but nevertheless in a way that is not banally repetitive. Every episode of *Columbo* is directed by a different author. The critical addressee is invited to pronounce a judgment on the best variation.

I used the term "variation" thinking of classical musical variations. They, too, were "serial products" that aimed very little at the naive addressee and that bet everything on an agreement with the critical one. The composer was fundamentally interested only in the applause of the critical listener, who was supposed to appreciate the fantasy displayed in his innovations on an old theme.

In this sense seriality and repetition are not opposed to innovation. Nothing is more "serial" than a tie pattern, and yet nothing can be so personalized as a tie. The example may be elementary, but that does not make it banal. Between the elementary aesthetics of the tie and the recognized "high" artistic value of the *Goldberg Variations* is a gradated continuum of repetitious strategies, aimed at the response of the "smart" addressee.

The problem is that there is not, on the one hand, an aesthetics of "high" art (original and not serial) and, on the other, a pure sociology of the serial. Rather, there is an aesthetics of serial forms that requires a historical and anthropological study of the different ways in which, at different times and in different places, the dialectic between repetition and innovation has been instantiated. When we fail to find innovation in the serial, it is perhaps a result less of the structures of the text than of our "horizon of expectations" and our cultural habits. We know very well that in certain examples of non-Western art, where we always see the same thing, the natives recognize infinitesimal variations and they feel the shiver of innovation. Where we see innovation, at least in the serial forms of the Western past, the original addressees were not at all interested in that aspect and conversely enjoyed the recurrences of the scheme.

3.4. THE SAGA

The entire *Human Comedy* by Balzac presents a very good example of a treelike saga, as much as *Dallas* does. Balzac is more interesting than *Dallas* because every one of his novels increases our knowledge of the society of his time, whereas every program of *Dallas* tells us the *same* thing about American society. But both use the same narrative scheme.

3.5. INTERTEXTUALITY

The notion of intertextuality itself has been elaborated within the framework of a reflection on "high" art. Notwithstanding, the examples given above have been taken up provocatively by the world of mass communication in order to show how even these forms of intertextual dialogue have by now been transferred to the field of popular production. It is typical of what is called postmodern literature and art (but did it not already happen thus with the music of Stravinsky?) to quote by using (sometimes under various stylistic disguises) quotation marks so that the reader pays no attention to the content of the citation but instead to the way in which the excerpt from a first text is introduced into the fabric of a second one. Renato Barilli (1984) has observed that one of the risks of this procedure is the failure to make the quotation marks evident, so that what is cited is accepted by the naive reader as an original invention rather than as an ironic reference.

We have so far put forward three examples of quotations of a previous topos: *Raiders of the Lost Ark, Bananas,* and *ET.* Let us look closer at the third case: the spectator who knows nothing of the production of the two films (in which one quotes from the other) cannot succeed in understanding why what happens does happen. By that gag the movie focuses both on movies and on the media universe. The understanding of this device is a condition for its aesthetic enjoyment. Thus this episode can work only if one realizes that there are quotation marks somewhere. One can say that these marks can be perceived only on the basis of an extratextual knowledge. Nothing in the film helps the spectator to understand at what point there ought to be quotation marks. The film presupposes a previous world knowledge on the part of the spectator. And if the spectator does not know? Too bad. The effect gets lost, but the film knows of other means to gain approval.

These imperceptible quotation marks, more than an aesthetic device, are a social artifice; they select the happy few (and the mass media usually hope to produce millions of the happy few). To the naive spectator of the first level the film has already given almost too much; that secret pleasure is reserved, for that time, for the critical spectator of the second level.

The case of *Raiders* is different. If the critical spectator fails (does not recognize the quotation) there remain plenty of possibilities for the naive spectator, who at least can enjoy the fact that the hero gets the best of his adversary. We are here confronted by a less subtle strategy than in the preceding example, a mode inclined to satisfy the urgent need of the producer, who, in any case, must sell his product to whomever he can. While it is difficult to imagine *Raiders* being seen and enjoyed by those spectators who do not grasp the interplay of quotations, it is always possible that such will happen, and the work is clearly open to that possibility.

I do not feel like saying which of the two texts cited pursues the "more aesthetically noble" ends. It is enough for me (and perhaps for the moment I have already given myself much to think about) to point out a critically relevant difference in the functioning and use of textual strategy.

We come now to the case of *Bananas.* On that staircase there descend, not only a baby carriage, but also a platoon of rabbis and I do not remember what else. What happens to the spectator who has not caught the quotation from *Potemkin* mixed up with imprecise fancies about

Fiddler on the Roof? I believe that, because of the orgiastic energy with which the scene (the staircase with its incongruous population) is presented, even the most naive spectator may grasp the symphonic turbulence of this Brueghel-like kermis. Even the most ingenuous among the spectators "feels" a rhythm, an invention, and cannot help but fix his attention on the way it is put together.

At the extreme other end of the pole of the aesthetic interest I would like to mention a work whose equivalent I have not succeeded in finding in the contemporary mass media. It is not only a masterpiece of intertextuality but also a paramount example of narrative metalanguage, which speaks of its own formation and of the rules of the narrative genre: I refer to *Tristram Shandy*.

It is impossible to read and enjoy Sterne's antinovel without realizing that it is treating the novel form ironically. *Tristram Shandy* is so aware of its nature that it is impossible to find there a single ironic statement that does not make evident its own quotation marks. It brings to a high artistic resolution the rhetorical device called *pronuntiatio* (that is, the way of imperceptibly stressing the irony).

I believe that I have singled out a typology of "quotation marking" that must in some way be relevant to the ends of a phenomenology of aesthetic value, and of the pleasure that follows from it. I believe further that the strategies for matching surprise and novelty with repetition, even if they are semiotic devices, in themselves aesthetically neutral, can give place to different results on the aesthetic level.

Each of the types of repetition that we have examined is not limited to the mass media but belongs by right to the entire history of artistic creativity; plagiarism, quotation, parody, the ironic retake are typical of the entire artistic-literary tradition.

Much art has been and is repetitive. The concept of absolute originality is a contemporary one, born with Romanticism; classical art was in vast measure serial, and the "modern" avant-garde (at the beginning of this century) challenged the romantic idea of "creation from nothingness," with its techniques of collage, mustachios on the Mona Lisa, art about art, and so on.

The same type of repetitive procedure can produce either excellence or banality; it can put the addressees into conflict with themselves and with the intertextual tradition as a whole; thus it can provide them with easy consolations, projections, identifications. It can establish an agreement with the naive addressee, exclusively, or exclusively with the smart one, or with both at different levels and along a continuum of solutions which cannot be reduced to a rudimentary typology.

Nevertheless, a typology of repetition does not furnish the criteria that can establish differences in aesthetic values. Yet, since the various types of repetition are present in the whole of artistic and literary history, they can be taken into account in order to establish criteria of artistic value. An aesthetics of repetition requires as a premise a semiotics of the textual procedures of repetition.

4. A radical or "postmodern" aesthetic solution

I realize that all I have said until now still represents an attempt to reconsider the various forms of repetition in the media in terms of the "modern" dialectic between order and innovation. The fact, however, is that when one speaks today of the aesthetics of seriality, one alludes to something more radical, that is, to a notion of aesthetic value that wholly escapes the "modern" idea of art and literature (cf. Costa 1983; Calabrese 1987).

It has been observed that with the phenomenon of television serials we find a new concept of "the infinity of the text"; the text takes on the rhythms of that same dailiness in which it is produced and which it mirrors. The problem is not one of recognizing that the serial text works variations indefinitely on a basic scheme (and in this sense it can be judged from the point of view of the "modern" aesthetics). The real problem is that what is of interest is not so much the single variations as "variability" as a formal principle, the fact that one can make variations to infinity. Variability to infinity has all the characteristics of repetition, and very little of innovation. But it is the "infinity" of the process that gives a new sense to the device of variation. What must be enjoyed— suggests the postmodern aesthetics—is the fact that a series of possible variations is potentially infinite. What becomes celebrated here is a sort of victory of life over art, with the paradoxical result that the era of electronics, instead of emphasizing the phenomena of shock, interruption, novelty, and frustration of expectations, would produce a return to the continuum, the Cyclical, the Periodical, the Regular.

Omar Calabrese (1983) has thoroughly looked into this: from the point of view of the "modern" dialectic between repetition and innovation, one can recognize easily how, for example, in the *Columbo* series, on a basic scheme some of the best names in American cinema have worked variations. Thus it would be difficult to speak, in such a case, of pure repetition: if the scheme of the detection and the psychology of the protagonist actor remains unchanged, the style of the narrative changes each time. This is no small thing, especially from the point of view of the "modern" aesthetics. But it is exactly on a different idea of style that Calabrese's paper is centered. In these forms of repetition "we are not so much interested in what is repeated as we are in the way the components of the text come to be segmented and then how the segments come to be codified in order to establish a system of invariants: any component that does not belong to the system can be defined as an *independent variable*" (29). In the most typical and apparently "degenerated" cases of seriality, the independent variables are not all together the more visible, but the more microscopic, as in a homeopathic solution where the potion is all the more potent because by further "succussions" the original particles of the medicinal product have almost disappeared.

This is what permits Calabrese to speak of the *Columbo* series as an "exercice de style" à la Queneau. We are thus facing a "neobaroque aesthetics" that is instantiated not only by the "cultivated" products but even, and above all, by those that are most degenerated. Apropos of *Dallas* one can say that "the semantic opposition and the articulation of the elementary narrative structures can migrate in combinations of the highest improbability around the various characters" (35).

Organized differentiations, policentrism, regulated irregularity—such would be the fundamental aspects of this neobaroque aesthetic, the principal example of which is the Baroque musical variations. Since in the epoch of mass communications "the condition for listening . . . it is that for which all has already been said and already been written . . . as in the Kabuki theater, it may then be the most minuscule variant that will produce pleasure in the text, or that form of explicit repetition which is already known" (38). It seems to me that these remarks apply perfectly to a typical Baroque corpus such as *Der Fluyten Lust-hof* by Jacob van Eyck (first half of the seventeenth century). For every composition the basic melody is given by a psalm, a folk dance, or a folk song that contemporary listeners were supposed to know by heart. Each of the customary three or more variations follows a fixed pattern. The pleasure is given both by the recurrence of the same patterns on different melodies and by the skill with which the player is supposed to interpret the many possibilities of reinventing the pieces by a variety of portatos, nonlegatos, staccatos, and so on.

What results from these reflections is clear. The focus of the theoretical inquiry is displaced. Before, mass mediologists tried to save the dignity of repetition by recognizing in it the possibility of a traditional dialectic between scheme and innovation (but it was still the innovation that accounted for the value, the way of rescuing the product from degradation). Now, the emphasis must be placed on the inseparable scheme-variation knot, where the variation is no longer more appreciable than the scheme.

As Giovanna Grignaffini (1983:45–46) observes, "the neobaroque aesthetics has transformed a commercial constraint into a 'formal principle.' " Consequently "any idea of unicity becomes destroyed to its very roots." As happened with Baroque music, and as (according to Walther Benjamin) happens in our era of "technological reproduction," the message of mass media can and must be received and understood in a "state of inattention."

It goes without saying that the authors I have quoted see very clearly how much commercial and "gastronomical" consolation there is in putting forward stories that always say the same thing and in a circular way always close in on themselves. But they not only apply to such products a rigidly formalistic criterion; they also suggest that we ought to conceive of a new audience which feels perfectly comfortable with such a criterion. Only by presupposing such agreement can one speak of a new aesthetics of the serial. Only by such an agreement is the serial no longer the poor relative of the arts, but the form of the art that can satisfy the new aesthetic sensibility, indeed, the post-postmodern Greek tragedy.

We would not be scandalized if such criteria were to be applied (as they have been applied) to abstract art. And in fact, here we are about to outline a new aesthetics of the "abstract" applied to the products of mass communication. But this requires that the naive addressee of the first level disappear, by giving place only to the critical reader of the second level. In fact, there is no conceivable naive addressee of an abstract painting or sculpture. If there is one who—in front of it—asks, "But what does it mean?" this is not an addressee of either the first or second level; he is excluded from any artistic experience whatever. Of abstract works there is only a critical "reading": what is formed is of no interest; only the way it is formed is interesting.

Can we expect the same for the serial products of television? What should we think about the birth of a new public that, indifferent to the stories told (which are in any case already known), only relishes the repetition and its own microscopic variations? Despite the fact that today the spectator still weeps in the face of the Texan families' tribulations, ought we to expect for the near future a true and real genetic mutation?

If it should not happen that way, the radical proposal of the postmodern aesthetics would appear singularly snobby: as in a sort of neo-Orwellian world, the pleasures of the smart reading would be reserved for the members of the Party; and the pleasures of the naive reading, reserved for the proletarians. The entire industry of the serial would exist, as in the world of Mallarmé (made to end in a Book), with its only aim being to furnish neobaroque pleasure to the happy few, reserving pity and fear to the unhappy many who remain.

5. Some questions in the guise of conclusions

According to this hypothesis, we should think of a universe of new consumers uninterested in what really happens to J.R. and bent on grasping the neobaroque pleasure provided by the form of his adventures. However, one could ask whether such an outlook (even though warranting a new aesthetics) can be agreed to by an *old* semiotics.

Baroque music, as well as abstract art, is "asemantic." One can discuss, and I am the first to do so, whether it is possible to discriminate so straightforwardly between purely "syntactic" and "semantic" arts. But may we at least recognize that there are figurative arts and abstract arts? Baroque music and abstract painting are not figurative; television serials are.

Until what point shall we be able to enjoy as merely musical those variations that play upon "likenesses"? Can one escape from the fascination of the possible worlds that these "likenesses" outline?

Perhaps we are obliged to try a different hypothesis. We can say then that the neobaroque series brings to its first level of fruition (impossible to eliminate) the pure and simple myth. Myth has nothing to do with art. It is a story, always the same. It may not be the story of Atreus and it may be that of J.R. Why not? Every epoch has its mythmakers, its own sense of the sacred. Let us take for granted such a "figurative" representation and such an "orgiastic" enjoyment of the myth. Let us take for granted the intense emotional participation, the pleasure of the reiteration of a single and constant truth, and the tears, and the laughter—and finally the catharsis. Then we can conceive of an audience also able to shift to an aesthetic level and to judge the art of the variations on a mythical theme—in the same way as one succeeds in appreciating a "beautiful funeral" even when the deceased was a dear person.

Are we sure that the same thing did not happen even with the classical tragedy? If we reread Aristotle's *Poetics* we see that it was possible to describe the model of a Greek tragedy as a serial one. From the quotations of the Stagirite we realize that the tragedies of which he had knowledge were many more than have come down to us, and they all followed (by varying it) one fixed scheme. We can suppose that those that have been saved were those that corresponded better to the canons of the

ancient aesthetic sensibility. But we could also suppose that the decima-
tion came about on the basis of political-cultural criteria, and no one
can forbid us from imagining that Sophocles may have survived by virtue of a political maneuver, by sacrificing better authors (but "better"
according to what criteria?).

If there were many more tragedies than those we know and if they all
followed (with variations) a fixed scheme, what would happen if today
we were able to see them and read them all together? Would our evalua-
tions of the originality of Sophocles or Aeschylus be different from what
they are currently? Would we find in these authors variations on topical
themes where today we see indistinctly a unique (and sublime) way of
confronting the problems of the human condition? Perhaps where we
see absolute invention the Greeks would have seen only the "correct"
variation on a single scheme, and sublime appeared to them not the
single work but precisely the scheme. It is not by chance that Aristotle
dealt mainly with schemes before all else and mentioned single works
only for the sake of example.

At this point I am engaging in what Peirce called "the play of musement" and I am multiplying the hypotheses in order to find out, maybe
later, a single fruitful idea. Let us now reverse our experiment and look
at a contemporary TV serial from the point of view of a future neo-
romantic aesthetics which, supposedly, has again assumed that "originality is beautiful." Let us imagine a society in the year A.D. 3000, in
which ninety percent of all our present cultural production had been
destroyed and of all our television serials only *one* episode of *Columbo*
had survived.

How would we "read" this work? Would we be moved by such an
original picture of a little man in the struggle with the powers of evil,
with the forces of capital, with an opulent and racist society dominated
by WASPs? Would we appreciate this efficient, concise, and intense representation of the urban landscape of an industrial America? When—in
a single piece of a series—something is simply presupposed by the audience which knows the whole series, would we speak perhaps of an art of
synthesis of a sublime capacity of telling through essential allusions?

In other words, how would we read a piece of a series if the whole of
the series remained unknown to us?

6

Interpreting Drama

According to Jorge Luis Borges, Abulgualid Mohammed Ibn Ahmed Ibn Mohammahd Ibn Rushd, better known as Averroes, was thinking—something like eight or nine centuries ago, more or less—about a difficult question concerning Aristotle's *Poetics*. As you probably know, Averroes was a specialist on Aristotle, mainly on the *Poetics*. As a matter of fact, Western civilization had lost this book and had rediscovered it only through the mediation of Arab philosophers. Averroes did not know about theater. Because of the Muslim taboo on representation, he had never seen a theatrical performance. At least, Borges, in his short story "The Quest of Averroes," imagines our philosopher wondering about two incomprehensible words he had found in Aristotle, namely, "tragedy" and "comedy." A nice problem, since Aristotle's *Poetics* is nothing else but a complex definition of those two words, or at least of the first of them.

The novel of Borges is long and fanciful. Let me quote only two episodes. In the first one, Averroes is disturbed by some noise coming from downstairs. On the patio a group of boys are playing. One of them says, "I am the Muezzin," and climbs on the shoulders of another one, who is pretending to be a minaret. Others are representing the crowd of believers. Averroes only glances at this scene and comes back to his book, trying to understand what the hell "comedy" means.

In the second episode, Averroes and the Koranist Farach are talking

A longer version of this chapter was published in *The Drama Review* 21, no. 1 (March 1977).

with the merchant Albucasim, who has just come back from remote countries. Albucasim is telling a strange story about something he has seen in Sin Kalan (Canton): a wooden house with a great salon full of balconies and chairs, crowded with people looking toward a platform where fifteen or twenty persons, wearing painted masks, are riding on horseback, but without horses, are fencing, but without swords, are dying, but are not dead. They were not crazy, explains Albucasim, they were "representing" or "performing" a story. Averroes does not understand, and Albucasim tries to explain it. "Imagine," he says, "that someone shows a story instead of telling it." "Did they speak?" asks Farach. "Yes, they did," answers Albucasim. And Farach remarks, "In such a case they did not need so many persons. Only one teller can tell everything, even if it is very complex." Averroes approves. At the end of the story, Averroes decides to interpret the words "tragedy" and "comedy" as belonging to encomiastic discourse.

Averroes touched twice on the experience of theater, skimming over it without understanding it. Too bad, since he had a good theoretical framework ready to define it. Western civilization, on the contrary, during the Middle Ages, had the real experience of theatrical performance but had not a working theoretical net to throw over it.

Once Peirce wondered what kind of sign could have been defined by a drunkard exposed in a public place by the Salvation Army in order to advertise the advantages of temperance. He did not answer this question. I shall do it now. Tentatively. We are in a better position than Averroes. Even though trying to keep a naive attitude, we cannot eliminate some background knowledge.

We know Sophocles and Gilbert and Sullivan, *King Lear* and *I Love Lucy*, *Waiting for Godot* and *A Chorus Line*, *Phèdre* and *No, No Nanette*, *The Jew of Malta* and *Cats*. Therefore, we immediately suspect that in that sudden epiphany of intoxication lies the basic mystery of (theatrical) performance.

As soon as he has been put on the platform and shown to the audience, the drunken man has lost his original nature of "real" body among real bodies. He is no more a world object among world objects—he has become a semiotic device; he is now a sign, something that stands to somebody for something else in some respect or capacity—a physical presence referring to something absent. What is our drunken man referring to? To a drunken man. But not to *the* drunk who he is, but to *a* drunk. The present drunk—insofar as he is the member of a class—is referring us back to the class of which he is a member. He stands for the category he belongs to. There is no difference, in principle, between our intoxicated character and the word *drunk*.

Apparently this drunk stands for the equivalent expression, *There is a drunken man,* but things are not that simple. The physical presence of the human body along with its characteristics could stand either for the phrase *There is a drunken man in this precise place and in this precise moment* or for the phrase *Once upon a time there was a drunken man;* it could also mean *There are many drunken men in the world.* As a matter of fact, in the example I am giving, and according to Peirce's suggestion, the third alternative is the case. To interpret this physical presence in one or in another sense is a matter of convention, and a more sophisticated theatrical performance would establish this convention by means of other semiotic media—for instance, words. But at the point we are, our tipsy sign is open to any interpretation: he stands for all the existing drunken men in our real world and in every possible world. He is an open expression meaning an open range of possible contents.

Nevertheless, there is a way in which this presence is different from the presence of a word or of a picture. It has not been actively produced (as one produces a word or draws an image)—it has been *picked up* among the existing physical bodies and it has been shown or *ostended*. It is the result of a particular mode of sign production (Eco 1976:3.6). Ostension is one of the various ways of signifying, consisting in de-realizing a given object in order to make it stand for an entire class. But ostension is, at the same time, the most basic instance of performance.

You ask me, *How should I be dressed for the party this evening?* If I answer by showing my tie framed by my jacket and say, *Like this, more or less,* I am signifying by ostension. My tie does not mean my actual tie but your possible tie (which can be of a different stuff and color) and I am "performing" by representing to you the you of this evening. I am prescribing to you how you should look this evening. With this simple gesture I am doing something that is theater at its best, since I not only tell you something, but I also am offering you a model, giving you an order or a suggestion, outlining a utopia or a feasible project. I am not only picturing a given behavior, I am also in fact eliciting a behavior, emphasizing a duty, mirroring your future. In Jakobsonian terms, my message is at the same time a referential, a phatic, an imperative, an emotive—and (provided I move gracefully) it is aesthetic. By picturing your future way of dressing (through my present one) I have, however, added the verbal expression *more or less.* My performance, which was eminently visual and behavioral, has been accompanied by a verbal metalinguistic message establishing some criteria of pertinence. *More or less* signified *making an abstraction from the particular stuff, color, and size of* MY tie. It was a rather important device; it helped you to de-realize the object that was *standing for* something else. It was reducing the pertinent features of the vehicle I used to signify "tie" to you, in order to make it able to signify all the possible ties you can think of.

The same happens with our intoxicated man. It is not necessary that he have a specific face, a specific eye color, a moustache or a beard, a jacket or a sweater. It is, however, necessary (or at least I think so) that his nose be red or violet; his eyes dimmed by a liquid obtuseness; his hair, his moustache or beard ruffled and dirty; his clothes splashed with mud, sagging and worn-out. I am thinking of the typical Bowery character, but when I think of him I am ready to make abstractions from many features, provided that some essential characteristics are conserved and emphasized. The list of these characteristics is established by a social code, a sort of iconographic convention. The very moment our Salvation Army sergeant has chosen the right drunk, he has made recourse to a socialized knowledge. His choice has been semiotically oriented. He has been looking for the right man as one looks for the right word.

Nevertheless, there is something that distinguishes our drunkard from a word. A word is a sign, but it does not conceal its sign quality. We conventionally accept that through words someone speaks about reality, but we do not confuse words with things (except in cases of mental illness). When speaking, we are conscious that something impalpable (*flatus vocis*) stands for something presumably palpable (except in cases of lying). But not every sign system follows the same rules as the others. In the case of our elementary model of mise-en-scène, the drunk is a sign, but he is a sign that pretends not to be such. The drunkard is playing a double game: In order to be accepted as a sign, he has to be recognized as a "real" spatiotemporal event, a real human body. In theater, there is a "square semiosis." With words, a phonic object stands for other objects made with different stuff. In the mise-en-scène, an object, first recognized as a real object, is then assumed as a sign in order to refer to another object (or to a class of objects) whose constitutive stuff is the same as that of the representing object.

Our drunk is representing drunkenness. His red nose has been selected as a natural unintentional event able to represent intentionally (the intention belongs to the Salvation Army, not to him) the devastating effects of intemperance. But what about his teeth? There is no specific convention establishing that an average drunken man lacks his incisors or has a set of black teeth. But if our intoxicated man possesses those characteristics, this would work very well. Insofar as the man becomes a sign, those of his characteristics that are not pertinent to the purposes of representation also acquire a sort of vicarious representative importance. The very moment the audience accepts the convention of the mise-en-scène, every element of that portion of the world that has been framed (put on the platform) becomes significant. I am thinking of the sociopsychological *frame analysis* proposed by Erving Goffman in his latest book. Goffman imagines two situations, both concerning a mirror and a lady. First situation: The mirror is in a beauty parlor, and the lady, instead of using it to adjust her hairdo, inspects the quality of its frame. That seems irregular. Second situation: The mirror is exhibited in an antiques shop, and the lady, instead of considering the quality of the frame, mirrors herself and adjusts her hair. That seems irregular. The difference in the mode of framing has changed the meaning of the actions of the characters in play. The contextual frame has changed the meaning of the mirror's carved frame—that is, the frame as situation has given a different semiotic purport to the frame as object. In both cases, however, there is a framing, an ideal platforming or staging, that imposes and prescribes the semiotic pertinence both of the objects and of the actions, even though they are not intentional behavior or nonartificial items.

I should, however, stress that, until now, I have incorrectly put together natural and unintentional signs. I have done it on purpose because it is a kind of confusion frequently made by many semioticians. But we should disambiguate it.

On one hand, I can produce a false natural event, as when I purposely produce a false imprint in order to fool somebody. I can produce a false symptom by painting red spots on my face to pretend I have measles. On the other hand, I can produce unintentionally what usually is conceived to be intentional (the most typical examples are psychoanalytic slips of the tongue or those common errors that everybody makes when speaking a foreign language), but I also can produce intentionally what is usually believed to be unintentional. For instance, his pronunciation shows that a man is, let me say, a Frenchman speaking English. The choice of English words is an intentional act, the way of pronouncing them, even though semiotically important (it means *to me* "Frenchman") is unintentional.

But what about an actor who purposefully and caricaturally emits English phonemes with a French accent in order to tell his audience that he pretends (theatrically) to be a Frenchman who pretends (in theatrical reality) to be an American? The elementary mechanisms of human interaction and the elementary mechanisms of dramatic fiction are the same. This is not a witty idea of mine: from Goffman to Bateson and from the current researches in ethnomethodology to the experiences of a Palo Alto group (think also of Eric Berne's behavioral games models in *Games People Play*), everyday life is viewed as an instance of theatrical performance. This finally explains why aesthetics and criticism have always suspected that theatrical performances were instances of everyday life. It is not theater that is able to imitate life; it is social life that is designed as a continuous performance, and because of this there is a link between theater and life.

Let me outline an elementary matrix considering eight possible types of interaction in emitting and receiving unintentional behavior as signs. Let me list under E the intention of the emitter (with + meaning that the behavior is intentional and − that it is not), under A the intentionality or the unintentionality of the reaction of the addressee, and under I the intention that the addressee attributes (or does not attribute) to the emitter:

	E	A	I
1	+	+	+
2	+	+	−
3	+	−	(+)
4	+	−	(−)
5	−	+	+
6	−	+	−
7	−	−	(+)
8	−	−	(−)

Case 1: An actor hobbles along, pretending to be a lame person. The addressee understands that he is doing it voluntarily.

Case 2: I simulate a limp in order to make the addressee believe that I am lame. The addressee consciously receives this piece of information, believing that my behavior is unintentional. This represents the typical case of successful simulation.

Cases 3 and 4: In order to get rid of a boring visitor, I drum on the desk with my fingers to express nervous tension. The addressee receives this as a subliminal stimulus that irritates him; he is unable to attribute to me either intentionality or unintentionality, although later he might (or might not) realize what happened and attribute plus or minus intentionality to my act.

Cases 5 and 6: Being bored by the same visitor, I unintentionally drum with my fingers. The visitor realizes the situation and attributes plus or minus intention to me.

Case 6 is also the one of the patient emitting an involuntary slip of the tongue during a conversation with his psychoanalyst, who understands the sign and recognizes that it was not intentionally emitted.

Cases 7 and 8 are variations of cases 3 and 5, with a different misunderstanding strategy.

In fact, one can get from this matrix all the basic plots of Western comedy and tragedy, from Menander to Pirandello, or from Chaplin to Antonioni. But the matrix could be further complicated by adding to it a fourth item, that is, the intention that the emitter wishes that the addressee attribute to him. *I tell you p so that you believe that I am lying and that, in fact, I meant q while p is really the case.* Remember the Jewish story reported by Lacan: *Why are you telling me that you are going to Krakow so that I believe that you are going to Lenberg, while as a matter of fact you are really going to Krakow and, by telling it explicitly, you are trying to conceal it?* The new matrix would have sixteen rows. Paola Pugliatti (1976) has applied this matrix to the well-known *nothing* uttered by Cordelia, examining the different interplay of interpretations and misunderstandings taking place between Cordelia and King Lear, Cordelia and France, King Lear and Kent and so on. But Paolo Valesio (1980) has further complicated this analysis by interpreting the *nothing* of Cordelia as a witty rhetorical device aiming not to convince Lear but rather to inform France about her mental disposition and rhetorical ability.

Coming back to our poor tipsy guinea pig (who, I believe, is rather tired from having been kept standing on his platform for an untenable amount of time): his presence could be reconsidered in the light of the matrix above. In any case, we could concentrate in this bare presence the whole set of problems discussed by Austin and Searle apropos of *speech acts,* and all the questions raised by the logic of natural languages or epistemic and doxastic logic apropos of all those expressions such as "I want you to believe," "I believe that you believe," "I am asserting that," "I am promising that," "I am announcing that," and so on. In the very presence of that drunken man, we are witnessing the crucial antinomy that has haunted the history of Western thought for two thousand years, that is, the "liar paradox": *Everything I am saying is false.*

In the same way, should the drunken man open his devastated mouth and utter something like *I love liquor* or *Don't trust alcohol. . . .* Well, we ought to face at that precise moment the linguistic and logical set of problems concerning the difference between the *sujet de l'énonciation* and the *sujet de l'énoncé*. Who is speaking, *qui parle?* That intoxicated individual? The class he is representing? The Salvation Army?

Luis Prieto has pointed out that in theater (as well as in cinema) words are not transparent expressions referring to their content (and through it to things). They are expressions referring to other expressions, namely, to a class of expressions. They are phonic objects taken as objects and ostended as such. The statement *I love liquor* does not mean that the subject of the utterance loves liquor—it means that there is somewhere somebody who loves liquor and who says that. In theater and cinema, verbal performances refer back to verbal performances about which the mise-en-scène is speaking.

In a certain sense every dramatic performance (be it on the stage or on the screen) is composed by two speech acts. The first is performed by the actor who is making a performative statement—*I am acting.* By this implicit statement the actor tells the truth since he announces that from that moment on he will lie. The second is represented by a pseudo statement where the subject of the statement is already the character, not the actor. Logically speaking, those statements are referentially opaque. When I say *Paul has said that Mary will come,* I am responsible for the truth of the proposition *Paul has said p,* not with the truth of p. The same happens in a dramatic performance: because of the first performative act, everything following it becomes referentially opaque. Through the decision of the performer (*I am another man*) we enter the possible world of performance, a world of lies in which we are entitled to celebrate the suspension of disbelief.

There is a difference between a narrative text and a theatrical performance. In a narrative, the author is supposed to tell the truth when he is speaking as subject of the acts of utterance, and his discourse is recognized as referentially opaque only when he speaks about what Julien Sorel or David Copperfield have said. But what about a literary text in which Thomas Mann says *I* and the *I* is not Thomas Mann but Serenus Zeitblom telling what Adrian Leverkuhn has said? At this moment, narrative becomes very similar to theater. The author implicitly begins his discourse by saying performatively *I am Serenus.* (As in the case of the drunk, it is not necessary that he assume all the properties of Serenus. It is enough that he reproduce certain pertinent features, namely, certain stylistic devices able to connote him as a typical German humanist, a cultivated and old-fashioned middle bourgeois.)

Once this is said—once the methodological standpoint that both fiction and living reportage are instances of mise-en-scène—it remains to ask, "How does a character who acts as an element of a mise-en-scène speak?" Do his words have a univocal meaning? Do they mean one thing only and nothing else?

In 1938 Bogatyrev, in a fundamental paper on signs in theater, pointed out that signs in theater are not signs of an object but signs of a sign of an object. He meant that, beyond their immediate denotation, all the objects, behaviors, and words used in theater have an additional *connotative* power. For instance, Bogatyrev suggested that an actor playing a starving man can eat some bread as bread—the actor connoting the idea of starvation but the bread eaten by him being denotatively bread. But under other circumstances, the fact of eating bread could mean that this starving man eats only a poor food, and therefore the piece of bread stands not only for the class of all possible pieces of bread but also for the idea of poverty.

However, our drunken man does something more than standing for drunkenness. In doing so, he is certainly realizing a figure of speech, a metonymy, since he stands for the cause of his physical devastation. He also realizes an antonomasia, since he, individually taken, stands for his whole category—he is the drunken man par excellence. But (according to the example of Peirce) he is also realizing an irony by antonymy. He, the drunk, the victim of alcoholism, stands ironically for his contrary; he celebrates the advantages of temperance. He implicitly says *I am so, but I should not be like this, and you should not become like me.* Or, at another level, *Do you see how beautiful I am? Do you realize what a kind of glorious sample of humanity I am representing here?* But in order to get the irony, we need the right framing: in this case, the standards of the Salvation Army surrounding him.

Since we have approached the rhetorical level, we are obliged to face the philosophical one. Our drunken man is no longer a bare presence. He is not even a mere figure of speech. He has become an ideological abstraction: temperance vs. intemperance, virtue vs. vice. Who has said that to drink is bad? Who has said that the spectacle of intoxication has to be interpreted as an ironic warning and not as an invitation to the most orgiastic freedom? Obviously, the social context. The fact that the drunk has been exposed under the standards of the Salvation Army obliges the audience to associate his presence with a whole system of values.

What would have happened had the drunk been exposed under the standard of a revolutionary movement? Would he still have signified "vice" or, rather, "the responsibility of the system," "the results of a bad administration," "the whole starving world"? Once we have accepted that the drunk is also a figure of speech, we must begin to look at him also as an ideological statement. A semiotics of the mise-en-scène is constitutively a semiotics of the production of ideologies.

All these things, this complex rhetorical machinery, are, moreover, made possible by the fact that we are not only looking at a human body endowed with some characteristics—we are looking at a human body standing and moving within a physical space. The body could not stagger if there were not an environing space to give it orientation—up and down, right and left, to stand up, to lie down. Were the bodies two or more, space would establish the possibility of associating a given meaning with their mutual distances. In this way we see how the problems of the mise-en-scène refer to the problems of many other semiotic phenomena, such as proxemics or kinesics. And we realize that the same semiotic parameters can be applied to the semiotics of theater, of cinema, of architecture, of painting, of sculpture.

From the idiosyncratic character of the theatrical phenomenon we have arrived at the general problems of semiotics. Nevertheless, theater has additional features distinguishing it from other forms of art and strictly linking it with everyday conversational interaction—for instance, the audience looking at the drunk can laugh, can insult him and he can react to people's reactions. Theatrical messages are shaped also by the feedback produced from their destination point.

So the semiotics of theatrical performance has shown its own *proprium,* its distinguishing and peculiar features. A human body, along with its conventionally recognizable properties, surrounded by or supplied with a set of objects, inserted within a physical space, stands for something else to a reacting audience. In order to do so, it has been framed within a sort of performative situation that establishes that it has to be taken as a sign. From this moment on, the curtain is raised. From this moment on, anything can happen—Oedipus listens to Krapp's last tape, Godot meets La Cantatrice Chauve, Tartuffe dies on the grave of Juliet, El Cid Campeador throws a cream cake in the face of La Dame aux Camélias.

But the theatrical performance has begun before—when Averroes was peeping at the boy who was saying, *I am the Muezzin.*

7

Interpreting Animals

How, how much, why, and in which way did a dog bark in the Middle Ages? The question is not so whimsical as it seems.

In the course of their discussions on language, many medieval grammarians and logicians were usually quoting, as an example of pseudo language, the *latratus canis.* Not only the bark of the dog, indeed, but also the sounds of the horse, of the pigeon, of the cow and, it goes without saying, the language of parrots and magpies.

Animals in the Middle Ages "said" many things, but mostly without knowing it. In the Bestiaries they show up as living signs of something else. Characters of a book *scriptus digito dei,* they did not produce a language but were themselves "words" of a symbolic lexicon.

Philosophers and grammarians were interested in the *latratus* as a linguistic phenomenon, however, and they mention it in relation to the *gemitus infirmorum* and to other kinds of interjections. What aroused our curiosity was the fact that—if one extrapolates from each of these discourses a sort of taxonomic tree—one realizes that in certain trees the *latratus* goes along with the *gemitus infirmorum,* whereas in some others it occupies a different node.

We thus realized that perhaps such a marginal question would have

This chapter simply summarizes and elaborates upon some aspects of a broader study I made in 1983 in collaboration with three other authors: U. Eco, R. Lambertini, C. Marino, A. Tabarroni, "On Animal Language in the Medieval Classification of Signs," *VS* 38/39 (May/December 1984): 3–38 (now in U. Eco and C. Marmo, eds., *On the Medieval Theory of Signs* [Amsterdam: Benjamins, 1989]). First published as "Latratus canis" in *Tijdschrift voor Filosofie* 47 (1985), no. 1.

helped us to understand better certain imperceptible differences concealed by these discussions that, as it usually happens with medieval stuff, at first glance look like the stubborn repetition of the same archetypical model.

Medieval scholars were not lacking texts on animal behavior. Only late Schoolmen knew Aristotle's *Historia animalium,* but, through the mediation of Pliny and of Ammonius, they knew various discussions about the natural characteristics of dogs, not to mention the problem of the voice of fishes and birds (including parrots and magpies).

Likewise, something must have filtered down from the discussion which took place among Stoics, Academicians, and Epicureans about the possibility of an "animal *logos.*" Sextus Empiricus says (*Pyrr.* 1.1.65–67) that the dogs manifest, through their behavior, various capacities of reflection and apprehension. Sextus quotes an observation of Crysippus, according to which, when a dog follows his prey and arrives at a place where three roads meet, having sniffed the two ways by which its victim has not passed, makes a perfect dialectical syllogism: "the beast has passed either by here, or by there or by some other part." It is controversial whether Sextus was known by the Middle Ages or not, but it is worth noticing that the same argument can be found in the Bestiary of Cambridge. That the idea does not appear in Isidore or in the *Physiologus* means that a great part of the Greek discussion had filtered in some way through other secondary sources.

All this mass of "naturalistic" observation survived in some way in the work of philosophers tied, through the mediation of Augustine, to the Stoic legacy. However, in general, every appearance of the dog is dependent on that page of Aristotle's *De interpretatione* (16a and following), which influenced enormously the whole medieval discussion on human and animal language. Thus the dog circulates in the philosophical and linguistic literature mainly as a barking animal, making noise along with parrots, cocks—sometimes along with the *gemitus infirmorum,* sometimes under a separate heading. The barking of the dog, born as a topos, a topos remains. Nevertheless, the authority has a nose of wax, and below and beyond any literal appearance, every time the topos is quoted again, one is entitled to suspect that a slight shift of perspective has taken place.

1. Signs and words

To justify the embarrassing position of the *latratus canis* in the medieval theories of language, one should remember that Greek semiotics, from the Corpus Hippochraticum up to the Stoics, made a clear-cut distinction between a theory of verbal language (names, *onomata*) and a theory of signs (*semeia*). Signs are natural events that act as symptoms or indexes, and they entertain with that which they designate a relation based on the mechanism of inference (if such a symptom, then such a sickness; if smoke, then fire). Words stand in a different relation with the thing they designate (or with the passions of the soul they signify or, in Stoic terms, with the proposition—*lekton*—they convey), and this relation is based on mere equivalence and biconditionality (as it appears also in the influential Aristotelian theory of definition).

As I have tried to stress elsewhere (Eco 1984, ch. 1), the fusion between a theory of signs and a theory of words (albeit vaguely foreseen by the Stoics) is definitely sanctioned only by Augustine, who is the first explicitly to propose "general semiotics," that is, a general science of *signa,* the sign being the genus of which both words and natural symptoms are species. In doing so, not even Augustine resolves definitely the dichotomy between inference and equivalence, and the medieval tradition is left with two lines of thought which are not yet unified. This is a crucial observation because one of the main reasons why the *latratus canis* occupies different positions in different classifications of signs depends on whether they are classifications of signs in general (in the Stoic and Augustinian mode) or of *voces,* in the Aristotelian mode of a theory of spoken language.

2. Aristotle

The detonator of the controversy about the *latratus canis* is the passage of *De interpretatione* (16–20a), where Aristotle, with the intention of defining nouns and verbs, makes some marginal statements about signs in general. To summarize the result of an unending discussion among interpreters of this passage, Aristotle basically says that nouns and verbs are cases of *phoné semantiké katà synthéken,* that is, in medieval terms, *vox significativa ad placitum.* Aristotle says that words are symbols of the affections of the soul (or, if you want, of concepts), just as the written words are symbols of the spoken ones. He takes "symbol" in the sense of Peirce, as a conventional device, and that is why symbols are not the same for every culture. On the contrary, the passions of the soul are the same for all, since they are images (we could say "icons") of the things. But in speaking of the passions of the soul, Aristotle adds (rather parenthetically) that words are, of these passions, "before all else" *signs.*

Is that an instance of mere redundancy in which the word "sign" is synonymous with "symbol"? Certainly not, because when Aristotle speaks expressly of signs (*semeia*) in the *Rhetoric,* he means symptoms, natural events from which one can infer something else. Aristotle is simply saying that, even though words are conventional symbols, insofar as they are uttered they can *also* (or *in first instance*) be taken as symptoms of the evident fact that the one who speaks has something to say in his mind.

All this becomes clearer a few sentences below, where Aristotle remarks that, since even vocal sounds can be taken as signs (or symptoms), also inarticulate noises, like those emitted by animals, can act as symptoms. He says "noises" (*agràmmatoi psòphoi*), not "sounds," because, as Ammonius and all the subsequent commentators will explain, he is also thinking of certain animals, such as fishes, which do not emit sounds but make some noise ("quidam enim pisces non voce, sed branchiis sonant"—will say Boethius—"et cicada per pectum sonum mittit"). Aristotle says that these noises manifest (*deloûsi*) something.

Now, what happens with the first influential translation of *De interpretatione,* made by Boethius? Boethius translates both "symbol" and "sign" with *nota,* so that the Aristotelian nuance gets lost. Moreover, he translates *deloûsi* not as "they show," but with *significant* (they signify).

Aristotle spoke of the noises of animals, and lexically distinguished a noise from a sound. Unfortunately, from Boethius onward, the medieval commentators translated the Aristotelian *phoné* (sound) with *vox,* and *psòphos* (noise) with *sonus.* Thus from the medieval commentators animals without lungs emit sounds, but animals with lungs emit voices, and *voces* can be *significativae.* The road is open for a significant bark of the dog.

3. Boethius Latrans

The bark of the dog appears for the first time in Ammonius, and in the Latin world with Boethius as an example of *vox significativa* not *ad placitum* (by convention) but rather *naturaliter* (see figure 7.1). Thus a sound that for Aristotle was a sign is placed under the headings of *vox significativa,* where also stand words or symbols. In the same category Boethius places the *genitus infirmorum,* the whinny of the horse, and even the sounds of animals without lungs that "tantu sonitu quodam concrepant." Why do these sounds signify *naturaliter?* Evidently because one is able to know, through them, their cause by a symptomatic inference.

BOETHIUS

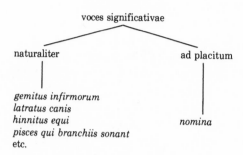

Figure 7.1

Boethius, however, disregards two important differences: (i) the difference, which the Stoics acknowledged clearly, between natural events which "happen" but are not emitted by living beings, such as smoke from fire or a medical symptom, and sounds brought forth by animated creatures; (ii) the difference between sounds emitted intentionally and sounds emitted unintentionally—the infirm wail unintentionally and so do dogs when barking. Or do dogs have an intention to communicate? Boethius says of the horse that "hinnitus quoque eorum saepe alterius equi consuetudinem quaerit," that is, the horse whinnies to call another horse, intentionally and, I suspect, with a precise sexual purpose. Boethius also says that frequently animals emit voices "aliqua significatione preditas," that is, sounds endowed with some meaning. But endowed by whom? By the animal that emits them or by the man who listens? Boethius disregards this question because he has disregarded the difference (i). When one interprets a natural event as a sign, it is the human intention that takes it as something signifying something else.

Thus the dog is put in a very embarrassing situation. It emits *voces* but emits them naturally. Its voice stands ambiguously midway between a natural event and an intentional utterance: if the dog barks intentionally, it is not clear whether in doing so it intentionally talks to another dog or to a human—which, in zoosemiotical terms, is not a minor question. Moreover, does human understand dog (or horse) because human has a natural disposition to interpret symptoms, or because human has a natural disposition to understand the canine language?

4. Aquinas

Thomas Aquinas will not distance himself from Boethius's classification: his will only become a more complex taxonomy. He deals with the problem in more than one page of his commentary on *De Interpretatione* and with some ambiguities. The Thomistic classification echoes various influences. In some passages Aquinas, along Augustinian lines, calls *signum* every *vox significativa,* in some other passages *signum* is quoted also as the sound of a military trumpet (*tuba*) which, evidently,

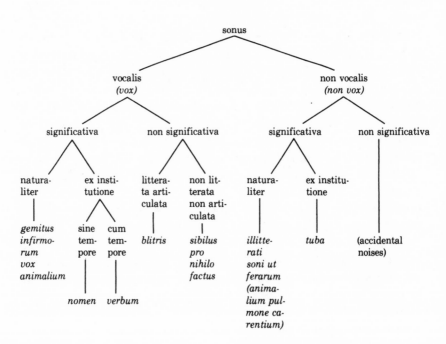

Figure 7.2

does not represent a case of *vox vocalis*. It seems that for him *signum* is every utterance endowed with meaning, whether it is vocal or non-vocal. But he does not take into account the *signa naturalia* (the *semeia*), even though natural signs will play an important role both in the theory of sacraments and in the theory of analogy.

However, let me try to summarize his views (see figure 7.2). For Aquinas, the main difference between human and animal sounds does not, however, consist in the opposition "intentional vs. unintentional" but rather in another one, as he stresses in an interesting passage of the commentary on *Politics:* both men and animals have modes of signifying according to some intention (dogs bark and lions roar to tell to their interspecific mates their feelings) in the same way as men emit interjections. An infirm person can wail (unintentionally) and can utter intentionally interjections signifying his or her pain. But the real opposition is that between interjections (which cannot express concepts) and linguistic sounds, able to convey abstractions, and this is why only by language men are able to establish social institutions ("*domum et civitatem*").

5. The Stoic legacy: Augustine

The embarrassment we have found in the interpreters of *De interpretatione* is absent from thinkers who, as happened to Augustine, were not exposed to such an influence and were more directly dominated by the Stoic tradition.

In *De doctrina christiana,* Augustine (after having given his celebrated definition "signum est enim res praeter speciem, quam ingerit sensibus, aliud aliquid ex se faciens in cogitationem venire") works out the distinction between *signa naturalia* and *signa data*. Natural signs are those that "sine voluntate atque ullo appetitu significandi praeter se aliquid aliud ex se cognoscere faciunt" (such as the smoke which reveals the fire and the face of the enraged which reveals anger without any intention). *Signa data* are those exchanged by living beings in order to convey "motus animi" (which are not necessarily concepts and can be sensations or psychological states).

With a stroke of genius Augustine places, among the *signa data,* without a tremor of doubt, both the words of the Holy Scriptures and the signs produced by animals (see figure 7.3): "Habent enim bestiae inter se signa, quibus produnt appetitus animi sui. Nam et gallo gallinaceus reperto cibo dat signum vocis gallinae, ut accurrat; et columba

AUGUSTINE

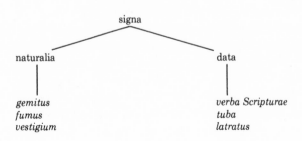

Figure 7.3

gemitu columbam vocat, vel ab ea vicissim vocatur." However, Augustine remains doubtful about the nature of such an animal intention.

6. Abelard

The problem will be solved originally by Abelard. In his *Dialectica* his classification of signs can be traced back to the Boethian one and divides *voces significativae* between these signifying *naturaliter* and these signifying *ex impositione* (by convention). In the *Summa Ingredientibus* Abelard adds a new opposition: the one between *voces significativae* and *voces significantes,* and this opposition is given by the difference between speaking *ex institutione* or *sine institutione* (see figure 7.4).

The *institutio* is not a convention (like the *impositio*); it is rather a decision which precedes both the human convention and the natural meaningfulness of animal sounds. One can see this "institution" as very close to an intention. Words are meaningful by virtue of the institution of the human will which orders them *ad intellectum constituendum* (to produce something, perhaps less than a concept, as Augustine maintained, in the mind of the hearer). The bark of the dog has equally some meaning, even though a natural one, and the institution (the intentionality) of his expression is provided by God, or by nature. In this sense the bark is as *significativus* as a human word. And in this sense it must be distinguished by these phenomena, which are only *significantia* and therefore merely symptomatic. The same bark can be emitted *ex institu-*

ABELARD

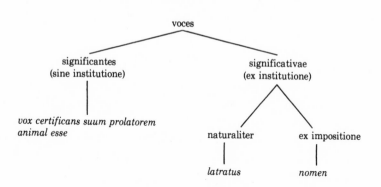

Figure 7.4

tione (and be therefore *significativus*), or can be heard from afar, so allowing one simply to infer that "down there, there is a dog."

It is clear that Abelard, in an Augustinian vein, is following the Stoic line of thought and distinguishes between signs (*significantia*) and words or pseudo-natural words (*significativa*). The same bark can act as a symptom (where the intentionality stands only on the part of the interpreter and the event has not been instituted for this purpose) or as a naturally signifying utterance which the dog utters in order to *constituere intellectum*. This does not mean that the dog "wants" to do what he is doing; his intention (*institutio*) is not his own but rather a "natural" intention impressed by nature, so to speak, on the neural circuits of the whole species. We are curiously witnessing here the proposal of a sort of Agent Will, molded on the Agent Intellect of Avicenna—an interpretation which can be supported by an analogous suggestion provided by Albert the Great in *De anima*. Thus the agent is not individual, but it is nonetheless intentional.

7. Bacon

Not forgetting the provocation of Augustine, there now comes Roger Bacon. The classification which can be extrapolated from his *De signis* is hardly homogeneous (see figure 7.5). His natural signs seem those of

Augustine, emitted without intention, but we could lose a lot of time wondering about the criteria followed on the left side of the classification. For the present purpose it is enough to remark that the signs of the right side are, as in Abelard, those produced by an intention of the soul, and on this side we, as in Abelard, find again the distinction between a voluntary intention and a natural one.

It is definitely interesting that, once again, there is a difference between the crow of the cock taken as a symptom of the presence of the cock and the crow of the cock taken as a somewhat intentional sound emitted in order to communicate. When it appears among the signs *ordinata ab anima,* it is called *cantus galli;* when it appears among *signa naturalia,* it is defined by an infinitive construction: "*gallum cantare,*" the fact that the cock crows. It is, as the Stoics would have said, an "incorporeal," a symptomatic sequence of events. As such it can be interpreted by human beings: "cantus galli nihil proprie nobis significat tamquam vox significativa sed gallum cantare significat nobis horas."

Bacon does not arrive where Augustine dared to, that is, he is not putting the barking of the dog and the word of God under the same headings. But as Abelard did, he does not consider the voice uttered by the animal (when the animal communicated by a natural impulse) only as a mere symptom. His description of animal language is as sensitive as the Augustinian one: dogs, hens, and pigeons, in his examples, are not mere topoi but "real" animals observed with naturalistic interest in their usual behavior.

The Baconian classification mirrors a new attitude toward nature and direct experience. Bacon has a sharp feeling for the relativity of human languages, but also for the necessity of learning languages. He is strongly convinced that cocks crow and dogs bark in order to communicate to their interspecific mates. Perhaps we do not understand their language in the very sense in which a Greek does not understand a Latin, and vice versa, but the ass is understood by the ass, the lion by the lion. For humans it is enough to have a little training and, as Latins understand Greeks, it will be possible to understand the language of beasts: such a conclusion is reached a little later by the Pseudo-Marsilius of Inghen.

Thus the night of the Middle Ages seems to be haunted by a crowd of barking dogs and crying sick people: the landscape designed by so many theoretical pages cannot but suggest a more real landscape of stray dogs running through the streets of medieval cities while people, not yet comforted by aspirin, celebrated with uncontrolled lamenta-

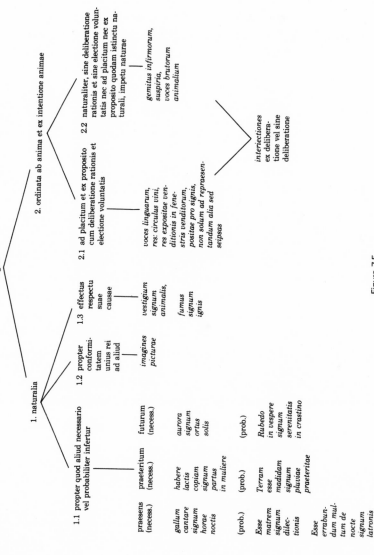

BACON

Figure 7.5

tions the approach of Judgment Day. In this landscape hens and parrots scratch about but, as far as I know, no cats show up. They were probably reserved for more intimate sorcery parties and could not be recognized as usual inhabitants of the "official" city.

8

A Portrait of the Elder
as a Young Pliny

1.

In his Letter 6, XVI, 1, C. Pliny the Younger (hereafter the Younger) writes to Tacitus about the death of his uncle Pliny the Elder (hereafter the Elder), who perished during the eruption of Vesuvius at Pompeii, 79 A.D.

The letter is written to provide Tacitus with material for his *Historiae*. As can be understood from the letter, the Younger had firsthand evidence of the first part of the events and firsthand reports about the circumstances of the death of his uncle. This fact is very important for the purpose of the following analysis: at the beginning of the letter there is an implicit Ego (the Younger) writing presumably around 104 A.D. to his addressee, and the only true proposition one could identify in this text is *I, Pliny, am writing in this moment to you Tacitus saying p*. The whole set of propositions labeled as *p* should be referentially opaque. But the letter implies a sort of performative mode, as if it said: *I swear that p is true*. There is a sort of authentication agreement (Greimas [1979] would say *contract de veridiction*) between the Younger and Tacitus, by force of which Tacitus—and any other possible addressee of the letter—must take *p* as pure matter of fact. Besides, Tacitus asked the

A first version of this chapter was presented at the Symposium Synopsis 2: Narrative Theory and Poetics of Fiction, Porter Institute, Tel Aviv–Jerusalem, June 1979, and subsequently published under the same title as this chapter in *VS* 35/36 (1983). The translation is reproduced from Pliny 1969. I have eliminated the footnotes and stressed with italics certain relevant expressions for purposes of analysis.

Younger for reliable information just because he thought and assumed that his correspondent would tell a true story. As far as we know, the story is true indeed; in any case, it mirrors the only historical truth we recognize as such, since it has contributed (along with some other texts) to what our cultural encyclopedia records as truth.

But we have improperly defined what the Younger says as a set of propositions labeled as *p*. As a matter of fact, the Younger narrates something, but his narration, as every other narration, is made up of two components, the underlying *fabula* (or story) and the vehicular *discourse* (or plot, or discursive arrangement of events).

The aim of the present analysis is to show that the story (once it has been isolated by a reader in the form of a series of macropropositions chronologically ordered) says something. However, the discourse says, if not something else, at least something more, in such a way that it is difficult to isolate the two levels clearly.

This *double jeu* is evident in the opening lines of the letter: Tacitus asked for a description of facts, but the Younger understands very well that what is at stake is an account for posterity—that is, a cultural monument.

1. *Petis* ut *tibi* avunculi *mei* exitum *scribam*, quo verius tradere posteris possis. Gratias ago; nam *video* morti eius si celebretur a te immortalem gloriam esse propositam. Quamvis enim pulcherrimarum clade terrarum, ut populi ut urbes memorabili casu, quasi semper victurus occiderit, quamvis ipse plurima opera et mansura condiderit, multum tamen perpetuitati eius scriptorum tuorum aeternitas addet. Equidem beatos puto, quibus deorum munere datum est aut facere scribenda aut scribere legenda, beatissimos vero quibus utrumque. Horum in numero avunculus meus et suis libris et tuis erit. Quo libentius suscipio, *deposco* etiam quod iniungis.

1. Thank *you* for asking *me* to send you a description of my uncle's death so that you can leave an accurate account of it for posterity; *I know* that immortal fame awaits him if his death is recorded by you. It is true that he perished in a catastrophe which destroyed the loveliest regions of the earth, a fate shared by whole cities and their people, and one so memorable that it is likely to make his name live for ever: and he himself wrote a number of books of lasting value: but you write for all time and can still do much to perpetuate his memory. The fortunate man, in my opinion, is he to whom the gods have granted the power either to do something which is worth recording or to write what is worth reading, and most fortunate of all is the man who can do both. Such a man was my uncle, as his own books and yours will prove. So you set me a task I would choose for myself, and *I am* more than willing to start on it.

Pliny the Younger is explicit: Tacitus can provide immortal glory to the Elder by representing him as a scientific hero. Such an introduction can be taken in two ways. It looks as if the Younger were saying, "I provide you with the facts, and they will speak for themselves—all the rest is up to you." On the other hand, the Younger is providing facts and comments, or fact wrapped with comments. Only he is not so naive as to put forth comments as comments. He follows a different persuasive strategy.

2. *Erat* Miseni classemque imperio praesens regebat. Nonum kal. Septembres hora fere septima mater mea indicat ei adparere nubem inusitata et magnitudine et specie. Usus ille sole, mox frigida, gustaverat iacens studebatque; poscit soleas, ascendit locum ex quo maxime miraculum illud conspici poterat. Nubes—incertum procul intuentibus ex quo monte (*Vesuvium fuisse postea cognitum est*)—oriebatur, cuius similitudinem et formam non alia magis arbor quam pinus expresserit. Nam longissimo velut trunco elata in altum quibusdam ramis diffundebatur, credo quia recenti spiritu evecta, dein senescente eo destituta aut etiam pondere suo victa in latitudinem vanescebat, candida interdum, interdum sordida et maculosa *prout terram cineremve sustulerat*. Magnum propiusque noscendum ut eruditissimo viro visum. Iubet liburnicam aptari; *mihi* si venire una vellem facit copiam; respondi studere me malle, et forte ipse quod scriberem dederat. Egrediebatur domo; accipit codicillos Rectinae Tasci *imminenti periculo exterritae* (nam villa eius subiacebat, nec ulla nisi navibus fuga): ut se tanto discrimini eriperet orabat. Vertit ille consilium et *quod studioso animo incohaverat obit maximo*. Deducit quadriremes, ascendit ipse non Rectinae modo sed multis (erat enim frequens amoenitas orae) laturus auxilium. Properat illuc unde alii fugiunt, *rectumque cursum recta gubernacula in periculum tenet adeo solutus metu,* ut omnes illius mali motus omnes figuras ut deprenderat oculis dictaret enotaretque.

Iam navibus cinis incidebat, quo propius accederent, calidior et densior; iam pumices etiam nigrique et ambusti et fracti igne lapides; iam vadum subitum ruinaque montis litora obstantia. Cunctatus paulum

2. My uncle *was* stationed at Misenum, in active command of the fleet. On 24 August, in the early afternoon, my mother drew his attention to a cloud of unusual size and appearance. He had been out in the sun, had taken a cold bath, and lunched while lying down, and was then working at his books. He called for his shoes and climbed up to a place which would give him the best view of the phenomenon. It was not clear at that distance from which mountain the cloud was rising (*it was afterwards known to be Vesuvius*); its general appearance can best be expressed as being like a pine rather than any other tree, for it rose to a great height on a sort of trunk and then split off into branches, I imagine because it was thrust upwards by the first blast and then left unsupported as the pressure subsided, or else it was borne down by its own weight so that it spread out and gradually dispersed. Sometimes it looked white, sometimes blotched and dirty, *according to the amount of soil and ashes it carried with it*. My uncle's scholarly acumen saw at once that it was important enough for a closer inspection, and he ordered a boat to be made ready, telling *me I* could come with him if I wished. I replied that I preferred to go on with my studies, and as it happened he had himself given me some writing to do.

As he was leaving the house he was handed a message from Rectina, wife of Tascus, whose house was at the foot of the mountain, so that escape was impossible except by boat. *She was terrified* by the danger threatening her and implored him to rescue her from her fate. He changed his plans, and *what he had begun in a spirit of inquiry he completed as a hero*. He gave orders for the warships to be launched and went on board himself with the intention of bringing help to many more people besides Rectina, for this lovely stretch of coast was thickly populated. He hurried to the place which everyone else was hastily leaving, *steering his course straight for the danger zone. He was entirely fearless,* describing each new movement and phase of the portent to be noted down exactly as he observed them. Ashes were already falling, hotter and thicker as the ships drew near, followed by bits of pumice and blackened stones, charred and cracked by the flames:

an retro flecteret, mox gubernatori ut ita faceret monenti *"Fortes"* inquit *"fortuna iuvat*: Pomponianum pete."* Stabiis erat diremptus sinu medio (nam sensim circumactis curvatisque litoribus mare infunditur); ibi *quamquam nondum periculo adpropinquante,* conspicuo tamen et cum cresceret proximo, sarcinas contulerat in naves, certus fugae si contrarius ventus resedisset. Quo tunc avunculus meus secundissimo invectus, complecitur trepidantem consolatur hortatur utque timorem eius sua securitate leniret, deferri in balineum iubet; lotus accubat cenat, aut hilaris aut (quod aeque magnum) similis hilari. Interim e Vesuvio monte pluribus locis latissimae flammae altaque incendia relucebant, quorum fulgor et claritas tenebris noctis excitabatur. Ille agrestium trepidatione ignes relictos desertasque villas per solitudinem ardere, in remedium formidinis dictitabat. Tum se quieti dedit et quievit verissimo quidem somno; nam meatus animae, qui illi propter amplitudinem corporis gravior et sonantior erat, ab iis qui limini obversabantur audiebatur. Sed area ex qua diaeta adibatur ita iam cinere mixtisque pumicibus oppleta surrexerat, ut si longior in cubiculo mora, exitus negaretur. Excitatus procedit, seque Pomponiano ceterisque qui pervigilaverant reddit. In commune consultant, intra tecta subsistant an in aperto vagentur. Nam crebris vastisque tremoribus tecta nutabant, et quasi emota sedibus suis nunc huc nunc illuc abire aut referri videbantur. Sub dio rursus quamquam levium exesorumque pumicum casus metuebatur, quod tamen periculorum collatio elegit; et apud illum quidem ratio rationem, apud alios timorem timor vicit. Cervicalia capitibus imposita linteis constringunt; id munimentum adversus incidentia fuit. Iam dies alibi, illic nox omnibus noctibus nigrior densiorque; quam tamen faces

then suddenly they were in shallow water, and the shore was blocked by the debris from the mountain. For a moment my uncle wondered whether to turn back, but when the helmsman advised this he refused, telling him that *Fortune stood by the courageous* and they must make for Pomponianus at Stabiae. He was cut off there by the breadth of the bay (for the shore gradually curves round a basin filled by the sea) so that *he was not as yet in danger,* though it was clear that this would come nearer as it spread. Pomponianus had therefore already put his belongings on board ship, intending to escape if the contrary wind fell. This wind was of course full in my uncle's favour, and he was able to bring his ship in. He embraced his terrified friend, cheered and encouraged him, and thinking he could calm his fears by showing his own composure, gave orders that he was to be carried to the bathroom. After his bath he lay down and dined; he was quite cheerful, or at any rate he pretended he was, which was no less courageous.

Meanwhile, on Mount Vesuvius, broad sheets of fire and leaping flames blazed at several points, their bright glare emphasized by the darkness of night. My uncle tried to allay the fears of his companions by repeatedly declaring that these were nothing but bonfires left by the peasants in their terror, or else empty houses on fire in the districts they had abandoned. Then he went to rest and certainly slept, for as he was a stout man his breathing was rather loud and heavy and could be heard by people coming and going outside his door. By this time the courtyard giving access to his room was full of ashes mixed with pumice-stones, so that its level had risen, and if he had stayed in the room any longer he would never have got out. He was wakened, came out, and joined Pomponianus and the rest of the household, who had sat up all night. They debated whether to stay indoors or take their chance in the open, for the buildings were now shaking with violent shocks, and seemed to be swaying to and fro as if they were torn from their foundations. Outside, on the other hand, there was the danger of falling pumice-stones, even though these were light and porous; however, after comparing the risks they chose the latter. In my uncle's case one reason outweighed the other, but for the others it was a choice of fears. As a protection against falling objects they put pillows on their heads tied down with cloths.

multae variaque lumina solvebant. Placuit egredi in litus, et ex proximo adspicere, ecquid iam mare admitteret; quod adhuc vastum et adversum permanebat. Ibi super abiectum linteum recubans semel atque iterum frigidam aquam poposcit hausitque. Deinde flammae flammarumque praenuntius odor sulpuris alios in fugam vertunt, excitant illum. Innitens servolis duobus adsurrexit et statim concidit, ut ego colligo, crassiore caligine spiritu obstructo, clausoque stomacho qui illi natura invalidus et angustus et frequenter aestuans erat. Ubi dies redditus (is ab eo quem novissime viderat tertius), corpus inventum integrum inlaesum opertumque ut fuerat indutus: habitus corporis quiescenti quam defuncto similior.

3. Interim Miseni ego et mater—sed nihil ad historiam, nec tu aliud quam de exitu eius scire voluisti. *Finem ergo faciam.* Unam adiciam, omnia me quibus interfueram quaeque statim, cum maxime vera memorantur, audieram, persecutum. Tu potissima excerpes; *aliud est enim epistulam aliud historiam, aliud amico aliud omnibus scribere.* Vale.

Elsewhere there was daylight by this time, but they were still in darkness, blacker and denser than any night that ever was, which they relieved by lighting torches and various kinds of lamp. My uncle decided to go down to the shore and investigate on the spot the possibility of any escape by sea, but he found the waves still wild and dangerous. A sheet was spread on the ground for him to lie down, and he repeatedly asked for cold water to drink. Then the flames and smell of sulphur, which gave warning of the approaching fire, drove the others to take flight and roused him to stand up. He stood leaning on two slaves and then suddenly collapsed, I imagine because the dense fumes choked his breathing by blocking his windpipe which was constitutionally weak and narrow and often inflamed. When daylight returned on the 26th—two days after the last day he had seen—his body was found intact and uninjured, still fully clothed and looking more like sleep than death.

3. Meanwhile, my mother and I were at Misenum, but this is not of any historic interest, and you only wanted to hear about my uncle's death. *I will say no more,* except to add that I have described in detail every incident which I either witnessed myself or heard about immediately after the event, when reports were most likely to be accurate. It is for you to select what best suits your purpose, *for there is a great difference between a letter to a friend and history written for all to read.*

The first impression one receives in reading this letter is that the Elder was indeed a hero of science who lost his life sailing courageously to the source of the eruption because of his sense of duty and of his erudite curiosity. The acknowledgment of such an effect is not only a matter of intuition. Unfortunately, we do not know how Tacitus, as an empirical reader, reacted to the letter, since his *Historiae* stops at 70 A.D. and its second part is lost. But we know how other readers reacted, since our encyclopedia records the fate of the Elder as a paramount example of scientific holocaust.

Nevertheless, if one puts the underlying *fabula* into a sequence of propositions, the crude facts are the following: the Elder moves toward the eruption before knowing that it is an eruption (moreover, at that time nobody considered Vesuvius an active volcano and the same Pliny the Elder, in his *Naturalis historia* 3.62, describes Vesuvius as a pleasant and harmless component of the Neapolitan landscape; see Sherwin-Withe 1966: 372–375). Even when he arrives at Pomponianus's home in Stabiae, he is still unaware of the proportions of the disaster, understanding neither its format nor its definitive effects. He says with nonchalance that the flames raging on the mountain are only bonfires left by the peasants. It is true that, according to the Younger's interpretation, he says so in order to allay the fears of his companions; but afterward he *really* goes to sleep without realizing that he was risking burial by ashes had somebody not awakened him. When he finally understands that there is no escape and that the situation is really dramatic, it is too late. He dies as quickly as possible, because he was also asthmatic, as some commentators suggest.

When one carefully reconsiders the bare *fabula,* one gets the impression of reading the story of a very narcissistic and narrow-minded Roman admiral, completely unable to cope with the situation (in short, this efficient rescuer not only did not help anybody but also succeeded in depriving the fleet of its commander in chief, just when some efficiency was needed from the local military authority). Pliny the Younger does not conceal anything; if Tacitus had wished, he could have extrapolated the real story (perhaps he did) precisely as we are now doing. The Tacitus we are interested in, however, is not the "real" Tacitus; it is the planned addressee of Pliny's letter, that is, what I have elsewhere called the Model Reader of a text (Eco 1979a).

Pliny's letter is a text which, as any other text, is not empirically addressed to an empirical addressee: it builds up, by a discursive strategy, the type of reader who is supposed to cooperate in order to actualize the text such as the Model Author (that is, the objective textual strategy) wants it to be. We can refuse to play the role of the Model Reader, as we are presently doing; but we must recognize the kind of reader that the text not only presupposes but also produces through the use of given linguistic strategies.

To read the discursive maneuvers of the Younger at a metatextual level means to acknowledge the way in which the text gives its Model Reader the appropriate instructions as to how to realize a certain persuasive effect. This letter not only aims at saying something "true" (in an assertive mode); it also wants to make Tacitus (or every other possible reader) believe that the Elder was a hero, as well as wanting Tacitus to write that the Elder was one. Greimas would speak of modalities: *faire croire* and *faire faire.* Or, how to do things with words.

In order to produce the "right" cooperation of his Model Reader, Pliny the Younger plays upon a complicated gamut of discursive operations, mainly temporal shifts in and out (*embragages* and *débrayages*, according to Greimas's terminology) and a planned confusion between the subject of the speech act and the subject of the narrative utterance (the *instance de l'énonciation* suddenly intruding the course of *l'énoncé*). Moreover, as we shall see, the *fabula* concerns not only the world of events but also the epistemic worlds (or the propositional attitudes) of the characters, and these epistemic worlds continually overlap with the supposed epistemic world of the Model Reader (different propositional attitudes are thus *focalized* at the same moment). The final result is that the reader does not understand (provided he or she does not perform a metatextual analysis) *who* is speaking in a given moment (for such a dialectics of *voices,* see also Genette 1972).

2. A portrait of the young Pliny as an old reporter

At the beginning of the letter (§1) there is an implicit *Ego* (the subject of *scribam*) which clearly refers to an individual, Pliny the Younger, author of that letter, presumably in 104 A.D. Let us define *this* Pliny as P_1, writing at a time-moment t_0 in a world W_0 conventionally taken as the real world. This oversimplification is due to the fact that we assume that the letter is not a piece of fiction but of "natural" narrativity (like a newspaper article). If it were a piece of fiction (like the letters of *Clarissa* or of *Les liaisons dangereuses*), we would assume that there is another subject (a P_0), the empirical producer of the speech act, while the *Ego* of the discourse is a fictive subject, not to be identified with the author. In other cases (fiction written in the third person), the subject of the speech act can interfere with the discourse as a semifictive subject, an *Ego* who comments on the facts and who can or cannot be identified with the empirical author (see, for instance, the comments provided in the first person by Fielding or by Manzoni throughout *Tom Jones* or *The Betrothed*).

In our case we can assume that the "historical" Pliny and the Ego speaking from §1 to §3 can be taken as the same entity, the Sender of the letter whose Addressee is Tacitus.

However, from §2 onward, P_1 tells Tacitus a story concerning P_2, that is, what happened to himself twenty-five years before, at Misenum, in A.D. 79, on August 24. Thus we have a letter written in t_0 which tells about another time, or a given series of temporal states that we shall register as follows:

t_{-3} = August 24, afternoon, when the cloud appears and the Elder decides to sail;

t_{-2} = the lapse of time or the series of temporal states occurring from the departure of the Elder to his death (the evening of the 24th and the following day, the 25th);

t_{-1} = August 26, when the Younger receives fresh news about what happened.

The moment in which P_1 shifts out to the time of the *fabula* (t_{-3}) is marked by the passage from present to the imperfect tense (*erat Miseni . . . regebat*). The narrative mood is also stressed by the insertion of chrononyms (*Nonum kal. Septembres*) and by the introduction of individuals belonging to a former temporal state (the uncle, the mother—the former as the implicit subject of *erat* and by the attribution of some functional properties as *regat classem*). All these grammatical devices mark clearly the passage between the introductory part, where the Younger speaks as P_1, and the second one, where the explicit or implicit Ego is P_2.

One should notice in the diagram (figure 8.1) that the third box, embedded in the second one, does not necessarily represent the level of the *fabula* as opposed to the level of discourse. As a matter of fact, the *fabula* of P_2 is still told in a discursive form and must be extrapolated from the discourse by the cooperative reader.

What the reader extrapolates are different states of the same narrative sequence, that is, different states of the same narrative world. According to the definitions proposed in Eco 1979a (8.6), passing from one state to another the individuals of such a world change some of

TEXT

| P_0 The historical Pliny the Younger subject of the speech act *(sujet de l'énonciation)* | P_1 Narrator. Pliny the Young as the subject of the uttered discourse, in t_0. *Enonciation énoncé* or spoken speech act | P_2 as one of the characters of the narration along with:
E   the Elder
M   the mother ...
All in $t_{-3} \ldots t_{-1}$ |

Figure 8.1

their *accidental* properties without changing their *essential* properties. Thus, in the narrative state corresponding to the time t_{-3}, the Elder is a living Roman admiral, in t_{-2} he is the same Roman admiral undertaking certain unpleasant experiences, and in t_{-1} he is a Roman admiral who has accidentally died.

Nevertheless, what interests us is not a comparison between these different states of the same narrative world (which incidentally coincide, as far as we know, with the "real" world as it has been recorded by our encyclopedical competence). What interests us is that P_1, as the subject of the uttered discourse in t_0, shares with Tacitus (as his Model Reader) some knowledge apropos of the death of the Elder. At the same time, P_1, telling Tacitus what happened in t_{-3}, attributes to the Elder and to himself a different sort of knowledge.

We are thus concerned with two epistemic worlds: the world W_0 of the beliefs shared by P_1, Tacitus, and ourselves as contemporary readers; and the W_{Nct-3} of the knowledge attributed by P_1, as narrator, to the characters of the narrated events—P_1 is telling the story of himself and of his uncle who, twenty-five years before, saw a strange cloud and believed p (p being the content of the epistemic world W_{Nct-3}).

In plainer words, the Younger in 104 A.D. knew what he himself and his uncle could not know on August 24, 79 A.D., namely, that the cloud of unusual size came from the eruption of Vesuvius and that it was made of poisonous ashes and other harmful materials. To P_2 the cloud was an amazing phenomenon (and so it was to E), whereas for P_1 (and for Tacitus) it was, in short, Death.

This means that the *fabula* should tell about certain individuals of a given narrative world W_{Nt-3}, the individuals being P_2, E, M, along with C (the cloud) and V (Vesuvius), this world hosting at least one narrative subworld W_{Nc}, representing the beliefs of the characters of the story (since it happens that at that moment the Younger, the Elder, and the Mother share the same epistemic world). In such a subworld W_{Nct-3}, the cloud is not yet linked with the volcano, is still amazing but not necessarily harmful, and, what is more important, is not supposed to represent the element that will kill the Elder.

On the contrary, the epistemic world of P_1 and of his Model Reader contains at t_0 the same individuals but endowed with rather different properties: E is a dead scientist, the cloud has a volcanic origin, Vesuvius was the cause of the disaster, the disaster (or Vesuvius itself) was the agent

It is important to maintain the difference between these worlds, since in t_{-3} the Elder believes that the cloud is harmless, does not suspect that Vesuvius had something to do with the phenomenon he is watching, and does not know that he will die—all elements that make his decision to go a little less courageous than if he had known what was to be the further course of events.

Let us assume that we are dealing with two narrative worlds: W_{Nct-3} is the world of the narrated beliefs of the characters of the story told by P_1—for the sake of economy we shall consider only the beliefs of the Elder that coincide with those of both the Younger and his mother, at that time. On the contrary, W_{0t0} is the world of the story such as it is known by P_1 and Tacitus.

From this point of view we can consider these two worlds as structured according to S-necessary properties (Eco 1979a:8.7.3), that is, those that link the individuals of the *fabula* by strict textual interdependence, so that one individual can be defined only in the terms of another.

Thus we can outline two world matrices in terms of the following individuals and of their S-necessary properties, where

E = Elder
C = Cloud
V = Vesuvius
cRe = the relation defining a cloud as the one actually perceived by the Elder in t_{-3}
cRv = the relation defining a cloud as being produced by the eruption of Vesuvius
vRe = the relation defining Vesuvius as the fatal agent of the Elder's death

The resulting matrices will then be as shown (figure 8.2).

One then realizes that none of the individuals of the first world shares the same S-necessary properties of the homonymous individuals of the second one. Thus the individuals are designated by the same names but they are not the same: the cloud of the second world is the one perceived by the Elder and at the same time the one produced by Vesuvius, whereas in the first world, had there been by chance a cloud with the property of being erupted by Vesuvius, it would not have been the same as C_1. And so on.

Two possible narrative worlds furnished with individuals sharing different S-necessary properties are not narratively accessible. In the same way, a heretic Gospel telling the story of a man called Jesus who is

$W_{Nc}t_{-3}$	cRe	cRv	vRe
C_1	+	−	
E_1	+		−
V_1		−	−

W_0t_0	cRe	cRv	vRe
C_2	+	+	
E_2	+		+
V_2		+	+

Figure 8.2

not the Son of the Father does not speak about the same theological character as the Canonic Gospels. Such is the difference between the epistemic world of P_1 (and of Tacitus) and the epistemic world of P_2 (and of the Elder).

3. A portrait of the old Pliny the Younger as a young informant

Now we can come back to the discursive surface of the story of P_2 told by P_1. Notice that P_1 should make it clear that P_2 and the Elder shared the epistemic world $W_{Nc}t_{-3}$. A good narrator interested in the psychology of his or her characters and in the dialectics between reality and illusion should insist on this gap. (Think of the energy with which Sophocles shows Oedipus blinded by a set of propositional attitudes that do not correspond to the real course of past events; see Eco 1979a:243–345).

Which is, on the contrary, the discursive strategy of P_1? In §1 the *Ego* who speaks in t_0 reminds Tacitus of what he is supposed to know very well, namely, that the Elder perished in that catastrophe, that the catastrophe was memorable, and that because of this his name will live forever. Why such an insistence on this piece of encyclopedic information? The Younger is clearly preparing his Model Reader to think of the Elder in terms of W_0t_0.

In §2 the Younger operates a temporal shifting-out: the change of tense produces—so to speak—a flashback and puts the Model Reader in a previous state of the same world. But in this previous state of the same world the characters nourished propositional attitudes which cannot cope with those of the Model Reader. The Younger is prima facie very honest. He says that neither he (twenty-five years before) nor his uncle knew where the cloud was coming from. But immediately afterward he opens a parenthesis and reminds Tacitus that it was coming from Vesuvius: the parenthesis marks a new temporal and epistemic shifting-in (an *embrayage*, a return to t_0), expressed by the use of different tenses—*cognitum est postea . . . Vesuvium fuisse.* But, though the move is grammatically correct, from both the semantic and the syntactic point of view, its pragmatic effect is quite different: it reintroduces into the core of the epistemic world of P_2 and of E the epistemic world of P_1 and of Tacitus. The cloud is without any shadow of doubt the one that the Model Reader is supposed to know as cRv (knowing also that vRe).

The following move is more interesting: P_2 and E are watching a cloud which is *candida interdum, interdum sordida* (sometimes white, sometimes dirty) and these are indeed the accidental properties of cRe, the cloud such as the Elder witnessed it in t_{-3}. But the Younger (who in this case seems to be the *Ego* P_2 but who in fact, by a sudden shifting in t_0, is P_1) says that the cloud looked so *prout terram cineremve sustulerat* (according to the amount of soil and ashes it carried with it): a property that could not be scored as belonging to C_1 since it was typical of C_2, the cloud of the later epistemic world of P_1, the cloud coming from Vesuvius, the dangerous one, the one that *now* (in $W_0 t_0$) everyone knows as the mythical co-agent of the subsequent disgrace.

This time the Younger has not signaled his shifting-in by a parenthesis; on the contrary, he has further confused the temporal situation, using a pluperfect (*sustulerat*) against the imperfect of the surrounding discourse (*diffundebatur, vanescebat*). He thus stresses the obvious fact that (from the point of view of the logic of events) the presence of soil and ashes was prior to the spreading out of the cloud. Which is correct from the point of view of the *fabula,* not from the point of view of the epistemic world of P_2, who knew all this only *afterward.* P_1 is telling *his* truth, which also happens to be the truth of the Reader but which was not the truth of P_2 and of his unfortunate uncle. The reader could become conscious of this subtle operation, if he or she wanted. But how can he or she want it since the reader is so cordially invited to disregard this sudden *embrayage-débrayage*?

At this point it becomes difficult for a generously cooperating reader to avoid the conviction that the Elder in t_{-3} is courageously facing his *evident* destiny. The *double jeu* of shifting has, so to speak, projected onto a mirror, or a screen, the future that the encyclopedia has definitely recorded: the Model Reader is the only one able to watch that mirror, but he nourishes the impression that the Elder is watching with him.[1]

Thus it is very easy for P_1 (always acting as P_2) to say that, since Rectina is "terrified," the Elder "*vertit . . . consilium and quod studioso animo incohaverat obit maximo*" (the translator, caught in the trap displayed by the text, emphasizes, and writes "as a hero"). One can suspect that, from the moment the Elder receives Rectina's message, he already knows that cRv. In any case, he does not know that vRe. But the text is shameless: the Elder "*rectumque cursum recta gubernacula in periculum tenet adeo sloutus metu,*" hurries to the danger (his own danger!), steering his course straight, entirely fearless (fearless of *his* incumbent death!). The same Elder who, according to P_1, after his arrival, goes peacefully to bed! The Model Reader, confused by a double flickering mirror where two epistemic worlds collide and vanish one into another, may now admire the sublime decision of the hero: *fortes fortuna iuvat,* let us proceed, I don't care about *my* death!

In a hiccup of honesty, P_2 cannot avoid telling the truth: "*quamquam nondum periculo appropinquante,*" the Elder does not feel himself in any immediate danger, Pomponianus's spot where the Elder lands is still relatively safe. . . . But the Reader *knows* that this spot is exactly the one where the Elder will lose his life. The Elder has sailed from W_{NcT-3} toward W_{0t0} as if he knew everything about the furniture of that world, as if he were Ulysses crossing the Pillars of Hercules.

This story of temporal shiftings-in and -out is also a story of rapid switchings in focalization. It happens as if a moving light spot were throwing its rays, alternately, on two different epistemic worlds so that, by a sort of optical effect, one never realizes which world is being focused on; or as happens in so-called three-card monte, where the trickster maneuvers his cards at such a speed that the victim can no longer understand which card is where. A paramount example of discursive manipulation determining the extrapolation of the *fabula*'s level. Really Pliny the Younger (or his text) is *doing* things with words.

The last instruction of Tacitus (after having again shifted in at t_0; see §3) is a masterpiece of hypocrisy. "*Finem faciam,*" "I stop representing P_2 and the Elder in t_{-3} as I did until now (what a supreme lie!), let me come back to the present, notice, my dear Tacitus, that until now we were in another world, let us return to our own which has never interfered with that one" (such is indeed the rhetorical function of *finem faciam*). "What I, P_1, have said until now is only what I have witnessed at *that* time, what I knew at *that* time, what I believed along with my uncle at *that* time, what I have heard from my firsthand informants" (who obviously, let me add, knew a little more than the Elder knew at t_{-3}). "Now, Tacitus, it is you who must transform my honest report into a cultural monument, because there is a difference between writing a letter to a friend and writing history for posterity." In fact, as we well know, the letter was already written for posterity, but to become effective (as it did) it had to conceal its purpose from its Model Readers.

Fortunately, every text is always, more or less consciously, conceived for two kinds of Model Reader. The first is supposed to cooperate in actualizing the content of the text; the second is supposed to be able to describe (and enjoy) the way in which the first Model Reader has been textually produced. One wonders whether Pliny the Younger would have preferred a Reader accepting his glorious product (monument to the Elder) or a Reader realizing his glorifying production (monument to the Younger).

NOTE

1. Naturally, the Model Reader foreseen by the Younger is the Naive or Semiosic one (see above, ch. 3, section 4).

9

Joyce, Semiosis, and Semiotics

1. Introductory remarks

During the last years many critics have tried to apply semiotic tools to Joyce, and with interesting results (for further bibliographical information, see Bosinelli et al. 1986). But I am convinced that, if one were to look at a complete Joycean bibliography of the last twenty years, one would remark that those critics represent a generous but modest percentage. A parallel inquiry into a complete bibliography of theoretical semiotics, narratology, and text pragmatics would lead to the same results: despite many interesting exceptions, only a modest percentage of theoretical semioticians have drawn their examples and evidence from Joyce's works. Among the "pilgrim fathers" of semiotics, Roland Barthes has subtly analyzed Balzac; Greimas has carefully scrutinized Maupassant; Jakobson has carried out acute analyses of Baudelaire and Shakespeare; and others similarly have analyzed Faulkner, Becket, and Borges. Literary semiotics has left little territory unviolated, but Joyce has been confined to a region where only a few courageous pioneers have dared to venture.

Naturally, reasons can be sought for this silence. The first is that much of traditional Joycean criticism, even while uninterested in semiotic theory, working on an author who has put into question the very structure of language and all the rules of narrativity, had already made a

A longer version of this chapter was presented at the James Joyce Society Symposium, Venice, 1988.

noteworthy contribution toward the clarification of many semiotic problems. To take only one example, Wolfgang Iser has largely based his semiotic theory of the Implied Reader upon the researches of Joycean criticism.

The second reason is that semiotics in its first phase of development usually analyzed isolated sentences, dialogues, newspaper stories, *trivialliteratur*, and even when it has approached texts with aesthetic ends, it has preferred to work on more traditional narrative works. This is so because a semiotics of literature was first of all interested in acknowledging rules, codes, and systems of conventions. In order to analyze works such as those of Joyce, which question rules, codes, and systems of conventions, it is first necessary to have clear ideas on what is being questioned. In other words, it would seem that to establish a semiotics of the avant-garde it would first be useful to establish a semiotics of tradition.

2. Semiotic problems in Joyce

I think, on the contrary, that the whole opus of Joyce is a paramount playground for semiotic research.

Since linguistics isolates and analyzes, alongside grammatical sentences, also the ungrammatical ones, Joyce is able to offer endless examples of deviations from phonological, lexical, syntactic, and narrative rules.

Text semiotics, for example, is interested in the rules of coherence and cohesiveness of a given text. It seems problematic to say what is wrong in the expression *John came home very late. Napoleon died in St. Helena*. Such texts are usually scored as grammatically correct but textually incoherent. Naturally, linguists and semioticians know that similar texts can become coherent if they are seen as a part of a larger textual environment that in some way makes the lateness of John relevant to the death of Napoleon, or vice versa. But the problem of text semiotics is to ascertain by which strategies a context signals its topic or its aboutness. Now, every instance of stream of consciousness in *Ulysses* is the paramount playing ground for this kind of analysis.

In text pragmatics, scholars are puzzled by the different truth value of metaphors and symbols. A metaphor is easily recognizable as such because, if it were taken literally, it would not tell the truth (since it is not true that Achilles was a lion). The symbolic mode is, on the contrary, instantiated when a text describes behaviors, objects and events that make sense literally but when, nevertheless, the reader feels them to be pragmatically inexplicable because the context does not succeed in justifying their intrusion. The standard reaction to any instantiation of the symbolic mode is a sort of uneasiness felt by the reader when witnessing a sort of semantic waste, a surplus of possible and still imprecise significations conveyed by something that—in terms of conversational or narrative economy—should not be there. Well, every example of epiphany in the early works of Joyce, as well as the whole of *Ulysses*, are a seminal source for studying this type of textual strategy (see Eco 1962b, 1984:4.5).

There is an immense literature on Joyce's puns, and there is an immense literature on the semiotic revisitation of Rhetoric. In its *Rhétorique générale* (1970), Groupe μ has widened the field of rhetorical figures by distinguishing four types of operations which usually arise and work on both the level of expression (signifier) and that of content (signified) of the semiotic system, as well as on both lexical unities and synctatic chains. Therefore, such figures as alliteration, apocope, and metathesis are cases of metaplasm. Metaphors which act upon the content are metasememes: figures such as hypallage or hystheron proteron, which play on the syntactic structure of the expression, are metasyntagm, whereas a figure of thought, such as irony, is a metalogism. (See figure 9.1.)

All the puns of *Finnegans Wake* are metaplasm with a metasememic effect, where the structure of the linguistic expression is acted upon in order to produce alterations also at the level of content, similar to those which operate in metaphors. A metaphor substitutes one expression for another in order to produce an expansion (or a "condensation") of knowledge at the semantic level. The Joycean pun obtains analogous effects, but through two new procedures. On the one hand, it modifies the very structures of the expression: a pun such as *scherzarade* in fact

	unit	*syntagm*
content	metasemene	metalogism
expression	metaplasm	metasyntagm

Figure 9.1

produces a word which did not previously exist in the English lexicon. On the other hand, it produces a metaphor *in praesentia* because it does not annul one term, substituting it with another, but unites three preexisting words (*scherzo, charade,* and *Scheherazade*), in a sort of lexical *monstruum* (metaplasm), and in so doing it obliges us to see similarities and semantic connections between the joke (*scherzo*), the enigma (*charade*), and the narrative activity (*Scheherazade*).

3. Pun and unlimited semiosis

In Eco 1979 (2.4) I tried to show that each metaphor produced in *Finnegans Wake* (*FW*) is comprehensible because the entire book, read in different directions, actually furnishes the metonymic chains that justify it. I tested this hypothesis on the atomic element of *FW*, the pun, seen as a particular form of metaphor founded on subjacent chains of metonymies. Such a chain of metonymies is presupposed by the text as a form of background knowledge based on a network of previously posited cultural contiguities or psychological associations. But at the same time it is the text itself which, by a network of interconnected puns, makes the cultural background recognizable. I thus proposed to consider *FW* as a contracted model of the global semantic field.

Let us take the lexeme *Neanderthal* (not found as such in the text) and see what mechanism led the author to modify it into *meandertale*. Naturally, we could also follow the inverse process: we could take the pun found in the text and trace it back to its original components. But the very fact that we can conceive of two possible courses indicates that, in this case, the two moments coincide; it was possible to invent the pun because it is possible to read it; language, as a cultural base, should be able to allow both operations. It should be noted also that, for reasons of a simple operative convention, we will start from one of the component words of the pun in order to deduce the other; probably another one would serve our purpose equally well.

Our experiment thus has two senses: first, to see if, from a point outside Joyce's linguistic universe, we can enter into that universe; then, departing from a point internal to that universe, to see whether or not we can connect, through multiple and continuous pathways, as in a garden where the paths fork, all the other points. It will then come down to defining whether or not this entrance and this traversability are based on simple relationships of contiguity. For the moment, however, we will attempt to reason in terms—however imperfectly defined—of "association" (phonetic and semantic).

Let us take the word *Neanderthal*. In the schema (see figure 9.2) we will notice how the lexeme generates, through a phonetic association, three other lexemes—*meander, tal* (in German, "valley"), and *tale*—which combine to form the pun *meandertale*.

In the associative course, however, intermediate modes create themselves from terms that are all present in the text of *FW*. Here the associations can be of either a phonetic or a semantic type. It would be noted that all the lexemes mentioned here are only those which are to be found in the text of *FW*. The same psycholinguistic test might have generated, in another subject, other equally plausible responses. Here we have limited ourselves to this type of response, not only because it is the Joycean one (in which case the experiment would seek to understand only how the pun is born, not how it is read), but also for reasons of economy and, in addition, because the reader of *FW*, controlled by the text, is in

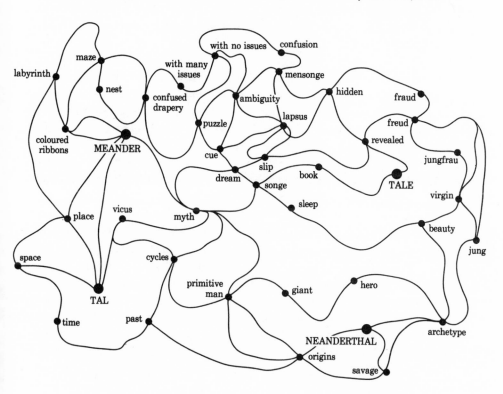

Figure 9.2

fact led into a game of associations that were previously suggested by the co-text (which means that every text, however "open" it is, is constituted, not as the place of all possibilities, but rather as a field of oriented possibilities).

The interconnections show, moreover, the way in which every lexeme can in turn become the archetype of an associative series which would amalgamate sooner or later, with the associative terminals of another lexeme. The whole diagram has a purely orientational value, in the sense that it impoverishes the associations in terms of both number and dimension: a bidimensional graph cannot reproduce the game of interconnections produced when lexemes are brought into contact with their respective sememes. We should consider as multidimensional, not only the game of interconnections produced in the global semantic system of real languages, but also the game of that Ersatz field—the literary work, the text (in our case *FW*, more open to interconnections than are many other texts and thus more fit for experimentation).

If we pass from the diagram to Joyce's text, we can see how all the associations have been developed. They actually produce the puns which define the book. The book is a *slipping beauty* (and thus a beautiful sleeper who, in sleeping, generates lapsus by semantic slippages, in remembering a flaw, and so on), a *jungfraud's messongebook* a psychoanalytic lie, a virginal trick, a young message, a dream and a confusion, and so on and so on, a labyrinth in which is found *a word as cunningly hidden in its maze of confused drapery as a fieldmouse in a nest of coloured ribbons*, and thus at last a *Meandertale*.

The pun-lexeme *meanderthaltale* becomes, in the end, the metaphoric substitution for everything that can be said about the book and that is said by the associative chains indicated in the diagram.

Thus, dealing with Joyce, semiotics is obliged to study as a specimen of object-language a work which is nothing else but an example of metalinguistic representation of the nature of language. The whole Joycean opus is a living example of a cultural universe ruled by the laws of Unlimited Semiosis. *FW* seems to instantiate such notions as "infinite regression" and "infinite series" or interpretation as "another representation to which the torch of truth is handed along" (Peirce 1934:1.339).

The universe of unlimited semiosis looks extraordinarily similar to the Joycean meandertale. One could say that the whole *FW* is only a metaphor for the semiosic universe, or that the theory of the semiosic universe is only a metaphor for *FW*. If it were only so, then the semiotic theory of unlimited semiosis would simply portray the very peculiar universe of a category of literary open works, to which *FW* belongs, whose aim is to stimulate an ideal reader affected by an ideal insomnia to perform free, uncontrolled, infinite readings. The problem is, however, more serious than that. The most recent studies in artificial intelligence show that the model of unlimited semiosis, even though duly tamed and reduced to local manageable formats, for experimental reasons, is the only one which can explain how language is produced and understood.

4. Joyce and the encyclopedia

Two semantic models are today competing to explain how human beings produce and understand texts: the dictionary model and the encyclopedia model. According to the dictionary model a language is a series of items explained by a concise definition, usually composed by a finite set of semantic universals, that cannot be further analyzed. In this perspective *man* means "animal human adult male." Such items can be combined according to a finite set of syntactical rules. A sentence such as *this man is a pig* is scored as nonsensical. The dictionary model is undoubtedly pretty artificial, but many linguists and analytical philosophers for a long time believed that, since it depicts the competence of an average stupid human being, it could at least work to give semantic instructions to intelligent machines. Unfortunately, the researches in AI have proved that, with a dictionary-like competence, the machines cannot emulate even a stupid human being. In order to understand a text, a machine must be provided with information structured in the format of an encyclopedia.

The encyclopedia model is based on the assumption that every item of a language must be interpreted by every other possible linguistic item which, according to some previous cultural conventions, can be associated with it. Every sign can be interpreted by another sign that functions as its interpretant. The interpretants of the verbal item *man* can be a synonym, a simple definition, a long explanation which takes into account the biological nature of human beings, the history of our species, every piece of information connected with the past, present, and future of mankind, every inference that can be drawn from the very idea of man. One of the first and more influential models proposed by AI was the model of Ross Quillian that I largely used in Eco 1976 (2.12 and p. 123), in order to suggest how our cultural competence should be postulated. Quillian's model was based on a mass of nodes interconnected by various types of associative links. For the meaning of every lexeme there has to exist, in the memory, a node which has as its "patriarch" the term to be defined, here called a *type*. The definition of a type A foresees the employment, as its interpretants, of a series of other lexemes which are included as tokens. The configuration of the meaning of the lexeme is given by the multiplicity of its links with various tokens, each of which, however, becomes in turn a type B, that is, the patriarch of a new configuration which includes as tokens many other lexemes, some of which were also tokens of type A and which can include as token the same type A. A token such as *grow* can become the type of a new branch (or plane) which includes among its tokens many of those which go with *plant* (as, for example, *air* or *water* and, indeed, *plant* itself). Thus the ideal structure of a complete memory would form an enormous aggregation of planes, each consisting entirely of token nodes except for its "head node."

This model is based on a process of unlimited semiosis. From a sign which is taken as a type, it is possible to penetrate, from the center to the farthest periphery, the whole universe of cultural units, each of which can in turn become the center and create infinite peripheries.

A similar model can still receive a bidimensional graphic configuration when one part of it is examined (and it is understood that in its mechanical simulation, thanks to the limited number of tokens included, it may be possible to confer on it a structure which can be described). But actually no graph is in a position to represent it in all its complexity. It must appear as a sort of polydimensional network, equipped with topological properties, in which the distances covered are abbreviated or elongated and each term acquires proximity with others by means of shortcuts and immediate contacts, meanwhile remaining linked with all the others, according to continually changing relationships.

We can imagine all the cultural units as an enormous number of marbles contained in a box; by shaking the box we can form different connections and affinities among the marbles. This box would constitute an informational source provided with high entropy, and it would constitute the abstract model of semantic association in a free state.

But we should think of magnetized marbles which establish a system of attraction and repulsion, so that some are drawn to one another and others are not. A similar magnetization would reduce the possibility of interrelation. Still better, we could consider every cultural unit in this Global Semantic Universe as emitting given wavelengths which put it in tune with a limited (though possibly very large) number of other units.

Except that we have to admit that the wavelengths can change according to new messages emitted and that therefore the possibilities of attraction and repulsion change in time. In effect, this model presupposes that the system can be nourished by fresh information and that further data can be inferred from incomplete data.

The maze-like structure that represents the ideal competence of a *Finnegans Wake* reader results in being very similar to the Quillian model—as well as to the most up-to-date models provided by the so-called new connectionism. When one tries to provide a machine with a sort of competence that can match our own way of thinking and speaking, one is obliged to conceive of a cultural universe structured more as *Finnegans Wake* than as a grammar made with a dictionary plus some syntactic algorithms.

If the model of our encyclopedic competence is an immense web of interpretants where from every single point of the net every other point can be reached, then one could reread the whole Joycean opus as the gigantic attempt of presupposing, as its own reading code, an encyclopedia.

The first intuition of a semiosic encyclopedia came to the young Joyce through a decadent heritage, as if the encyclopedia was something that only the poet could call into life from a previous chaos. Roughly encyclopedic is the idea of a tissue of events that the epiphanic intuition can correlate in different ways, finding out new meanings from an unheard-of correlation. Walter Pater was teaching Joyce that reality is a sum of forces and elements that fade away as soon as they arise, a world of incoherent, flashing, and unstable impressions. To isolate epiphanic events means to dissolve the most conventional entities into a network of new relationships. The poet alone "is capable of absorbing in itself the life that surrounds him and flinging it abroad amid planetary music" (*Stephen Hero*). The artistic activity consists in positing new relations between the elements of the "rhizome" of experience: "The artist who could disentangle the subtle sound of an image from the mesh of its defining circumstances most exactly and 're-embody' in artistic circumstances chosen as the most exact for it in its new office, he was the supreme artist" (*Stephen Hero*). One of the most probable sources for the invention of the stream of consciousness was James's argument according to which reality has a myriad of forms, experience is never limited and is never complete: it is like a kind of huge spiderweb of the finest silken threads suspended in the chamber of consciousness and catching every particle in its tissue.

Between the first novels and *Ulysses*, however, this idea of encyclopedia undergoes a substantial change. If in the early work this tissue was only something imprecise between our psychological activity and metaphysical structure (something midway between the impalpable structure of "reality" and the equally impalpable network of the creative imagination), in *Ulysses* it was more clearly referred to a supposed structure of the physical world as described by modern science.

With *Finnegans Wake* this semiotic process is definitely implemented; the tissue of events has become a tissue of linguistic entities. The encyclopedia underlying *Finnegans Wake* is a purely linguistic or semiotic one, a world of infinite semiosis where words (along with their meanings) "by the coincidence of their contraries reamalgamerge in that identity of undiscernible" (*FW*, p. 49).

5. Early Jesuit semiotics

It seems that in order to read and understand *Finnegans Wake* the "ideal reader affected by an ideal insomnia" ought to possess a sort of global index of all the knowledge ever expressed by language. It is curious to note that this idea of an encyclopedia index had been developed in the seventeenth century by a Baroque rhetorician of metaphor, the Italian Emanuele Tesauro, whom Joyce probably had never read. We cannot, however, underestimate the fact that Tesauro was a Jesuit, and that the search for a multiple combination of elements, the idea of an Ars Magna and of a total encyclopedia, obsessed many Jesuits during and after the Baroque era (see, first of all, Athanasius Kircher, but also Gaspar Schott and many others). I do not know whether someone has carefully studied the relationship between Joyce's cultural background and that very peculiar mainstream of Jesuit culture.

Tesauro wrote a treatise on metaphor, *Il cannocchiale aristotelico* (1655), in which he appears to be aware of the fact that, after Galileo, the way of looking at the universe had changed. Nevertheless, Tesauro wants to demonstrate that the Aristotelian notion of metaphor still represents a valid instrument (a telescope) with which to know, not the world of physical events, but that of human language and the possibilities within it for creation and knowledge.

Here we won't concern ourselves with the minutiae or with the enthusiasm with which the author extends the metaphorical mechanism to visual witticisms, painting, sculpture, actions, inscriptions, mottoes, maxims, broken sentences, laconic letters, mysterious characters, hieroglyphs, logogryphs, ciphers, hints, medals, columns, ships, garters, chimeras. Joyce shared with him the same taste for lists and inventories. What interests us is that Tesauro knows quite well that metaphors are not created by any inventive felicity but require labor, the mastery of which takes practice. The first exercise is the reading of catalogues, anthologies, collections of hieroglyphics, medals, reverses, and emblems: it might be called a clear invitation to intertextuality, to the imitation of the "already said." But the second exercise presupposes the apprehension of a combinational mode.

Tesauro speaks of a categorical index made with files and tables, that is, a model of an organized semantic universe. This proceeds from Aristotle's categories (substance, quantity, quality, relation, place, time, to be in a situation, to have, to act, to undergo), and then the various members that collect everything that can be ordered under the categories are systematized with them. Does one need a metaphor about a dwarf? One runs down the categorical index under the heading of Quantity, one identifies the concept Small Things, and all microscopic items that are found there will still be able to be divided into contextual selections: astronomy, human organism, animals, plants, and so on. But the index which proceeds according to substances should be integrated with a second index, in which every substance is analyzed for the particles that define the way in which the object in question manifests itself (in the category of Quantity one should then find "How large it is," "How much it weighs," "What parts it has;" in the category of Quality there will be: "Whether it is visible," "Whether it is not visible," and so on). This is obviously an actual and authentic system of content organized into an encyclopedia. At this point one will say of the dwarf that to calculate his tininess a geometric digit would be too vast a measure.

Using the categorical index, Tesauro creates and interprets not only metaphors but also neologisms and actual puns. Taking a linguistic invention as a departure point, he deduces an infinite number of others. He shows how from a witty invention one can arrive at an entirely infinite series of other inventions. The *Cannocchiale aristotelico* of Tesauro seems, in short, a manual with which to read *Finnegans Wake*. In point of fact, *Finnegans Wake* is an example of a categorical index put into practice, a sort of computer which has received the input of all available knowledge and which returns an output of new connections effected among the various elements of this knowledge. *Finnegans Wake* is the representation (even if in an artistic rather than theoretical form) of an encyclopedia in action.

6. The temptation of deconstruction

So far, it seems that the ideal Joycean reader affected by an ideal insomnia is a paramount model of a decontructionist reader for whom any text is an inexhaustible nightmare. For such a reader any true interpretation is a creative misprision, every reading of a text cannot but be a truly creative one. For such a reader there will be no critical interpretation of *Finnegans Wake* but, rather, an infinite series of original re-creations.

I think on the contrary that *Finnegans Wake* is a satisfactory image of the universe of unlimited semiosis just because it is a text in its own right. An open text is always a text, and a text can elicit infinite readings without allowing any possible reading. It is impossible to say what is the best interpretation of a text, but it is possible to say which ones are wrong. In the process of unlimited semiosis it is certainly possible to go from any one node to every other node, but the passages are controlled by rules of connection that our cultural history has in some way legitimated.

Every short circuit conceals a cultural network in which every association, every metonymy, every inferential link can be potentially displayed and proved. By setting the speakers free to establish an immense number of connections, the process of unlimited semiosis permits them to create texts. But a text is an organism, a system of internal relationships that actualizes certain possible connections and narcotizes others. Before a text is produced, every kind of text could be invented. After a text has been produced, it is possible to make that text say many things—in certain cases a potentially infinite number of things—but it is impossible—or at least critically illegitimate—to make it say what it does not say. Texts frequently say more than their authors intended to say, but less than what many incontinent readers would like them to say.

Independent of any alleged intention of the author is the intention of the text. But a text exists only as a physical object, as a Linear Text Manifestation. It is possible to speak of text intentions only as the result of a conjecture on the part of the reader. The initiative of the reader basically consists in making a conjecture about the text intention. A text is a device conceived in order to produce its Model Reader. Such a Model Reader is not the one who makes the only right conjecture. A text can foresee a Model Reader entitled to try infinite conjectures. But infinite conjecture does not mean any possible conjecture.

How to prove that a given interpretive conjecture is, if not the only right one, at least an acceptable one? The only way is to check it upon the text as a coherent whole: any interpretation given of a certain portion of a text can be accepted if it is confirmed, and must be rejected if it is challenged, by another portion of the same text. In this sense the internal textual coherence controls the otherwise uncontrollable drift of the reader.

7. Some final Joycean gossip

In the glorious *A Wake Newslitter* (October 1964, p. 13), Philip L. Graham suggests that the last historical event recorded in *Finnegans Wake* was the German-Austrian *Anschluss*. Ruth von Phul argues on the contrary that the latest historical allusion concerned the Munich Pact of September 3, 1938. While the reference to the *Anschluss* is proved by the presence of this word, the reference to the pact is a matter of clever conjectures. However, there is nothing repugnant in assuming that an author able to quote the *Anschluss* was also eager to quote the Munich Pact.

In the October 1965 issue, Nathan Halper argues that the conjecture about the Munich Pact can be challenged on the basis of a precise semantic analysis of the terms Joyce used, but he does not take a definite stand pro or con. He suggests, however, that Joyce could have used the word *Anschluss* in its customary and nonpolitical sense, and remarks that the political reading is not supported by the following context. If the strong conjecture about the *Anschluss* is weakened, then the weak one about the Munich Pact is seriously challenged. In order to show how easy it could be to find everything in Joyce, Halper makes the example of Beria:

> Beria, December 9, 1938 (based on "berial," 415.31). "The Tale of the Ondt and the Gracehoper" is preceded by the phrase "So vi et!" This relates to the communal ant-society. One page later there is an allusion to a "berial." This is a variant of "burial." There seems to be no reason why Joyce should use it (rather than "burial") unless he is making an additional reference to that society. This time, by a reference to the Soviet functionary, Lavrenti Beria. He was not known in the Western world before December 9, when he was named Commissar of Internal Affairs. Prior to this he was merely a minor functionary. Joyce wouldn't have known his name. Or, if he had, would have seen no point in using it. On this date the manuscript was at the printer's. But, instead of being a weakness, this is a strong point in the case. We know that he always made additions to the proofs. We would expect that some of the last-minute thoughts would come as a result of current events. It is not unlikely that the last historical event would be one he added in the proofs. All that remains is to check when it first appears. It is not present (though "So vi et" is) in *transition* 12, March 1928. Alas, it is

present in *Tales Told of Shem and Shaun*, August 1929. My case has a flaw that is worse, if anything, than the ones in Mrs. von Phul's—or even Mr. Graham's. "Berial" is not a reference to Beria. Query: Can anyone tell me why Joyce did use this particular spelling? . . . There is a theory that *FW* is prophetic. Thus, although "berial" appeared ten years earlier, it does refer to Beria. I think that this is nonsense. If we are going to go in for these prophecies, it becomes impossible to find a "last historical event."

In the issue of December 1965, von Phul struck again, but this time to support Halper's prudence:

About the spelling "berial" (415.31). The Fable of the Ondt and the Gracehoper in part does refer to regimented and authoritarian societies and, as Mr. Halper notes, it is preceded by "So vi et!" This is not only a reference to Russian Marxism; it is also the Amen given by members of authoritarian religious bodies. In close context to berial is another political reference: The Ondt (which means "evil" in Danish-Norwegian) says he will "not come to a party at that lopp's"—a lop is a flea—"for he is not on our social list. Nor to Ba's berial nether. . . . " The various political allusions are allegories for religious significances; the main meaning of the fable concerns the Gracehoper's often terrified rejection of the eschatology of an authoritarian religion and its prescribed rituals for salvation, the conflict between forms and rites (i.e. works) and grace (i.e. faith)—it is the latter on which the Gracehoper relies.

The Ba to be buried is the soul of the dead; in Egyptian mythology a bird-headed human figure. At 415.35–36, after praying in the manner of the *Book of the Dead* (and so anticipating the unmistakable Egyptian allusions at the end of the fable: 418.5 ff), the Ondt says: "As broad as Beppy's realm shall flourish my reign shall flourish!" Beppy is the Italian diminutive for Joseph. Here the Ondt sets himself up as a rival to Joseph, for berial is a suppressed allusion to that Joseph who was twice figuratively buried, in the pit and in prison, but rose to rule Egypt. In Egypt he begot Ephraim (Gen. 46.20) who begot Beriah (Douay, Beria) which means "in evil" a name chosen because "it went evil with his house" (I Chr. 7.23). Joseph's brother Asher also had a son Beriah (Gen. 45.30). The two "in evils" relate the "berial nether" both to the Ondt (evil) and to funerary practices in "Amongded" (418.6), Egypt. Possibly a reference to Ammon, but also to Amen, of which Amon is a variant. In a later generation of Joseph's family one Zophah had a son, Beri (I Chr. 7.36); this means "man of the well," an apparent allusion to Joseph and the pit, a dry well. (This characteristic confusion of identities and of generations is the theme of Thomas Mann's essay on the Well of the Past, the introductory chapter of the Joseph tetralogy. In 1933 Mann began the work by showing us a vision of the immemorial identification and atonement of sons with fathers that is the essential theme of the *Wake*.)

Beria is thus liquidated—once more after his death. The context privileges the biblical allusion. I love that discussion. All the participants proved to be smart enough to invent acrobatic interpretations, but both, in the end, were prudent enough to recognize that their brilliant innuendos were not supported by the context. They won the game because they let *Finnegans Wake* win.

Such an example of respect of the text as a system ruled by an internal coherence seems to me a good conclusive parable. To develop an ideal insomnia, the ideal Joyce Reader always has to keep semiotically awake.

10

Abduction in Uqbar

1.

If we subscribe to the writings of detective-story theorists (for example, the rules set forth by S. S. Van Dine), Borges and Casares's *Six Problems for Don Isidro Parodi* appears completely "heretical." It has been said that the stories constitute a parody of Chesterton, who, in turn, parodied the classic detective story from Poe on. The *Ouvroir de Littérature Potentielle* (Paris) recently determined a matrix of the previously conceived detective-story plots (murderer = butler, murderer = narrator, murderer = detective, and so on) and discovered that a book in which the murderer is the reader has yet to be written. I ask myself whether this scenario (revealing to the readers that they, or rather *we*, are the murderer) might not be at the heart of every great book, from *Oedipus Rex* to Borges's short stories. But it is certain that Borges and Casares, in 1942, found an empty space in Mendeleiev's table of detective-story plots: the detective is a prison inmate. Instead of solving the crime (committed in a closed room) from the outside, the detective, locked in a closed room, must now solve a series of crimes committed on the outside.

The idea of a detective who solves the case in his own mind, on the basis of a few clues provided by someone else, is part of the detective-story tradition: consider Rex Stout's Nero Wolfe, to whom Archie

First published in German as "Die Abduktion in Uqbar," Postscript to *Sechs Aufgaben für Don Isidro Parodi* (Munich: Hanser, 1983). The nonscholarly purpose of this postscript explains the reasons for a vulgarization of Peirce's idea of abduction. Translated by Juliann Vitullo and Guy Raffa from the Italian version in Eco 1985.

Goodwin brings information but who never budges from his house as he moves sluggishly from his study to the orchid greenhouse. But a detective such as Isidro Parodi, who cannot leave his cell and who receives information from imbeciles unable to follow the sequence of events they have witnessed, is unquestionably the product of a noteworthy narrative *tour de force*.

The reader gets the impression that just as Don Isidro makes fun of his clients, so too Biorges (as the exceptional tandem Bioy-Jorge has been named) make fun of their readers—and that in this similarity (and only in this) lies the interest of these short stories.

The genesis of these stories is already well known, and Emir Rodriguez Monegal tells it to us best in his monumental biography of Borges.[1] But let us allow Borges to speak for himself:

> It is always taken for granted in these cases that the elder man is the master and the younger his disciple. This may have been true at the outset, but several years later, when we began to work together, Bioy was really and secretly the master. He and I attempted many different ventures. We compiled anthologies of Argentine poetry, tales of the fantastic, and detective stories; we wrote articles and forewords; we annotated Sir Thomas Browne and Gracián; we translated short stories by writers like Beerbohm, Kipling, Wells, and Lord Dunsany; we founded a magazine, *Destiempo*, which lasted three issues; we wrote film scripts, which were invariably rejected. Opposing my taste for the pathetic, the sententious, and the baroque, Bioy made me feel that quietness and restraint are more desirable. If I may be allowed a sweeping statement, Bioy led me gradually to classicism.
>
> It was at some point in the early forties that we began writing in collaboration—a feat that up to that time I had thought impossible. I had invented what we thought was a quite good plot for a detective story. One rainy morning, he told me we ought to give it a try. I reluctantly agreed, and a little later that same morning the thing happened. A third man, Honorio Bustos Domecq, emerged and took over.
>
> In the long run, he ruled us with a rod of iron and to our amusement, and later to our dismay, he became utterly unlike ourselves, with his own whims, his own puns, and his own very elaborate style of writing. . . . Bustos Domecq's first book was *Six Problems for Don Isidro Parodi* [1942], and during the writing of that volume he never got out of hand. Max Carrados had attempted a blind detective; Bioy and I went one step further and confined our detective to a jail cell. The book was at the same time a satire on the Argentines. For many years, the dual identity of Bustos Domecq was never revealed. When it finally was, people thought that, as Bustos was a joke, his writing could hardly be taken seriously.[2]

Moreover, the Argentine public had other reasons to be upset, or at least to remain perplexed. The book even bears an introduction by one of its characters, Gervasio Montenegro. Now, a character should not write the introduction to the book that will give him or her life. But what is worse, every time that Montenegro appears in one of the book's stories, he looks like a fool. How can the reader take him seriously when he fervently praises his authors with flashy, pompous, academic rhetoric? We are confronted with the paradox of Epimenides of Crete: all the Cretans are liars, says Epimenides, but how can we believe him, given that he too is from Crete and therefore a liar? (By the way, Saint Paul, not a character invented by Borges, in his letter to Titus cites Epimenides's dictum as a reliable source concerning the deceitful nature of the Cretans, because [he notes] if the man who says it is from Crete—and therefore knows the Cretans—we have to trust him. . . .)

2.

But the reasons why *Six Problems* must have baffled the Argentines do not end here. In these stories, we find ourselves face to face with another game, one destined to lose force in translation, no matter how good the translator. The speeches of the characters who come to visit Don Isidro in his cell are a fireworks display of commonplace expressions, cultural tics, and Kitsch weaknesses and fads of the Argentine intelligentsia of the time. And even if translators do their best (but they would fail even in translating *this* Spanish into a Spanish dialect different from the one spoken among Lavalle, Corrientes, and la Boca), the various ironic references are bound to be lost because the readers, in any case, are different: they speak another language and they are not the Argentine readers of 1942. The readers, therefore, must make an effort to imagine this earlier Buenos Aires, as well as the parodic virulence that a book such as this could embody; a book in which (says Rodriguez Monegal) "the solemnity of spoken Argentine, with all its variations (working-class slang, the Frenchified speech of pseudo-intellectuals, the thick and obsolete Spanish of Spaniards, Italianate jargon) was exploded through characters who were less narrative figures than figures of speech. For the first time in Argentina a deliberate attempt to create narrative through the parody of narrative form and speech was successful" (368).

There comes to mind an etymological game, which I will mention with no guaranties to fans of Isidore (Isidro?) of Seville, Heidegger, or Derridean exercises on drift: the fact that Don Isidro's name is Parodi should not be surprising, since Parodi is a very common Italian name (from Liguria), and nothing is more common in Argentina than an Italian name (there's even a joke about an Argentine who comes to Italy and is amazed that Italians all have Argentine last names). However, there is very little distance between "parodi" and "parody." Is this a coincidence?[3]

Having said this, however, it seems that there are very few reasons for rereading these stories today. It is difficult to grasp the colloquial references and to appreciate detective stories that only mimic the true *detection* stories . . . and so? Isn't it better to read firsthand the great *detection* stories (or fake *detection*), the *ficciones* such as "Death and the Compass"?

In fact, the first impression of the reader who approaches the Don Isidro stories is that, apart from the incomprehensible slang and cultural allusions, the chatter of the various characters is totally mindless. The temptation is rapidly to skim their unending monologues, treating them as if they were a musical commentary, in order to get to the end right away and to find pleasure in Don Isidro's (untenable) solution. The reader suspects, therefore, that these stories are the pleasing solution to *false* riddles, just as in the well-known joke:

Problem: The ship is thirty meters long, the main mast is ten meters high, and there are four sailors. How old is the captain?

Solution: Forty. (Explanation of the solution: I know because he told me.)

But no. The six stories all follow a fundamental rule of detective fiction: all the clues that the detective uses to solve the case are made available to the reader. The chatter of the characters is full of *important* information.

The difference with the classic *detection* stories is that, when we reread them from the beginning, after having learned the solution, we say to ourselves: "That's right. How come I hadn't noticed that detail?" But when we reread Don Isidro's stories, we are left wondering: "Why should I have taken note of that detail instead of others? Why did Don Isidro concentrate on that event or piece of information and consider the others irrelevant?"

Carefully reread, for example, the fourth story, "Free will and the Comendador." One evening after dinner, the Comendador claims to have a terracotta *pumita* in the third drawer of his desk. The young girl, Pumita, is amazed. There shouldn't be any reason to highlight this fact as a clue. It is natural that a girl named Pumita might display curiosity at the mention of a *pumita*. Later on, Don Isidro learns from another informer (and the reader also acquires this information) that the Comendador had a terracotta serpent in the drawer. What authorizes us (what authorizes Don Isidro) to think that the Comendador had a serpent *instead* of a *pumita*? Why couldn't he have *two* terracotta statues? But let's suppose that this clue authorizes Don Isidro to think that the Comendador had lied that evening (and claimed to have a *pumita* when he actually had a serpent). What causes Don Isidro to think that the Comendador lied in order to discover whether Pumita had rummaged through his drawer?

That Don Isidro stories are full of such clues proves two things: (i) the chatter of the characters is not irrelevant and does not function solely as linguistic parody: it is structurally important; (ii) in order to know how to "read" into the chatter of the characters, Don Isidro must make use of a "key," or rather a very powerful hypothesis. What sort of key is involved?

You see right away that, for the above-mentioned reasons, reading the Don Isidro stories is both challenging and fun. The fact that they are enjoyable should be enough to justify the effort of reading them. Forgive the aesthetic crudeness of my statement; I'm one of those who still (or again) maintain that enjoyment is reason enough to read a story. But here we have a different problem.

The mechanism of the Don Isidro stories anticipates the fundamental mechanism of many of Borges's later stories, perhaps all of them. I will call this mechanism (and I will elaborate in the following section) *the mechanism of conjecture in a sick Spinozist universe.*

3.

Borges appears to have read everything (and even more, given that he has reviewed nonexistent books). Still, I imagine that he has never read the *Collected Papers* of Charles Sanders Peirce. I could be mistaken, but I trust Rodriguez Monegal, and Peirce's name does not appear in the Index of Names at the end of Rodriguez Monegal's biography of Borges. If I am wrong, I am in good company.

In any case, it does not matter to me whether Borges has or has not read Peirce. It seems a good Borgesan procedure to assume that books speak to one another, and so it isn't necessary that writers (who use books in order to speak—a hen is the device used by an egg to produce another egg) know one another's works. The fact remains that many of Borges's short stories are perfect exemplifications of that art of inference which Peirce calls abduction or hypothesis, and which is nothing but conjecture.

Peirce claims that we reason according to three modes: Deduction,

Induction, and Abduction. Let's try to understand these three modes by turning to one of Peirce's examples. I will summarize it without boring the reader with logical and semiotic technical jargon.

Let's suppose that on this table I have a sack full of white beans. I know that it is full of *white* beans (let's say I bought the sack in a store in which the merchant, whom I trust, sells sacks of white beans); consequently, I can assume the Rule "All the beans in this sack are white." Once I know the Rule, I produce a Case; I blindly take a fistful of beans from the sack (blindly: it's not necessary to look at them), and I can predict the Result: "The beans in my hand are white." Deduction from a (true) Rule, by means of a Case, predicts a Result with absolute certainty.

Alas, except for a few axiomatic systems, we can make very few safe deductions. Let's move now to Induction. I have a sack, and I don't know what's in it. I stick in my hand, pull out a handful of beans, and observe that they are all white. I put my hand in again, and still come up with white beans. I repeat this procedure x number of times (the number of trials depends on how much time I have, or on how much money I've received from the Ford Foundation to establish a scientific law about the beans in the sack). After a sufficient number of trials, I make the following assessment: all the Results of my trials produce a fistful of white beans; I can reasonably infer that all these outcomes are Cases of the same Rule—that is, all the beans in the sack are white. From a series of Results, inferring that they are Cases of the same Rule, I arrive at the inductive formulation of this (probable) Rule. As we know, all it takes is one trial in which one of the beans drawn from the sack is black, and my entire inductive effort vanishes into thin air. This is why epistemologists are so suspicious with regard to Induction.

Actually, since we don't know how many trials are necessary before an Induction can be considered a good one, we really don't know what a valid Induction is. Are ten trials enough? And why not nine? Or eight? And why not even one?

At this point, Induction moves over and makes room for Abduction. With Abduction, I find myself confronted by a strange and unexplainable Result. To keep to our example, I have a sack of beans on the table, and nearby, also on the table, is a bunch of white beans. I don't know how they've gotten there or who has placed them there, or even where they come from. Let's consider this Result a strange Case. Now I need to find a Rule such that, if it were true, and if the Result were considered a Case of that Rule, the Result would no longer be strange, but rather extremely reasonable.

At this point I make a conjecture: I theorize a Rule for which that sack contains beans and all the beans in the sack are white, and I try to consider the Result that I have before my eyes as a Case of that Rule. If all the beans in the sack are white and these beans come from that sack, it's natural that the beans on the table are white.

Peirce observes that the reasoning for Abduction is typical of all "revolutionary" scientific discoveries. Kepler learns from those who preceded him that the planets' orbits are circular. Then he observes Mars in two different positions and reveals that they touch two points (x and y) that cannot be two points of a circle. This Case is strange. It would no longer be strange if one were to assume that the planets trace an orbit that can be represented by another type of curve (noncircular). Kepler must, therefore, find a different rule. He could imagine that the orbits are parabolic or sinusoidal. . . . It doesn't matter to us (in this paper) why he thinks of an ellipse (he has his good reasons). Thus he makes his Abduction: if the orbits of the planets were elliptical and the two positions of Mars revealed (x and y) were a Case of this rule, the Result would no longer be surprising. Naturally, at this point he must test his Abduction by a new Deduction. If the orbits are elliptical (if at least the orbit of Mars is elliptical) one must wait for Mars at a point z, which is another point of the ellipse. Kepler waits for it, and finds it. In principle, the Abduction is proven. Now one must simply test and prove that the hypothesis cannot be negated. Naturally, I abbreviated and summarized the phases of the discovery. The fact is that the scientist does not need ten thousand inductive tests. He makes one hypothesis, perhaps daring, very similar to a bet, and he puts it to the test. As long as the test gives positive results, he has won.

Now, a detective does not proceed any differently. Rereading the declarations of method by Sherlock Holmes, one discovers that, when he (and with him Conan Doyle) talks of Deduction and Observation, in effect he's thinking about an inference similar to Peirce's Abduction.[4]

It's strange that Peirce used such a term as "abduction." He formulated it in analogy with *Deduction* and *Induction* (and also in reference to some Aristotelian terms). But we cannot forget that in English "abduction" also means kidnapping. If I have a strange Result in a field of phenomena not yet studied, I cannot look for a Rule in that field (if there were and if I did not know it, the phenomenon would not be strange). I must go and "abduct," or "borrow," a Rule from elsewhere. You could say that I must reason by analogy.

Let's reconsider the Abduction about the white beans. I find a fistful of beans on the table. On the table is a sack. What tells me that I need to connect the beans on the table with the sack? I could ask myself whether the beans come from a sack, whether someone brought them there and then left. If I focus my attention on the sack (and why on that sack?) it is because in my head a sort of plausibility appears, such as "It is logical that the beans come from the sack." But there is nothing which guarantees me that my hypothesis is the right one.

In any case, many of the great scientific discoveries proceed in this fashion, but also many of the discoveries of investigators and many of the hypotheses made by doctors, to understand the nature or origin of an illness (and many of the hypotheses of the philologist, to understand what could be in a text where the original manuscript is unclear or contains blanks). Reread (or read) the second story of Don Isidro. Everything that happens to Gervasio Montenegro on the Pan-American train is strange, stupefying, without logic. . . . Don Isidro resolves the problem (the clues that he knows constitute a Result) inferring that it might be the Case of a very different Rule, the Rule of mise-en-scène. If all that happened on the train had been a theatrical representation in which no one was really what he or she seemed to be, then the sequence of events would not have appeared so mysterious. Everything would have been very clear, elementary (Dear Watson). And in fact it was. Montenegro is a fool, and appropriates Don Isidro's solution with the following remark: "The cold speculative intelligence comes to confirm the brilliant intuitions of the artist." Even though he is a liar and a deceiver, he speaks the truth. There is something artistic in a scientific discovery and there is something scientific in that which the naive call "brilliant intuitions of the artist." What they share is the felicity of Abduction.

But in order to choose in a "felicitous" fashion the relevant clues in the tale of Montenegro, it is necessary to have already made a conjecture: that every element of the affair should be read as if it were directly taken from a mise-en-scène. Why does Don Isidro make this conjecture? If we succeed in explaining it to ourselves, we will understand something about the technique of abduction and of Borges's metaphysics.

There are three levels of Abduction. On the first level, the Result is strange and unexplainable, but the Rule already exists somewhere, perhaps inside the same field of problems, and one just must find it, and find it to be the most probable. On the second level, the Rule is difficult to identify. It exists elsewhere, and one must bet that it could be extended to this field of phenomena (this is the case of Kepler). On the third level, the Rule does not exist, and one must invent it: this is the case of Copernicus, who decides that the universe must not be heliocentric for reasons of symmetry and "good form."[5]

We might take another look together at the history of science, of police *detection*, of the interpretation of texts, of clinical medicine (and other fields) showing how and in which cases abductions of the second and third type intervene. But in all these instances, when the detectives, or the scientists, or the critics, or the philologists make an Abduction, they must bet that the solution that they found (the Possible World of their hypothetical imagination) corresponds to the Real World. And for this they must perform other tests and experiments.

In the detective stories, from Conan Doyle to Rex Stout, these tests are not necessary. The detective imagines the solution and "says" it as if it were the truth; and immediately Watson, the killer who is present, or someone else verifies the hypothesis. They say: "It happened just like that!" And the detective is sure of what he guessed. In the detective novels the author (who acts in the place of God) guarantees the correspondence between the Possible World imagined by the detective and the Real World. Outside the detective novels, abductions are riskier and are always exposed to failure.

Now, Biorges's stories are a parody of the detective story because Don Isidro does not need someone to tell him that things were as he had imagined them. He is completely sure, and Borges-Casares with him (and the reader with them). Why?

4.

To be sure that the mind of the detective has reconstructed the sequence of the facts and of the rules as they had to be, one must believe a profound Spinozistic notion that "ordo et connexio rerum idem est ac ordo et connexio idearum." The movements of our mind that investigates follow the same rules of the real. If we think "well," we are obligated to think according to the same rules that connect things among themselves. If a detective identifies with the mind of the killer, he cannot help but arrive at the same point at which the killer arrives. In this Spinozist universe, the detective will also know what the killer will do tomorrow. And he will go to wait for him at the scene of the next crime.

But if the detective reasons like that, the killer can reason like that as well: he will be able to act in such a way that the detective will go and wait for him at the scene of the next crime, but the victim of the killer's next crime will be the detective himself. And this is what happens in "Death and the Compass," and in practice in all of Borges's stories, or at least in the more disturbing and enthralling ones.

The universe of Borges is a universe in which diverse minds can't help but think through the laws expressed by the Library. But this is the Library of Babel. Its rules are not those of neopositivistic science; they are paradoxical rules. The logic (the same) of the Mind and that of the World are both an illogic. An iron illogic. Only under these conditions can Pierre Menard rewrite "the same" *Don Quixote*. But alas, only under these conditions the same *Don Quixote* will be a different *Don Quixote*.

What of the rigorously illogical does Borges's universe have and what is it that permits Don Isidro to reconstruct with rigorous illogic the processes of an external universe equally illogical? Borges's universe functions according to the laws of the mise-en-scène or of fiction.

Reread all six stories of Don Isidro. In every instance we do not have stories which unfold on their own, as happens (we believe) in life. Don Isidro always discovers that what his clients experienced was a sequence of events projected by another mind. He discovers that they were already moving in the frame of a story and according to the rules of storytelling, that they were unconscious characters of a play already written by someone else. Don Isidro discovers the "truth" because of both his fertile mind and the fact that the subjects of his investigation proceed according to the rules of fiction.

This seems to me an excellent key for reading other stories by Borges. One is never confronted by chance, or by Fate; one is always inside a plot (cosmic or situational) developed by some other Mind according to a fantastic logic that is the logic of the Library.

This is what I meant when I talked about a mechanism of conjecture in a sick Spinozist universe. Naturally, "sick" in respect to Spinoza, not to Borges. In respect to Borges, that universe in which the detective and the killer always meet each other at the last moment, because both of them reasoned according to the same illogical fantasy, is the healthiest and most truthful universe of all.

If we are convinced of this, Don Isidro Parodi's way of reasoning will no longer appear paradoxical to us. Don Isidro is a perfect inhabitant of Borges's world (to come). And it is normal that one locked in a cell can resolve all the cases. The disorder and the disconnection of the ideas is the same as the disorder and disconnection of the world, or even of things.

It is irrelevant whether one thinks about it in the world, examining the facts, or locked in a prison, examining the unconscious falsifications of stupid observers. On the contrary, a prison is better than the world: the mind can function without too much external "noise." The mind, tranquil, becomes one with things.

But what are things at this point? And what is literature in respect to things?

Ah, kind reader, you're asking too much of me. I only wanted to tell you that Biorges's Don Isidro is Borges's character, and for this reason it is worth reflecting on his method. Biorges isn't kidding. He's talking "seriously," that is, through Parodi/parody.

Does the world really work like this? I believe that Borges would greet this question with a smile. Paraphrasing Villiers de l'Isle Adam, reality is boring, let's let our servants live it for us.

NOTES

1. Emir Rodriguez Monegal, *Jorge Luis Borges: A Literary Biography* (New York: Dutton, 1978).

2. Jorge Luis Borges, "An Autobiographical Essay," in *The Aleph and Other Stories, 1933–1969* (New York: Dutton, 1970), pp. 245–246, as quoted in Rodriguez Monegal, pp. 365, 366.

3. I understand that such an instance of reading goes against all the appeals to interpretive prudence that I have disseminated throughout the present book. But, as I said in 3.8, it is frequently very hard to keep the boundaries between *use* and *interpretation*. Sorry.

4. For a series of studies on the relationship between Peirce's abduction, Sherlock Holmes's method, the scientific method, and literary hermeneutics, see U. Eco and T. A. Sebeok, eds., *The Sign of Three* (Bloomington: Indiana University Press, 1984).

5. See U. Eco "Guessing: From Aristotle to Sherlock Holmes," *Versus* 30 (1981):3–19; and M. Bonfantini and G. P. Proni, "To Guess or Not to Guess?" in Eco and Sebeok, eds., ibid.

11

Pirandello *Ridens*

1.

In 1907, Pirandello began to publish a series of essays and lectures on the theme of what he called "umorismo," which he later put out in a volume in 1908 and republished in 1920 with a polemical answer to objections raised by Benedetto Croce.[1]

Croce had easily dismissed Pirandello's attempt because he himself had defined Humor and the Comic once and for all. For Croce, Humor was a psychological mechanism that served to define certain human situations, not an aesthetic category that would stand in need of definition. Croce, as we have come to know him, was a past master at dismissing problems by defining them as pseudo problems. This allowed him to pose only those problems for which he had already found the answer.

It is rather easy to see how this kind of procedure would not suit Pirandello at all, for Pirandello was used to posing only those problems for which there can be no answer. By posing the problem of Humor, Pirandello could in fact be truly pleased with himself. From his point of view, the problem of the Comic—of which Humor is certainly a subspecies or variant—had the advantage of always having caused embarrassment to those philosophers who had tried to define it.

This is the text of a paper translated by Gino Rizzo and presented at the Pirandello Society section of the Modern Language Association, December 28, 1968, Denver, Colorado, and subsequently published in *Altro Polo: A Volume of Italian Studies* (University of Sydney, 1978).

In surveying the question, we can say that every philosophical definition of Humor and the Comic has the following common characteristics:

(1) We are dealing with a very imprecise experience, so much so that it goes under various names, such as the Comic, Humor, Irony, and so on. We are never sure whether it is a question of different experiences or of a series of variations on one fundamental experience. We start by believing that this experience has at least one physiological manifestation, which is laughter, only to realize that there exist several instances of the Comic that are not accompanied by laughter at all.

(2) The imprecision of every definition is such that every single study on the Comic and on Humor ends up by including also experiences that common sense tells us are not comic but tragic. And paradoxically, one of the components of the Comic is pity, or tears.

(3) Not one of those who have written on the Comic could be called a Comic writer. Among them we do not find, for instance, either Aristophanes or Lucian, or Molière or Rabelais—not even Groucho Marx. On the other hand, we come across the following:

    (a) as serious a thinker as Aristotle, who introduces the Comic precisely as a final explication of the Tragic. By a fluke of history, that part of the *Poetics* which deals with the Comic was lost. Was this a mere accident? At any rate, let me present my own "humorous" hypothesis: as a thinker, Aristotle was lucid enough to decide to lose a text in which he had not succeeded in being as lucid as he usually was;

    (b) a fussy, moralizing, austere philosopher such as Kant;

    (c) another philosopher who was just as austere, boring, and not at all inclined to joke, such as Hegel;

    (d) a romantic, morbid, whining—although reasonably desperate—poet such as Baudelaire;

    (e) a somewhat gloomy and existentially anguished thinker such as Kierkegaard;

    (f) a few psychologists with little sense of humor, as, for instance, the German Lipps;

(g) of all the contemporary French philosophers, not the amiable conversationalist Alain, but the metaphysician Bergson and the sociologist Lalo; and

(h) the father of neurosis, Sigmund Freud, who revealed the tragic aspects and the death wish lying at the bottom of our unconscious.

There are even more, but this list should be sufficient. Pirandello is in good company. We would all agree that if human existence were as Pirandello describes it, there wouldn't be much reason to laugh about it. And sure enough, here is Pirandello writing on Humor.

To understand why he would want to do that, all we have to do is to go back to one of Baudelaire's definitions: laughter is profoundly human; therefore, it must also be diabolical. Angels do not laugh (busy as they are standing in unbelievably large numbers on the head of a pin), but the devils do. They have time to waste, a whole eternity to give expression to their uneasiness. Now, it is precisely the uneasiness manifested by those who have theorized on the Comic that inclines us to think that the Comic must be somehow connected with uneasiness.

(4) One last characteristic of those who have discussed the problem of the Comic: either they have failed (as, for instance, have Freud and Bergson) to give us a definition that includes all of its possible manifestations, or they have given a definition that includes too many things, far more than those that common sense calls Comic. This is the case with Pirandello. His essay "Humor" becomes a metaphysical treatise that could be called *Everything (but Nothing Else)*. The only thing that the essay "Humor" does not define, as we shall see, is the Humor of Pirandello.

We are confronted, then, with an ambiguous text. At first it seems to aim at a definition of Humor, then it touches on some definitions of the Comic and Irony, only to end by giving a definition of Art in general, or at least of Pirandello's Art, and by being therefore a text of a writer's poetics; finally revealing its true essence, as I will show later, as a drama or play by Pirandello which has erroneously taken the form of an essay. Let us try to read this essay three times, in these three different ways:

(1) as an imprecise and insufficient definition of Humor;

(2) as the enunciation of Pirandello's own poetics; and

(3) as the grotesque drama of an impossible definition.

2. The definition of Humor

The essay's first part, in which Pirandello surveys the better-known theories and tries to apply them to an analysis of Humor in Italian literature, gives the impression that he is always missing the mark. He begins by discussing Humor, and he defines the Comic instead; he ends up with Irony. In the second part, he attempts a theoretical systematization. At the very moment in which he seems to have accomplished it, he practically abandons it because, as we shall see, he is defining something else—let us say Art and Life in general.

Let us try to pinpoint Pirandello's explanation of Humor as an aesthetic experience and the ways in which the Humorist's attitude enters into the process of artistic creation.

Art is created by the imagination, which organizes its own vision, giving to life a harmonious whole. If there exist any rules or preexisting structures (because of tradition, language, culture in general), imagination destroys them and rebuilds them with a kind of nonanalyzable impulse. The creation has a new, original, harmonious form like that of a living being. This entire process is ruled and accompanied by what Pirandello calls "conscience" or "reflection." Like a mirror, reflection gives to the imagination the critical image of its own process and aids it in controlling its own movements. In the creation of the Humorist, however, reflection takes the upper hand: it intervenes directly in the process itself; it explicitly and actively controls the imagination, fragmenting its movement into many parts—pedantically, minutely, and analytically. Reflection, in other words, constantly blocks the imagination as if saying to it, Look here, you thought that the things that you created were just as you imagined them to be—perfect. But they could also be entirely different. Reflection follows the imagination at every step of the way, showing it that everything could also be the opposite of what it appears to be. When in this process there arises only a "perception of the opposite," we have what Pirandello calls the Comic.

In this respect, his position falls within the classical theories of the Comic. For Aristotle, the Comic is something that has gone wrong, as occurs whenever in a sequence of events there appears an element that alters the normal order. For Kant, laughter arises when we arrive at an absurd situation that defies our initial expectations. But in order to laugh at this "error," it is also necessary that we not be involved in it and that we experience a feeling of superiority at the error of someone else (since it isn't we who are falling into that error). For Hegel, the essential element of the Comic is that whoever laughs feels so sure of his or her own rightness as to be able to experience a sense of superiority when observing the contradictions in others. The kind of rightness, which makes us laugh at the misfortune of someone who is inferior, is, of course, diabolical, and on this point Baudelaire had already said everything there was to say. The typical example of this species of the Comic is that of the *miles gloriosus* as he struts about and slips on a banana peel; we expected from him a somewhat different behavior; *we* have not slipped, we are delighted and diabolically surprised, and therefore we laugh.

Pirandello gives the example of a decrepit old woman who smears her face with makeup and dresses as a young girl. He says, I *notice* that this old woman is the opposite of what a respectable old woman should look like. This is the incident that breaks the normal sequence of expectation, and the sense of superiority that I experience (since I understand someone else's error) makes me laugh.

But at this point Pirandello adds that the "perception of the opposite" may become "the sentiment of the opposite." Reflection (artistic consciousness) undergoes here a new development: it attempts to understand the reason why the old woman masks herself under the delusion of regaining her lost youth. The character is no longer separate from me; in fact, I try to get inside the character. In so doing, I lose my own sense of superiority because I think that I could be she. My laughter is mixed with pity; it becomes a smile. I have moved from the Comic to Humor. Pirandello sees with great clarity that, in order to take this step, one must *give up detachment and superiority*—the classic characteristics of the Comic. Pirandello's best example is that of Cervantes: all that Don Quixote does is comic. But Cervantes does not limit himself to laughing at a madman who mistakes windmills for giants. Cervantes lets you understand that he too could be Don Quixote—in fact, he is: like Don Quixote, he has fought against the Turks, believing in an ideal which he now questions; he has lost a hand and personal freedom, and has not found glory. *Don Quixote* is, therefore, a great novel of Humor. *Orlando Furioso* is not, because Ariosto, once he has shown us Astolfo flying on the hippogryph—a heroic fairy-tale vision—limits himself to a "perception of the opposite": at nightfall, Astolfo dismounts and goes to sleep at an inn (the opposite of the heroic is the everyday; of the exceptional, the common; of a knight errant, the traveling salesman or the merchant).

If we were to improve Pirandello's definition, we could perhaps say the following: we have Humor when, given a comic situation, we reflect on it and attempt to understand why the original expectation has not been fulfilled; or when, given a situation that is not yet comic (the *miles gloriosus* is still strutting about and has not slipped yet), we anticipate the Comic that is potentially in it, in order to warn ourselves that our system of expectations can be defied at every step of the way.

Humor, then, would be the reflection that is exercised either *before* or *after* the Comic, maintaining the *possibility of the opposite*, but eliminating our *detachment* and our *superiority*. If, rather than detached from, we find ourselves *within* a comic event (if it is we who slip), then we respond, not with laughter, but with tears. Because of this, Humor should always deal either with our past or with our future. But then how could one say that it may deal also with our present, as Pirandello's work would seem to demonstrate? What may be necessary is to complete Pirandello's definition as follows: Humor may reintroduce both the detachment and the sense of superiority by speaking of a present event which we suffer as tragic, as if it had already occurred or were still to occur—in any event, as if it did not involve us. In the essay at least, Pirandello does not say this. But he does do it in his work. Curiously enough, the theoretician of this Pirandellian process was not Pirandello but Brecht: the problem is that of *Verfremdung*, or "estrangement." I must show what happens to me as if it didn't happen to me, or as if it were not true, or finally, as if it happened to somebody else. Now, what does Pirandello do in his work? He doubles up the character and the actor, he has true events happen while saying that they are part of the performance of the actors, or he has actors play a role while insinuating the suspicion that what they are acting out is actually happening to them.

At this point it might be useful to resort to a precision of classification that Pirandello lacks, and to distinguish better than he does a few categories of Humor and the Comic, thus revealing that it is the category of Pirandellian Humor which is not sufficiently discussed by Pirandello:

The Comic: Something contrary to the natural order of things is happening, and I laugh because it does not concern me (detachment) and because it allows me to feel superior. Example: the decrepit old woman heavily made up.

Humor I: Nothing Comic is happening, but I understand that it may very well happen: I see a beautiful woman and I humorously reflect on the fact that thirty years from now she may very well be a made-up old woman. This eventuality, which is contrary to my expectations, concerns not only this woman but also me and my own future. The comic situation of others is a mirror for the possibility of a comic situation involving me. Reflection has shown to my imagination the opposite of its momentary illusion.

Humor II: Something comic is happening, but I give up my own detachment and superiority as I try to understand the feeling of the person who appears comical (I understand the old woman; I understand Don Quixote, who is not a madman but the victim of a delusion so respectable that I myself could believe in it).

Humor III: I find myself in a tragic situation. I am a betrayed husband, a desperate father, a man with a flower in his mouth. I try to see myself as if I were somebody else. I "estrange myself." I see myself as an actor who plays my role. I use reflection as a mirror, reality as a mirror of reflection, the mirror of a mirror mirroring the mirror of another mirror. On the one hand, I am involved in this situation and therefore, although seeing it as comical, I consider it with Humor. On the other hand, I am not involved in it, and in a certain sense I become alien to it and superior. On this account I can describe it as if it were comical.

In his essay Pirandello does not explicitly present this third definition of Humor, perhaps because he has lost sight of its potential for Humor. As far as this playing with mirrors is concerned, Pirandello ends by defining Art in general—and Life—rather than defining Humor; and he defines least of all his own Humor.

3. Pirandello's poetics

In the first part of his essay, Pirandello presents Humor—seen in the popular, mock poetry of traditional literary themes—as a tool to be used against the canons of Rhetoric. In the traditional view that weighed heavily on Italian literature, Rhetoric was a code, a system of rules. How does Humor function with respect to traditional forms? Through an operation of disentanglement, disruption, and disconnection, it creates new forms out of the themes and materials of the old, traditional ones.

In the second part of the essay, however, the same distinction is no longer used in relation to Rhetoric and Humor, but in relation to old and new Art. What is the essential characteristic of traditional Art? Pirandello asks. In its attempt to mold Life, which is an elusive, undefinable flux of events, traditional Art rigidifies it (crystallizes it) in fixed and topical forms. In this, it falls into the same error perpetrated by logic in its attempt to provide rational explanations for something that is irrational and opposed to any form that rigidifies it once and for all.

"Art," Pirandello says, here obviously referring to Art-before-himself, "usually abstracts and synthesizes, capturing and representing the peculiar and characteristic essence of objects as well as of human beings." If Art truly operated like this, it would be clearly destined to become Rhetoric and therefore, again and again, a codified system of rules. On the other hand, how does Humor operate? Humor, which—*felix culpa*—is now taken to be Art *cum-* and post-Pirandello, breaks the rules; it looks at things in an unexpected way, lifting the mask of Logic and Types, and revealing beneath the mask the contradictions and multiplicity of life.

If for Coleridge Art implied a "suspension of disbelief," we could say that, for Pirandello, Humor—which is for him all the new and true art in general—implies the "suspension of the suspension of disbelief." Humor, then, eliminates the trust brought about by the suspension of disbelief and introduces a new doubt: Art is a continuous exercise in "disbelief"; it puts into question all existing codes, and therefore Life and the World; it says to us, "Look, the Emperor has no clothes."

But this is precisely a definition of Art, not of Humor. It is the definition of art which is being given by the poetics of our age: Art as ambiguity (from Empson to Jakobson); Art as synonymous with the information it provides (and therefore, as a wedge against all those systems of "polite" norm that are already codified by conventions); Art as a wedge against the established laws of language; Art as the disruption of all systems of expectation—just as it breaks them up, reflecting at the same time on why it does so—and therefore an Art that provides, not only the comic effect caused by the ensuing disorder, but also a critical reflection on the reasons behind the disorder that is being introduced.

Pirandello's definition of Humor is, for him, the true and only definition of Art. We may ask, What is left then in this definition of the common notion we have of "Humor"? At this point the essay becomes a treatise on metaphysical and/or existentialist philosophy. And with this we have reached our third and last point.

4. The essay as the grotesque drama of an impossible definition

In principle, the only way we could speak of life would be in terms of Humor, for being as it is the constant disruption of the expected order, life itself is comic. But if one could comprehend this principle, one would do nothing but give form to life, thereby repeating the error of which Art has always been guilty. For Pirandello, what is peculiar to the Humorist (and to the artist in general) is that he no longer knows where to stand. As he himself says, his uniqueness consists (145) in his own perplexity and irresolution of conscience: "Certainly the Humorist is far from being pleased with reality! If he were to like it a little, his own reflection would intervene at once in this pleasurable experience and spoil it" (146). But this Pirandellian definition could also be rendered as follows: "It is impossible for the Humorist to define life as Humor. If he were to define it as Humor his own reflection would intervene at once in this definition and spoil it!"

For reflection, Pirandello says, "insinuates itself everywhere, disarranging everything: every image, every feeling" —so, why not also Humor—Humor as the "sentiment of the opposite" (and as the ability to "comprehend," "to laugh at one's own thought," and "to laugh at one's own suffering")? But first of all, what is life for Pirandello? I know that such a silly, naive, and romantic question, echoing perhaps the question asked by poor Jauffré Rudel in Carducci's poem, should not be posed. I must say that the fault is not mine, but Pirandello's, since he poses it in the course of his essay (not in his plays, to be sure, where he looks at someone else who is attempting to define life). At any rate, let us see why life seems to be constructed just so as to justify the approach afforded by Humor:

(1) reality is illusory; and we ourselves are different from what we should or should like to be;

(2) life in society exacts from us dissimulation and falsehood;

(3) society often forces us to act in ways that are contrary to our will (volition);

(4) if we are not conditioned by the forces of society, we certainly are by the forces of our unconscious, which defeat the presumption of our reason and logic;

(5) therefore, we do not have just *one* mind and *one* personality, but many;

(6) and this is so because life is a continuous flux; because the conceptual forms of our logic are but attempts to stop this flux at the decisive moment they do not hold but, rather, reveal themselves for what they truly are—mere masks.

Please forgive the platitude of such philosophical statements. As he formulates them, Pirandello seems to be putting together an anthology and, unconsciously, to be parodying at least three-quarters of contemporary philosophy. Even at the stylistic level, his essay echoes quotations that extend in range from Walter Pater's *Essay on the Renaissance* to Michelstaedter's little-known *La Persuasione e la rettorica (Persuasion and the Art of Rhetoric)*. Be that as it may, that's the way life is. Well, then, what can the artist do about it? He must resort to Humor, which in disrupting conventions and lifting up the mask, acts as a metalinguistic idiom on the petrified idiom with which we usually represent and explain life to ourselves. Since normally we are covered by the masks of logic and morality, Humor reveals us to ours as opposite to what we think we are, and therefore as utterly comical.

But as there is no cause for laughter when we find ourselves *within* a comic situation, so there is very little cause for even a smile when art "alienates" us from the situation, as it doubles the man with the actor, the actor with the character. You can smile, if you so choose, but the reason you smile would also suffice to make you cry. And this is so because Humor reveals to us the mechanism of life, but without telling us why it is what it is. Therefore, Humor and the Comic cannot exist; or if they exist, they coincide with Tragedy.

There is certainly humor in defining Humor through its very opposite. Now, at the beginning of his essay, Pirandello quotes Rabelais as saying, "Pour ce que le rire est le propre de l'homme," without realizing that Rabelais is in turn quoting a *topos* of medieval Scholasticism. *Propre*, or *proprium*, is the characteristic that is being added to a definition by species and kind, in order to indicate more clearly and unmistakably certain members of a given species. Man, for instance, is an animal; among all animals, he is the rational one, but he has, as that which is *proprium* to him, the faculty of being also *ridens*—and no other animal, even admitting that there be some that are rational, can laugh.

In showing to us that man is an irrational animal, Pirandello should also demonstrate that man cannot laugh. Instead, he writes his essay "Humor" in order to prove that, of all the animals, man is precisely the one who *can* laugh (as in fact he so often does). The entire essay aims, in an unconscious and contradictory way, at proving that the only animal that can laugh is precisely the one that, because of its own irrationality and its own constant frustration in the attempt to rationalize it, has no reason to laugh at all. To put it even better, one laughs only, and especially, for very serious reasons.

Perhaps that's why man causes *others* to laugh at *him*. But if this is the

conclusion we must reach in reading Pirandello's essay, we must agree
that, rather than defining Humor, the essay itself must be viewed as
another—or perhaps the very first—of Pirandello's "humorous" plays.

NOTE

1. "L'umorismo," in *Saggi, poesie, scritti vari* (Milan: Mondadori, 1960).

12

Fakes and Forgeries

It seems that in terms of natural language everybody knows what a fake, a forgery, or a false document is. At most, one admits that it is frequently difficult to recognize a forgery as such, but one relies on experts, that is, on those who are able to recognize forgeries simply because they know how to tell the difference between a fake and its original.

As a matter of fact, the definitions of such terms as "fake," "forgery," "pseudepigrapha," "falsification," "facsimile," "counterfeiting," "spurious," "pseudo," "apocryphal," and others are rather controversial. It is reasonable to suspect that many difficulties in defining these terms are due to the difficulty in defining the very notion of "original" or of "real object."

1. Preliminary definitions

1.1. CURRENT DEFINITIONS

Here follow some definitions from *Webster's New Universal Unabridged Dictionary:*

The first version of this chapter was presented in September 1986 as the Opening Speech at the Congress on *Fälschungen im Mittelalter,* organized in Munich by *Monumenta Germaniae Historica* (*Fälschungen im Mittelalter,* Monumenta Germaniae Historica Schriften, Bd. 33, 1 [Hanover: Hahnsche, 1988]). The present version, published in *VS* 46 (1987), takes into account the discussion that followed in the course of a seminar on the semiotics of fakes held at the University of Bologna, 1986–87. The present version was already written when I had the chance to see *Faking It: Art and the Politics of Forgery,* by Ian Haywood (New York: Saint Martin's Press, 1987); references to this book are introduced into the notes.

Forgery: "the act of forging, fabricating or producing falsely; especially, the crime of fraudulently making, counterfeiting, or altering any writing, record, instrument, register, note and the like to deceive, mislead or defraud; as the forgery of a document or of a signature."

Fake (v.t.): "to make (something) seem real, satisfactory, etc., by any sort of deception; to practice deception by simulating or tampering with (something); counterfeit (Colloq.)."

Fake (n): "any copy or likeness."

Facsimile: "any copy or likeness."

Spurious: "illegitimate, bastard. . . . False; counterfeit; not genuine. . . . In botany: false, like in appearance but unlike in structure or function (*spurious primary* or *quill*: the outer primary quills when rudimentary or very short, as in certain singing birds). Syn.: counterfeit, fictitious, apocryphal, false, adulterate, bastard."

Pseudo: "fictitious, pretended, sham (as in pseudonym); counterfeit, spurious, as in pseudepigrapha; closely or deceptively similar to (a specified thing), as in pseudomorph; not corresponding to the reality, illusory. . . ."

Apocryphal: "various writings falsely attributed . . . of doubtful authorship or authenticity . . . spurious."

A short inspection in other linguistic territories does not offer any more satisfactory help. Moreover, the term "apocryphal" (etymologically: secret, occult) designated at the beginning of the Christian Era noncanonical books kept out of the New Testament, whereas Pseudo-epigrapha were writings falsely attributed to biblical characters. For Protestants, the Apocrypha are in general fourteen books of the Septuagint regarded as noncanonical. Since, however, Catholics accept in the Roman canon eleven of these fourteen books, calling them Deuterocanonical, and call apocrypha the remaining three, then for Protestants the Catholic deuterocanonical books are usually called apocrypha, and the Catholic apocrypha are called pseudepigrapha.[1]

It is evident that all these definitions can work only once one has duly interpreted such terms as "false," "deceiving," "misleading," "fictitious," "illusory," "noncorresponding to reality," "pretended," "fraudulent," "adulterated," as well as "genuine," "real," "satisfactory," "similar," and so on. Each of these terms is obviously crucial for a semiotic theory and all together they depend on a "satisfactory" semiotic definition of Truth and Falsity.

It seems, however, rather difficult to look for a definition of Truth and Falsity in order to reach (after some thousand pages of a complete revisitation of the whole course of Western and Eastern philosophy) a "satisfactory" account of fakes. The only solution is thus to try a provisional and commonsensical definition of /forgery/ and /fake/—in order to cast in doubt some of our definitions of Truth and Falsity.

1.2. PRIMITIVES

In order to outline a provisional definition of forgery and fake, we must take as primitives such concepts as similarity, resemblance, and iconism. (These concepts are discussed and defined in Eco 1976:3.5, 3.6.)

Another concept we shall take as a primitive is that of *identity* (as a criterion of identity of things, not of terms, concepts, or names). Let us assume as a starting point Leibniz's law of the *identity of indiscernibles*: if, given two objects A and B, everything that is true of A is also true of B, and vice versa, and if there is no discernible difference between A and B, then A is identical with B. Since many "things" can be true of any A and B, that is, innumerable "properties" can be predicated of the same object, let us assume that, rather than in the predication of those substantial properties advocated by Aristotle (*Met.* v. 9.1018a: "things whose matter is formally or numerically one, and things whose substance is one, are said to be the same"), we are interested in the predication of a crucial "accidental" property: two supposedly different things are discovered to be the same if they succeed in occupying at the same moment the same portion of space. (For space-temporal identity, see Barbieri 1987, 2. For transworld-identity, see Hintikka 1969; Rescher 1973; and Eco 1979:8.6.3.)

Such a test is, however, insufficient for forgeries because we normally speak of forgeries when something present is displayed as if it were the original while the original (if any) is elsewhere. One is thus unable to prove that there are two different objects occupying at the same time two different spaces. If by chance one is in the position of perceiving at the same time two different though similar objects, then one is certainly able to detect that each of them is identical with itself and that they are not indiscernibly identical, but no criterion of identity can help to identify the original one.

Thus, even if we start from the primitive concepts above, we shall be obliged to outline additional criteria for distinguishing authentic from fake objects. The many problems elicited by such an attempt will arouse some embarrassing suspicions about several current philosophical and semiotic notions, for example, originality and authenticity, as well as about the very concepts of identity and difference.

2. Replicability of objects

It appears from the current definitions given above that fakes, forgeries, and the like concern cases in which either (i) there is a physical object that, because of its similarity with some other object, can be mistaken for it, or (ii) a given object is falsely attributed to an author who is said to have made—or supposed to have been able to make—similar objects. It remains unprejudiced, however, whether these mistakes are caused by someone who had the intention of deceiving or are accidental and fortuitous (see section 3). In this sense, a forgery is not an instance of lie through objects. At most, when a fake is presented as if it were the original with the explicit intention of deceiving (not by mistake), there is a lie uttered about that object.

A semiotics of the lie is undoubtedly of paramount importance (see Eco 1976:0.1.3), but when dealing with fakes and forgeries we are not directly concerned with lies. We are first of all concerned with the possibility of mistaking one object for another because they share some common features.

In our everyday experience, the most common case of mistakes due to similarity is the one in which we hardly distinguish between two tokens of the same type, as when in the course of a party we have put our glass down somewhere, next to another one, and are later unable to identify it.

2.1. DOUBLES

Let us define as a *double* a physical *token* which possesses all the characteristics of another physical *token*, at least from a practical point of view, insofar as both possess all the essential attributes prescribed by an abstract *type*. In this sense two chairs of the same model or two pieces of typing paper are each the double of the other, and the complete homology between the two objects is established by reference to their type.

A double is not identical (in the sense of indiscernibility) with its twin, that is, two objects of the same type are physically distinct from one another: nevertheless, they are considered to be *interchangeable*.

Two objects are doubles of one another when for two objects Oa and Ob their material support displays the same physical characteristics (in the sense of the arrangement of molecules) and their shape is the same (in the mathematical sense of "congruence"). The features to be recognized as similar are determined by the type. But who is *to judge* the criteria for similarity or sameness? The problem of doubles seems to be an ontological one but, rather, is a pragmatic one. It is the user who decides the "description" under which, according to a given practical purpose, certain characteristics are to be taken into account in determining whether two objects are "objectively" similar and consequently interchangeable. One need only consider the case of industrially produced and commercially available fakes: the reproduction does not possess all the features of the original (the material used may be of lower quality, the form may not be precisely the same), but the buyer displays a certain flexibility in the evaluation of the essential characteristics of the original and considers—whether from thriftiness, snobbery, or indifference— the copy as adequate for his needs, either for consumption or for display. The recognition of doubles is a pragmatic problem, because it depends on cultural assumptions.

2.2. Pseudo doubles

There are cases in which a single token of a type acquires for some users a particular value, for one or more of the following reasons:

(i) Temporal priority. For a museum or for a fanatic collector, the first token of the Model T produced by Ford is more important than the second one. The coveted token is not different from the others, and its priority can be proved only on the grounds of external evidence. In certain cases there is a formal difference due to imperceptible (and otherwise irrelevant) features, for example, when only the first or a few early copies of a famous incunabulum are affected by a curious typographical imperfection that, since it was later corrected, proves the temporal priority of this or these copies.

(ii) Legal priority. Consider the case of two one-hundred-dollar bills with the same serial number. Clearly, one of them is a forgery. Suppose that one is witnessing a case of "perfect" forgery (no detectable differences in printing, paper, colors, and watermark). It should be ascertained which one was produced at a given precise moment by an authorized maker. Suppose now that both were produced at the same moment in the same place by the Director of the Mint, one on behalf of the Government and the other for private and fraudulent purposes. Paradoxically, it would be sufficient to destroy either and to appoint as legally prior the surviving one.

(iii) Evident association. For rare-book collectors, an "association copy" is one which bears the signature of the author or any owner's mark of a famous person (obviously, these evidences can be forged in their turn). Normally, two bank notes of the same denomination are considered interchangeable by ordinary people, but if a given bank note marked with the serial number x was stolen in the course of a bank robbery, this, and this one only, becomes significant for a detective who wants to prove someone guilty.

(iv) Alleged association. A token becomes famous because of its supposed (but not physically evident) connection with a famous person. A goblet which is in outward appearance interchangeable with countless others, but was the one used by Jesus Christ at the Last Supper, becomes the Holy Grail, the unique target of an unending Quest. If the Grail is merely legendary, the various beds in which Napoleon slept for a single night are real and are actually displayed in many places.

(v) Pseudo association. This is a case in which a double looks like a pseudo double. A great number of tokens of the same industrial type (be they bags, shirts, ties, watches, and so on) are coveted because they bear the emblem of a famous producer. Each token is naturally interchangeable with any other of the same kind. It can happen, however, that another minor company makes perfect tokens of the same type, with no detectable differences in form and matter and with a forged emblem reproducing the original one. Any difference should concern only lawyers (it is a typical case of merely legal priority), but many customers, when realizing that they have bought the "wrong" token, are as severely disappointed as if they had obtained a serial object instead of a unique one.

2.3. UNIQUE OBJECTS WITH IRREPRODUCIBLE FEATURES

There are objects so complex in material and form that no attempt to reproduce them can duplicate all the characteristics acknowledged as essential. This is the case with an oil painting done with particular colors on a particular canvas, so that the shades, the structure of the canvas, and the brush strokes, all essential in the appreciation of the painting as a work of art, can never be completely reproduced. In such cases a unique object becomes *its own type* (see section 5, and the difference between *autographic* and *allographic* arts). The modern notion of a work of art as irreproducible and unique assigns a special status both to the origin of the work and to its formal and material complexity, which together constitute the concept of *authorial authenticity*.

Frequently, in the practice of collectors, the temporal priority becomes more important than the presence of irreproducible features. Thus in statuary, where it is sometimes possible to cast a copy which possesses all the features of the original, temporal priority plays a crucial role, even though the original may have lost some of its features (for instance, the nose is broken) while the copy is exactly as the original originally was. In such cases one says that artistic fetishism prevails over aesthetic taste (see section 4.1.4, and the difference between the Parthenon of Athens and the one of Nashville).

3. Forgery and False Identification

From a legal point of view, even doubles can be forged. But forgeries become semiotically, aesthetically, philosophically, and socially relevant when they concern irreproducible objects and pseudo doubles, insofar as both possess at least one external or internal "unique" property. By definition, a unique object can have no double. Consequently, any copy of it is either honestly labeled as a facsimile or erroneously believed to be indiscernibly identical with its model. Thus a more restricted definition of forgery could be expressed so: any object which is produced—or, once produced, used or displayed—with the intention of making someone believe that it is indiscernibly identical to another unique object.

In order to speak of forgery, it is necessary but not sufficient that a given object look absolutely similar to another (unique) one. It could happen that a natural force shapes a stone so as to transform it into a perfect copy or an indistinguishable facsimile of Michelangelo's *Moses,* but nobody, in terms of natural language, would call it a forgery. To recognize it as such, it is indispensable that someone asserts that this stone is the "real" statue.

Thus the *necessary* conditions for a forgery are that, given the actual or supposed existence of an object Oa, made by A (be it a human author or whatever) under specific historical circumstances t1, there is a different object Ob, made by B (be it a human author or whatever) under circumstances t2, which under a certain description displays strong similarities to Oa (or with a traditional image of Oa). The *sufficient* condition for a forgery is that it be claimed by some Claimant that Ob is indiscernibly identical with Oa.

The current notion of forgery generally implies a specific intention on the part of the forger, that is, it presupposes *dolus malus.* However, the question whether B, the author of Ob, was guilty of *dolus malus* is irrelevant (even when B is a human author). B knows that Ob is not identical with Oa, and he or she may have produced it with no intention to deceive, either for practice or as a joke, or even by chance. Rather, we are concerned with any Claimant who claims that Oa is identical to Ob or can be substituted for it—though of course the Claimant may coincide with B.

However, not even Claimant's *dolus malus* is indispensable, since he or she may honestly believe in the identity he or she asserts.

Thus a forgery is always such only for an external observer—the Judge—who, knowing that Oa and Ob are two different objects, understands that the Claimant, whether viciously or in good faith, has made a false identification.

According to some scholars, the *Constitutum Constantini* (perhaps the most famous forgery in Western history) was initially produced, not as a false charter, but as a rhetorical exercise. As in the course of the following centuries it was mixed with other types of documents, it was step by step taken seriously by naive or fraudulent supporters of the Roman Church (De Leo 1974). While it was not a forgery for the former, it was such for the latter, as it was for those who later started challenging its authenticity.

Something is not a fake because of its internal properties, but by virtue of a *claim of identity*. Thus forgeries are first of all a pragmatic problem.

Naturally, the Judge, the Claimant, and both Authors are abstract roles, or *actants*, and it can happen that the same individual can play all of them at different times. For example, the painter X produces as Author A an Object A, then copies his first work by producing a second Object B, and claims that Object B is Object A. Later, X confesses his fraud and, acting as the Judge of the forgery, demonstrates that Object A was the original painting.

4. A pragmatics of False Identification

We should exclude from a topology of False Identification the following cases:

(i) Pseudonymity. To use a pen name means to lie (verbally) about the author of a given work, not to suggest identity between two works. Pseudonymity is different from pseudepigraphical identification (see section 4.3), where the Claimant ascribes a given work Ob to a well-known or legendary author.

(ii) Plagiarism. In producing an Ob which fully or partially copies an

Oa, B tries to conceal the similarity between the two objects and does not try to prove their identity. When a Claimant says that the two objects are identical, he or she acts as a Judge and says so, not in order to deceive anybody, but rather in order to uncover B's maneuver. When B makes his or her dependency on A's work evident, there is no plagiarism but rather parody, pastiche, homage, intertextual citation—none of these being an instance of forgery. A variation of these examples of pseudo plagiarism are the works made *à la manière de . . .* (see section 4.3).

(iii) Aberrant decoding (see Eco 1976:142): when a text O was written according to a code C1 and is interpreted according to a code C2. A typical example of aberrant decoding is the oracular reading of Virgil during the Middle Ages or the erroneous interpretation of Egyptian hieroglyphs by Athanasius Kircher. Here one is concerned, not with the identification between two objects, but rather with different interpretations of a single one.

(iv) Historical forgery. In diplomatics there is a distinction between *historical forgery* and *diplomatic forgery*. Whereas the latter is a case of forgery (see below, section 4.3.1), the former is a case of mere lie. Historical forgery occurs when in an original document, produced by an author who is entitled to do so, something is asserted which is not the case. A historical forgery is not dissimilar from a false piece of news published by a newspaper. In this case (see below, section 5), the phenomenon affects the content but not the expression of the sign function.[2]

Let us now consider three main categories of False Identification, namely, Downright Forgery, Moderate Forgery, and Forgery Ex-Nihilo.

4.1. DOWNRIGHT FORGERY

We must presuppose that Oa exists somewhere, that it is the unique original object, and that Oa is not the same as Ob. Certainly such assumptions sound rather committing from an ontological point of view, but in this section we are dealing with what the Claimant knows, and we must take such knowledge for granted. Only in Section 6 shall we escape such an ontological commitment by discussing the criteria of identification to be used by the Judge.

Additional requirements are these:

(i) The Claimant knows that Oa exists and knows—or presumes to know on the grounds of even a vague description—what Oa looks like (if a Claimant comes across *Guernica* and believes it is the *Mona Lisa*—which he or she has never seen or has no clear idea about—then one is witnessing a simple case of misnaming).

(ii) Claimant's addressees must share a more or less equivalent knowledge of Oa (if a Claimant succeeds in convincing someone that a pink dollar bill bearing the portrait of Gorbachev is good American currency, this would be, not forgery, but defrauding the mentally incapable).

These requirements being met, there is Downright Forgery when the Claimant claims, in good or bad faith, that Ob is identical with Oa, which is known to exist and to be highly valued.

4.1.1. Deliberate False Identification
The Claimant knows that Ob is only a reproduction of Oa. Nevertheless, he or she claims, with intent to deceive, that Ob is identical to Oa. This is forgery in the narrower sense—offering a copy of the *Mona Lisa* as the original, or putting forged bank notes into circulation.[3]

4.1.2. Naive False Identification
The Claimant is not aware that the two objects are not identical. Thus he or she, in good faith, takes Ob to be the genuine original. This is the case with those tourists who in Florence fetishistically admire outside Palazzo Vecchio the copy of Michelangelo's *David* (without knowing that the original is preserved elsewhere).

4.1.3. Authorial copies
After completing the object Oa, the same author produces in the same manner a perfect double Ob, which cannot outwardly be distinguished from Ob. Ontologically speaking, the two objects are physically and historically distinct, but the author—more or less honestly—believes that from the aesthetic point of view they both have equal value. One may think here of the polemics about the "forged" pictures by De Chirico, which in the opinion of many critics were painted by De Chirico himself. Such cases provoke a critical questioning of the fetishistic veneration of the artistic original.

4.1.4. Alteration of the original
A variant of the previous cases occurs when B alters Oa to Ob. Original manuscripts have been altered, old and rare books have been modified by changing indications of origin and possession, by adding false

colophons, by mounting pages from a later edition in order to make complete an incomplete copy of a first edition. Paintings and statues are restored in such a way as to alter the work; parts of the body which offend against censorship are covered up or eliminated; parts of the work are removed or a polyptych is separated into its component parts.[4]

Such alterations may be made in both good and bad faith, depending on whether one believes or does not believe that Ob is still identical with Oa, that is, that the object was altered in accordance with the *intentio auctoris*. In fact, we see as original and authentic ancient works which have been substantially altered by the course of time and by human intervention: we have to allow for loss of limbs, restoration, and fading colors. In this category belongs the neoclassical dream of a "white" Greek art, where in fact the statues and temples were originally brightly colored.

In a certain sense all works of art which have survived from Antiquity should be considered forgeries. But following this line of thought, since any material is subject to physical and chemical alteration, from the very moment of its production, every object should be seen as an instant forgery of itself. To avoid such a paranoiac attitude, our culture has elaborated flexible criteria for deciding about the physical integrity of an object. A book in a bookstore continues to be a brand-new exemplar even though opened by many customers, until the moment in which—according to the average taste—it is blatantly worn, dusty or crumpled. In the same vein, there are criteria for deciding when a fresco needs to be restored—even though the contemporary debate on the legitimacy of the restoration of the Sistine Chapel shows us how controversial such criteria are.

The weaknesses of these criteria provoke, in many cases, very paradoxical situations. For instance, from an aesthetic point of view, one usually asserts that a work of art can be recognized as authentically such, provided it maintains a basic integrity, and that if it is deprived of one of its parts it loses its organic perfection. But from an archaeological and historical point of view, one thinks that—even though the same work of art has lost some of its formal features—it is still authentically original, provided that its material support—or at least part of it—has remained indiscernibly the same through the years. Thus "aesthetic authenticity" depends on criteria that are different from those used in order to assert "archaeological genuineness." Nevertheless, these two notions of authenticity and genuineness interfere in various ways, frequently in an inextricable way. The Parthenon of Athens has lost its colors, a great deal of its original architectural features, and part of its stones; but the remaining ones are—allegedly—the same that the original builders set up. The Parthenon of Nashville, Tennessee, was built according to the Greek model as it looked at the time of its splendor; it is formally complete and probably colored as the original was intended to be. From the point of view of a purely formal and aesthetic criterion, the Greek Parthenon should be considered an alteration or a forgery of the Nashville one. Nevertheless, the half-temple standing on the Acropolis in Athens is considered both more "authentic" and more "beautiful" than the American structure.[5]

4.2. MODERATE FORGERY

As for Downright Forgery, we assume that Oa exists, or existed in the past, and that the Claimant knows something about it. The addressees know that Oa exists, or existed, but do not necessarily have clear ideas about it. The Claimant knows that Oa and Ob are different but decides that in particular circumstances and for particular purposes they are of equal value. The Claimant does not claim that they are identical but claims that they are interchangeable, since for both the Claimant and the addressees the lines between identity and interchangeability are very flexible.

4.2.1. Confusional enthusiasm

The Claimant knows that Oa is not identical with Ob, the latter having been produced later as a copy, but is not sensitive to questions of authenticity. The Claimant thinks that the two objects are interchangeable as regards their value and their function and uses or enjoys Ob as if it were Oa, thus implicitly advocating their identity.

Roman patricians were aesthetically satisfied with a copy of a Greek statue and asked for a forged signature of the original author. Some tourists in Florence admire the copy of Michelangelo's *David* without being bothered by the fact that it is not the original. At the Getty Museum in Malibu, California, original statues and paintings are inserted in very well reproduced "original" environments, and many visitors are uninterested in knowing which are the originals and which the copies (see Eco 1986b).

4.2.2. Blatant claim of interchangeability

This is generally the case with translations, at least from the point of view of the common reader. It was also the case with medieval copies from manuscript to manuscript, where the copyist frequently made deliberate alterations by abbreviating or censoring the original text (still in the belief to be transmitting the "true" message). In the bookstore of the Museum of the City of New York is sold a facsimile of the bill of sale of Manhattan. In order to make it seem really old, it is scented with Old Spice. But this Manhattan purchase contract, penned in pseudo-antique characters, is in English, whereas the original was in Dutch.

4.3. FORGERY EX-NIHILO

Let us rank under this heading (i) works made *à la manière de* . . . , (ii) apocrypha and pseudepigrapha, and (iii) creative forgery.[6]

We must assume (by temporarily suspending any ontological commitment; see section 4.1) that Oa does not exist—or, if according to uncertain report it existed in the past, it is by now irremediably lost. The Claimant claims—in good or bad faith—that Ob is identical with Oa. In other words, the Claimant falsely attributes Ob to a given author. In order to make this false attribution credible, one must know of a set a of different objects (Oa1, Oa2, Oa3 . . .) all produced by an author A who is famous and well regarded. From the whole set a can be derived an abstract type, which does not take into account all the features of the individual members of a but, rather, displays a sort of generative rule and is assumed to be the description of the way in which A produced every member of a (style, type of material used, and so on). Since Ob looks as if it has been produced according to this type, it is then claimed that Ob is a previously unknown product of A. When such an imitation ex-nihilo is openly admitted to be so—frequently as homage or parody—one speaks of a work made *à la manière de*. . . .

4.3.1. Diplomatic Forgery

In this case the Claimant coincides with author B, and there are two possibilities: (i) the Claimant knows that Oa never existed; (ii) the Claimant believes in good faith that Oa existed but knows that it is irremediably lost. In both cases, the Claimant knows that Ob is a brand-new production, but he or she thinks that Ob can fulfill all the functions performed by Oa, and consequently presents Ob as if it were the authentic Oa.

Whereas a historical forgery refers to a formally authentic charter, which contains false or invented information (as with an authentic confirmation of a false privilege), the diplomatic forgery offers a false confirmation of supposedly authentic privileges. Examples of this are the forged charters produced by medieval monks who wished to antedate the property claims of their monastery. We can assume that they did so because they strongly believed that their monastery had once genuinely received such confirmations. Medieval authors privileged tradition over documents and had a different notion of authenticity. The only form of credible document they possessed was the traditional notice itself. They could only rely on the testimony of the past, and this past had only vague chronological coordinates. Le Goff (1964:397–402) has observed that the form taken by medieval knowledge is that of folklore: "La preuve de vérité, à l'époque féodale, c'est l'existence 'de toute éternité.' " Le Goff adduces a legal dispute of 1252 between the serfs of the chapter of Notre Dame de Paris in Orly and the canons. The canons based their claim to the payment of tithes on the fact that Fama proved it; the oldest inhabitant of the region was questioned on the subject and he replied that it had been so "a tempore a quo non extat memoria." Another witness, the archdeacon John, said that he had seen old charters in the chapter house which confirmed the custom, and that the canons regarded these charters as authentic because of their script. No one thought it necessary to prove the existence of these charters, let alone investigate their contents; the report that they had existed for centuries was sufficient. In such a culture it was considered perfectly fair to provide a fake document in order to testify a "true" tradition.

4.3.2. Deliberate Ex-Nihilo Forgery

The Claimant knows that Oa does not exist. If the Claimant coincides with the author B, then the Claimant knows that Ob is of recent manufacture. In any case the Claimant cannot believe that Oa and Ob are the same. Nevertheless, the Claimant claims, fully aware that he or she is not entitled to do so, that the two objects—one real and one imaginary—are identical or that Ob is genuine, and does so with the intention to deceive. This is the case with modern charter forgeries, with many fake paintings (see the fake Vermeer painted in this century by van Meegeren), with forged family trees intended to demonstrate an otherwise unprovable genealogy, and with deliberately produced apocryphal writings (such as Hitler's diaries).[7]

It is also the case of the thirteenth-century poem De vetula, which was immediately ascribed to Ovid. One may suppose that the persons who brought the Corpus Dionysianum into circulation in the ninth century and ascribed it to a pupil of Saint Paul were well aware that the work was composed much later; nevertheless, they decided to credit it to an unquestionable authority. Slightly similar to the case listed in section 4.1.3 is the phenomenon of authorial stylistic forgeries, as when a painter, famous for his works of the twenties, paints in the fifties a work which looks like an unheard-of masterpiece of the early period.

4.3.3. False ascription in error

The Claimant does not coincide with B and does not know that Oa does not exist. The Claimant claims in good faith that Ob is identical with Oa (of which the Claimant has heard by uncertain report). This is what happened with those who received and took the *Corpus Dionysianum* for a work by a pupil of Saint Paul, with those who believed and still believe in the authenticity of the Book of Enoch, and with the Renaissance Neoplatonist who ascribed the *Corpus Hermeticum*, not to Hellenistic authors, but to a mythical Hermes Trismegistos, who was supposed to have lived before Plato in the time of the Egyptians and presumably to be identified with Moses. In this century, Heidegger wrote a commentary on a speculative grammar which he ascribed to Duns Scotus, though it was shown shortly afterward that the work was composed by Thomas of Erfurt. This seems also to be the case with the ascription of *On the Sublime* to Longinus.[8]

5. The fake as a fake sign

The topology presented above suggests some interesting semiotic problems. First of all, is a fake a sign? Let us first consider the cases of Downright Forgery (where Oa somewhere exists).

If a sign is—according to Peirce (1934:2.228)—"something which stands to somebody for something in some respects or capacity," then one should say that Ob stands to the Claimant for Oa. And if an icon— still according to Peirce (2.276)—"may represent its object mainly by its similarity," then one should say that Ob is an icon of Oa.

Ob succeeds in being mistaken with Oa insofar as it reproduces the whole of Oa's properties. Morris (1946:1.7) suggests that a "completely iconic sign" is no longer a sign because "it would be itself a denotatum." This means that a possibly completely iconic sign of myself would be the same as myself. In other words, complete iconism coincides with indiscernibility or identity, and a possible definition of identity is "complete iconism."

But in forgery there is only an alleged identity: Ob can have all the properties of Oa except that of being Oa itself and of standing at the same moment in the same place as Oa. Being incompletely iconic, can Ob be taken as a sign of Oa? If so, it would be a rather curious kind of sign: it would succeed in being a sign insofar as nobody takes it as a sign and everybody mistakes it for its potential denotatum. As soon as one recognizes it as a sign, Ob becomes something similar to Oa—a facsimile of Oa—but can no longer be confused with Oa. In fact, facsimiles are iconic signs but are not fakes.

How are we to define a sign that works as such only if and when it is mistaken for its own denotatum? The only way to define it is to call it a fake. A peculiar situation, indeed. What kind of semiotic object is a fake?

The question that the Claimant asks when facing Ob is not "What does it mean?" but, rather, "What is it?" (and the answer which produces a false identification is "It is Oa"). Ob is taken as the same as Oa because it is, or looks like, an icon of Oa.

In Peircean terms, an icon is not yet a sign. As a mere image, it is a Firstness. Only iconic representamens or hypoicons are signs, that is, instances of Thirdness. Although this point is in Peirce rather controversial, we can understand the difference in the sense that a mere icon is not interpretable as a sign. Obviously, Ob, in order to be recognized as similar to Oa, must be perceptually interpreted, but as soon as the Claimant perceives it, he or she identifies it as Oa. This is a case of *perceptual misunderstanding*.

There is a semiosic process which leads to the perceptual recognition of a given uttered sound as a certain word. If someone utters *fip* and the addressee understands *fi:p*, certainly the addressee mistakes *fip* with a token of the lexical type "*fi:p*." But we can hardly say that the uttered *fip* was a sign for the intended *fi:p*. The whole story concerns a phonetic muddle or, insofar as both utterances are words, an expression-substance to expression-substance mistake. In the same sense when Ob is mistaken, for reasons of similarity, for a token Oa (and in the case of Downright Forgery Oa is a token which is the type of itself), we are facing a phenomenon of expression-to-expression misunderstanding.

There are cases in semiosis in which one is more interested in the physical features of a token expression than in its content—for instance, when one hears a sentence and is more interested in ascertaining whether it was uttered by a certain person than in interpreting its meaning: or when, in order to identify the social status of the speaker, the hearer is more interested in the speaker's accent than in the propositional content of the sentence the speaker is uttering.

Likewise, in False Identification one is mainly concerned with expressions. Expressions can be forged. Signs (as functions correlating an expression to a content) can at most be misinterpreted.

Let us recall the distinction made by Goodman (1968:99ff) between "autographic" and "allographic" arts, Peirce's distinction among legisign, sinsign, and qualisign (2.243ff), and our own previous treatment of replicas (Eco 1976:178ff). There are (i) signs whose tokens can be indefinitely produced according to their type (books or musical scores), (ii) signs whose tokens, even though produced according to a type, possess a certain quality of material uniqueness (two flags of the same nation can be distinguished on the grounds of their glorious age), and (iii) signs whose token is their type (like autographic works of visual arts). From this point of view we are obliged to draw a straightforward distinction among different types of forgery. Let us mainly consider Downright Forgery and Forgery Ex-Nihilo (it will be evident in which sense Moderate Forgery stands in between).

Downright Forgeries affect only signs (ii) and (iii). It is impossible to produce a fake *Hamlet* unless by making a different tragedy or by editing a detectable censored version of it. It is possible to produce a forgery of its First Folio edition because in this case what is forged is not the work of Shakespeare but that of the original printer. Downright Forgeries are not signs: they are only expressions which look like other expressions—and they can become signs only if we take them as facsimiles.

On the contrary, it seems that phenomena of Forgery Ex-Nihilo are more semiosically complicated. It is certainly possible to claim that a statue Ob is discernibly the same as the legendary statue Oa by a great Greek artist (same stone, same shape, same original connection with the hands of its author); but it is also possible to attribute a written document Ob to an author A without paying attention to its expression substance. Before Aquinas, a Latin text, known to be translated from an Arab version, *De Causis,* was attributed to Aristotle. Nobody falsely identified either a given parchment or a given specimen of handwriting (because it was known that the alleged original object was in Greek). It was *the content* that was (erroneously) thought to be Aristotelian.

In such cases, Ob was first seen as a sign of something in order to recognize this something as absolutely interchangeable with Oa (in the sense examined above, section 4.2.2). In Downright Forgery (and in the case of autographic arts), the Claimant makes a claim about the authenticity, genuineness, or originality of the expression. In Forgeries Ex-Nihilo (which concern both autographic and allographic arts) the Claimant's claim can concern either the expression or the content.

In Downright Forgeries, the Claimant—by virtue of a perceptual misunderstanding concerning two expression substances—believes that Ob is the same as the allegedly authentic Oa. In the second case, the Claimant—in order to identify Ob with the legendary Oa—must first of all believe (and prove) that Ob is authentic (if it is an instance of autographic work) or that Ob is the expression of a given content which in itself is the same as the genuine and authentic content of the legendary allographic expression Oa.[9]

In both cases, however, one feels something uncanny. A naive approach to fakes and forgeries makes one believe that the problem with fakes is to take for granted or to challenge the fact that something is the same as an allegedly authentic object. After a more accurate inspection, however, it seems that the real problem is to decide what one means by "authentic object." Ironically, the problem with fakes is not whether Ob is or is not a fake but, rather, whether Oa is authentic or not, and on which grounds such a decision can be made.

It seems that the crucial problem for a semiotics of fakes is not the one of a typology of the mistakes of the Claimant, but rather of a list of the criteria by which the Judge decides whether the Claimant is right or not.

6. Criteria for acknowledging authenticity

The task of the Judge (if any) is to verify or falsify the claim of identity made by the Claimant. The Judge can basically face two alternatives:

(i) Downright Forgery. Oa is largely known to exist, and the Judge has only to prove that Ob is not identical with it. In order to do so, the Judge has two further alternatives: either succeed in putting Ob in front of Oa, thus showing that they are not indiscernibly identical, or compare the features of Ob with the celebrated and well-known features of Oa in order to show that the former cannot be mistaken for the latter.

(ii) Ex-Nihilo Forgery. The existence of Oa is a mere matter of tradition and nobody has ever seen it. When there are no reasonable proofs of the existence of something, one can assume that it probably does not exist or has disappeared. But the newly found Ob is usually presented by the Claimant as the expected proof of the existence of the Oa. In this case the Judge should prove or disprove that the Ob is authentic. If it is authentic, then it is identical with the allegedly lost original Oa. However, the authenticity of something allegedly similar to a lost original can be demonstrated only by proving that Ob is the original.

The second case seems more complicated than the first. In case (i) it seems that—in order to demonstrate the authenticity of Ob—it was enough to show that Ob was identical with the original Oa—and that the original Oa represented a sort of unchallengeable parameter. In case (ii) there is no parameter. However, let us further consider case (i).

A Judge can know beyond doubt that Oa and Ob are not identical only if someone shows a perfect copy—let us say—of the *Mona Lisa* while standing in front of the original in the Louvre and claims (crazily) that the two objects are indiscernibly identical. But even in this implausible case there would be a shadow of doubt remaining: perhaps Ob is the genuine original and Oa is a forgery.

Thus here we are facing a curious situation. Forgeries are cases of false identification. If the Judge proves that the objects are two and challenges the false claim of identification, the Judge has certainly proved that there was a case of forgery. But the Judge has not yet proved which one of the two objects is the original one. It is not sufficient to prove that the identification is impossible. The Judge must provide *a proof of authentication* for the supposed original.

At first glance case (ii) looked more difficult because, in the absence of the presumed original, one should demonstrate that the suspected fake is the original. In fact, case (i) is far more difficult: when the original is present, one must still demonstrate that the original is the original.

It is not sufficient to say that the Ob is a fake because it does not possess all the features of the Oa. The method by which the Judge identifies the features of any Ob is the same as that with which the Judge makes a decision about the authenticity of the Oa. In other words, in order to say that a reproduction is not the genuine *Mona Lisa,* one must have examined the genuine *Mona Lisa* and confirmed its authenticity with the same techniques as one uses to say that the reproduction differs from the original. Modern philology is not content with the testimony that, let us say, the *Mona Lisa* was hung in the Louvre by Leonardo as soon as he had completed it. This claim would have to be proved by documents, and this in turn would raise the question of the documents' authenticity.

In order to prove that an Ob is a fake, a Judge must prove that the corresponding Oa is authentic. Thus the Judge must examine the presumably genuine painting *as if it were a document,* in order to decide whether its material and formal features allow the assumption that it was authentically painted by Leonardo.

Modern scholarship proceeds, therefore, from the following assumptions:

(i) A document confirms a traditional belief, not the other way around.

(ii) Documents can be (a) objects produced with an explicit intention of communication (manuscripts, books, gravestones, inscriptions, and so on), where one can recognize an expression and a content (or an intentional meaning); (b) objects which were not primarily intended to communicate (such as prehistoric finds, objects of everyday use in archaic and primitive cultures) and which are interpreted as signs, symptoms, traces of past events; (c) objects produced with an explicit intention of communicating x, but taken as nonintentional symptoms of y—y being the result of an inference about their origin and their authenticity.

(iii) Authentic means historically original. To prove that an object is original means considering it *as a sign of its own origins.*

Thus if a fake is not a sign, for modern philology the original, in order to be compared with its fake copy, must be approached as a sign. False identification is a semiosic web of misunderstandings and deliberate lies, whereas any effort to make a "correct" authentication is a clear case of semiosic interpretation or of *abduction.*

6.1. PROOFS THROUGH MATERIAL SUPPORT

A document is a fake if its material support does not date back to the time of its alleged origin. This kind of proof is a rather recent one. Greek philosophers looking for the sources of an older, Oriental wisdom rarely had any chance of dealing with original texts in their original language. The medieval translators generally worked with manuscripts which stood at a considerable distance from the archetype. As for the artistic marvels of Antiquity, people in the medieval period knew only either crumbling ruins or vague rumors about unknown places. The judgments passed in the early Middle Ages on whether a document produced in evidence in a lawsuit was genuine or not were at best restricted to investigating the authenticity of the seal. Even during the Renaissance, the same scholars who started studying Greek and Hebrew, when the first manuscript of the *Corpus Hermeticum* was brought to Florence and was attributed to a very remote author, did not wonder at the fact that the sole physical evidence they had—the manuscript—dated to the fourteenth century.

Nowadays, there are recognized physical or chemical techniques for determining the age and the nature of a medium (parchment, paper, linen, wood, and so on), and such means are considered fairly "objective." In these cases, the material support—which is an instance of the substance of the expression—must be examined in its physical structure, that is, as a form (see Eco 1976:3.7.4 on the "overcoding of the expression"). In fact, the generic notion of material support must be further analyzed into subsystems and subsystems of subsystems. For instance, in a manuscript, writing is the substitute of the linguistic substance, inking is the support of the graphemic manifestation (to be seen as a form), the parchment is the support of the inked manifestation (to be seen as a form), the physico-chemical features of the parchment are the support of its formal qualities, and so on and so forth. In a painting, brush strokes are the support of the iconic manifestation, but they become in turn the formal manifestation of a pigmentary support, and so on.

6.2. PROOFS THROUGH LINEAR TEXT MANIFESTATION

The Linear Text Manifestation of a document must conform to the normative rules of writing, painting, sculpting, and so on, holding at the moment of its alleged production. The Linear Text Manifestation of a given document must thus be compared with everything known about the system of the form of the expression in a given period—as well as with what is known of the personal style of the alleged author.

Augustine, Abelard, and Aquinas were confronted with the problem of determining the credibility of a text from its linguistic characteristics. However, Augustine, whose knowledge of Greek was minimal and who knew no Hebrew, advises in a passage on *emendatio* that when dealing with biblical texts one should compare a number of different Latin translations, in order to be able to conjecture the "correct" translation of a text. He sought to establish a "good" text, not an "original" text, and he rejected the idea of using the Hebrew text because he regarded this as having been falsified by the Jews. As Marrou (1958:432–434) remarks, "ici réapparait le grammaticus antique. . . . Aucun de ses commentaires ne suppose un effort préliminaire pour établir critiquement le texte. . . . Aucun travail préparatoire, nulle analyse de la tradition manuscrite, de la valeur précise des différents témoins, de leur rapports, de leur filiation: saint Augustin se contente de juxtapose sur la table le plus grand nombre de manuscrits, de prendre en considération dans son commentaire le plus grand nombre de variants." The last word lay, not with philology, but with the honest desire to interpret and with the belief in the validity of the knowledge so transmitted. Only in the course of the thirteenth century did scholars begin to ask converted Jews in order to obtain information on the Hebrew original (Chenu 1950:117–125, 206).

Saint Thomas paid attention to the *usus* (by which he understood the lexical usage of the period to which a given text refers; see *Summa*

Th. I.29.2 ad 1). By considering the *modus loquendi,* he argued that in particular passages Dionysius and Augustine used particular words because they were following the practice of the Platonist. In *Sic et Non,* Abelard argued that one should mistrust an allegedly authentic text where words are used with unusual meanings, and that textual corruption can be a sign of forgery. But practice fluctuated, at least until Petrarch and the protohumanists.

The first example of philological analysis of the form of expression is provided in the fifteenth century by Lorenzo Valla (*De falso credita et ementita Constantini donatione declamatio,* xiii) when he shows that the use of certain linguistic expressions was absolutely implausible at the beginning of the fourth century A.D. Likewise, at the beginning of the seventeenth century, Isaac Casaubon (*De rebus sacris et ecclesiasticis exercitationes* XIV) proved that the *Corpus Hermeticum* was not a Greek translation of an ancient Egyptian text because it does not bear any trace of Egyptian idioms. Modern philologists demonstrate that the Hermetic *Asclepius* was not translated, as assumed before, by Marius Victorinus because Victorinus in all his texts consistently put *etenim* at the beginning of the sentence, whereas in the *Asclepius* this word appears in the second position in twenty-one cases out of twenty-five.

Today we resort to many paleographic, grammatical, iconographic, and stylistic criteria based upon a vast knowledge of our cultural heritage. A typical example of modern technique for attributing paintings was that of Morelli (see Ginzburg 1983), based on the most marginal features, such as the way of representing fingernails or the ear lobe. These criteria are not irrefutable but represent a satisfactory basis for philological inferences.

6.3. PROOF THROUGH CONTENT

For such proofs it is necessary to determine whether the conceptual categories, taxonomies, modes of argumentation, iconological schemes, and so on, are coherent with the semantic structure (the form of the content) of the cultural milieu of the alleged authors—as well as with the personal conceptual style of these authors (extrapolated from their other works).

Abelard tried to establish when the meaning of words varies with particular authors and recommended—as had Augustine in *De Doctrina Christina*—the use of contextual analysis. But this principle is restricted by the parallel recommendation to give preference to the more important authority in cases of doubt.

When Aquinas questioned the false ascription of *De Causis* to Aristotle, he (by confronting it with a recent translation of Proclus's *Elementatio Theologica*) discovered that the content of the allegedly Aristotelian text is in fact apparently Neoplatonic. This philosophical attitude was undoubtedly very mature, but Aquinas usually did not ask whether people thought and wrote according to the world view of their times but, rather, whether it was "correct" to think and write in such a way and therefore whether the text could be ascribed to doctrinal authorities who were never wrong.

Aquinas repeatedly used the term *authenticus,* but for him (as for the Middle Ages in general) the word meant, not "original," but "true." *Authenticus* denotes the value, the authority, the credibility of a text, not its origin: of a passage in *De causis* it is said "ideo in hac materia non est authenticus" (*Il Sent.* 18.2.2 ad 2). But the reason is that here the text cannot be reconciled with Aristotle.

As Thurot (1869:103–104) says, "an expliquant leur test les glossateurs ne cherchent pas à entendre la pensée de leur auteur, mais à enseigner la science elle-même que l'on supposait y être contenue. Un auteur *authentique,* comme on disait alors, ne peut ni se tromper, ni se contredire, ni suivre un plan défectueux, ni être en désaccord avec un autre auteur authentique."

On the contrary, one can find a modern approach to the content form in Lorenzo Valla, when he shows that a Roman emperor such as Constantine could not have thought what the *Constitutum* (falsely attributed to him) said. Likewise, Issac Casaubon's argument against the antiquity of the *Corpus Hermeticum* is that, if in these texts were to be found echoes of Christian ideas, then they had been written in the first centuries of our era.

However, even today, such criteria (though based on an adequate knowledge of the world views prevailing in different historical periods) are naturally dependent to a large extent on suppositions and abductions which are open to challenge.

6.4. PROOF THROUGH EXTERNAL EVIDENCES (REFERENT)

According to this criterion, a document is a fake if the external facts reported by it could not have been known at the time of its production. In order to apply this criterion, one must display adequate historical knowledge but must also hold that it is implausible that the alleged ancient author had the gift of prophecy. Before Casaubon, Ficino and Pico della Mirandola had read the *Corpus Hermeticum* by breaching this principle: they considered the Hermetic writings divinely inspired simply because they "anticipated" Christian conceptions.

In the Middle Ages, some opponents of the Donation of Constantine tried to reconstruct the facts and reject the text as apocryphal because it contradicted what they knew about the past. In a letter to Frederick Barbarossa in 1152, Wezel, a follower of Arnold of Brescia, argued that in the Donation was a *mendacium* because it contradicted other witnesses of the period, which showed that Constantine had been baptized under other circumstances and at a different time. The criticism became more rigorous in the early Humanistic era: for example, in the *Liber dialogorum hierarchie subcelestis* of 1388 and in the *De concordantia Catholica* by Nicholas of Cusa, the author tries to establish historical truth by careful evaluation of all the sources.

Lorenzo Valla displayed more indisputable historical proofs: for instance, he proved that the Donation speaks of Constantinople as a patriarchate when, at the supposed time of composition, Constantinople did not exist under that name and was not yet a patriarchate.

Recent study of an alleged exchange of correspondence between Churchill and Mussolini has shown that, despite the genuineness of the paper used, the correspondence must be rejected and considered a forgery because it contains evident factual contradictions. One letter is dated from a house in which Churchill had not at that time lived in for years; another deals with events which occurred after the date of the letter.

7. Conclusions

It thus seems that our modern culture has outlined "satisfactory" criteria for proving authenticity and for falsifying false identifications. All the aforementioned criteria, however, seem useful only when a Judge is faced with "imperfect" forgeries. Is there a "perfect forgery" (see Goodman 1968) which defies any given philological criterion? Or are there cases in which no external proofs are available while the internal ones are highly arguable?

Let us imagine the following:

In 1921, Picasso asserts that he has painted a portrait of Honorio Bustos Domeq. Fernando Pessoa writes that he has seen the portrait and praises it as the greatest masterpiece ever produced by Picasso. Many critics look for the portrait but Picasso says that it has been stolen.

In 1945, Salvador Dali announces that he has rediscovered this portrait in Perpignan. Picasso formally recognizes the portrait as his original work. The painting is sold to the Museum of Modern Art, under the title "Pablo Picasso: *Portrait of Bustos Domeq, 1921.*"

In 1950, Jorge Luis Borges writes an essay ("El Omega de Pablo") in which he maintains that:

1. Picasso and Pessoa lied because nobody in 1921 painted a portrait of Domeq.

2. In any case, no Domeq could have been portrayed in 1921 because such a character was invented by Borges and Bioy Casares during the 1940s.

3. Picasso actually painted the portrait in 1945 and falsely dated it 1921.

4. Dali stole the portrait and copied it (masterfully). Immediately afterward, he destroyed the original.

5. Obviously, the 1945 Picasso was perfectly imitating the style of the early Picasso and Dali's copy was indistinguishable from the original. Both Picasso and Dali used canvas and colors produced in 1921.

6. Therefore, the work exposed in New York is the deliberate authorial forgery of a deliberate forgery of a historical forgery (which mendaciously portrayed a nonexistent person).

In 1986, there is found an unpublished text of Raymond Queneau, asserting that:

1. Bustos Domeq really existed, except that his real name was Schmidt. Alice Toklas in 1921 maliciously introduced him to Braque as Domeq, and Braque portrayed him under this name (in good faith), imitating the style of Picasso (in bad faith).

2. Domeq-Schmidt died during the saturation bombing of Dresden, and all his identity papers were destroyed in those circumstances.

3. Dali really rediscovered the portrait in 1945 and copied it. Later, he destroyed the original. A week later, Picasso made a copy of Dali's copy; then the copy by Dali was destroyed. The portrait sold to the MOMA is a fake painted by Picasso imitating a fake painted by Dali imitating a fake painted by Braque.

4. He (Queneau) has learned all this from the discoverer of Hitler's diaries.

All the individuals involved in this story are by now dead. The only object we have at our disposal is that hanging in the MOMA.

It is evident that none of the philological criteria listed in 6 can help us in ascertaining the truth. Even though it is possible that a perfect connoisseur can distinguish some imponderable differences between the hand of Dali and the hand of Picasso, or between the two hands of Picasso in different historical periods, any assertion of this kind could be challenged by other experts.

Such a story is not so paradoxical as it might seem. We are still wondering whether the author of the Iliad was the same as the author of the Odyssey, whether one of them (at least) was Homer, and whether Homer was a single person.

The current notion of fake presupposes a "true" original with which the fake should be compared. But we have seen that every criterion for ascertaining whether something is the fake of an original coincides with the criteria for ascertaining whether the original is authentic. Thus the original cannot be used as a parameter for unmasking its forgeries unless we blindly take for granted that what is presented to us as the original is unchallengeably so (but this would contrast with any philological criterion).

Proofs through material support tell us that a document is a fake if its material support does not date back to the time of its alleged origin. Such a test can clearly prove that a canvas produced by a mechanical loom cannot have been painted during the sixteenth century, but it cannot prove that a canvas produced in the sixteenth century and covered with colors chemically similar to those produced at that time was really painted during the sixteenth century.

Proofs through Linear Text Manifestation tell us that a text is fake if its Linear Text Manifestation does not conform to the normative rules of writing, painting, sculpting, and so on, holding at the moment of its alleged production. But the fact that a text meets all those requirements does not prove that the text is original (this proves at most that the forgerer was very skilled).

Proofs through content tell us that a text is a fake if its conceptual categories, taxonomies, modes of argumentation, iconological schemes, and so on, are not coherent with the semantic structure (the form of the content) of the cultural milieu of the alleged author. But there is no way to demonstrate that a text was originally written before Christ only because it does not contain Christian ideas.

Proofs through external evidences tell us that a document is a fake if the external facts reported by it could not have been known at the time of its production. But there is no way to demonstrate that a text which reports events that happened at the time of its alleged production is—for that sole reason—original.

Thus a semiotic approach to fakes shows how theoretically weak are our criteria for deciding about authenticity.

Despite this, even though no single criterion is one-hundred-percent satisfactory, we usually rely on reasonable conjectures on the grounds of some balanced evaluation of the various tests. Thus we cast in doubt the socially accepted authenticity of an object only when some contrary evidence comes to trouble our established beliefs. Otherwise, one should test the *Mona Lisa* every time one goes to the Louvre, since without such an authenticity test there will be no proof that the *Mona Lisa* seen today is indiscernibly identical with the one seen last week.

But such a test would be necessary for every judgment of identity. As a matter of fact, there is no ontological guarantee that the John I meet today is the same as the John I met yesterday. John undergoes physical (biological) changes much more so than a painting or a statue. Moreover, John can intentionally disguise himself in order to look like Tom.

However, in order to recognize John, our parents, husbands, wives, and sons every day (as well as in order to decide that the Trump Tower I see today is the same as the one I saw last year) we rely on certain instinctive procedures mainly based on social agreement. They prove to be reliable because by using them our species has succeeded in surviving for millions of years and we are world-adapted beings. We never cast in doubt these procedures because it is very rare for a human being or a building to be forged (the rare exceptions to this rule are interesting subject matter only for detective stories or science fiction). But, in principle, John is no more difficult to forge than the *Mona Lisa*; on the contrary, it is easier to disguise successfully a person than to copy successfully the *Mona Lisa*.

Objects, documents, bank notes, and works of art are frequently forged, not because they are particularly easy to forge, but for mere economic reasons. However, the fact that they *are* so frequently forged obliges us to ask so much about the requirements an original should meet in order to be defined as such—while we do not usually reflect on all other cases of identification.

The reflection on these most commonly forged objects should, however, tell us how hazardous are our general criteria for identity and how much such concepts as Truth and Falsity, Authentic and Fake, Identity and Difference circularly define each other.

NOTES

1. See also Haywood 1987:10–18.

2. Cf. ibid., ch. 2, on literary forgeries. In this sense every novel which is presented as the transcription of an original manuscript, a collection of letters, and so on, could be intended as a form of historical forgery. But on this line of thought, every novel, insofar as it is presented as a report about real events, would be a historical forgery. What usually prevents novels from being so is the whole series of more or less perceptible "genre signals" that transform any pretended assertion of authenticity into a tongue-in-cheek statement.

3. See in ibid., p. 91ff, the question of the fake fossilized remains.

4. See ibid., p. 42ff, on editorial interference.

5. Goodman (1968) says: "A forgery of a work of art is an object falsely purporting to have the history of production requisite for the (or an) original of the work" (122). Thus the Parthenon of Nashville would be a forgery (or at least a mere copy) because it does not have the same story as the one of Athens. But this would not be sufficient in order to evaluate it aesthetically, since Goodman admits that architecture can be considered an allographic art. Given a precise plan (type) of the Empire State Building, there would be no difference between a token of that type built in Midtown Manhattan and another token built in the Nevada desert. In fact, the Greek Parthenon is "beautiful" not only because of its proportions and other formal qualities (severely altered in the course of the last two thousand years) but also because of its natural and cultural environment, its location on the top of a hill, all the literary and historical connotations it suggests.

6. See Haywood (ch. 1) for apocrypha and creative forgeries.

7. On van Meegeren, see ibid., ch. 5; Goodman 1968; Barbieri 1987; and the bibliography in Haywood.

8. See the chapter devoted by Haywood to the Schliemann case as a complex web of different cases of Ex-Nihilo Forgery. "Not only had Schliemann not uncovered Priam's fabled city (but a much earlier one)—but it has recently been revealed that Schliemann's discovery of the fabulous treasure which became world famous was a hoax. . . . Most of the treasure was genuine in the sense of being genuinely old. . . . The treasure was a forgery because its provenance was false. Schliemann even inserted the fictitious tale of discovery into his own diary. . . . The parts were genuine but the whole was fictional. Schliemann forged authentication and invented a context" (91–92).

9. If an Author B copies a book Oa and says, "This is Oa, made by Author A," then he or she says something true. If, on the contrary, the same Author B copies a painting or a statue Oa and says, "This is Oa, made by Author A," then he or she certainly says something false. (If both say that Ob is their own work, they are guilty of plagiarism.) But is it true that an Author B who has masterly

copied an Oa and presents it as his or her own work is asserting something blatantly false? Autographic works being their own type, to imitate them perfectly provides the imitation with a proper aesthetic quality. The same happens with Ex-Nihilo Forgery, for instance, when an Author B produces a painting *à la manière de.* . . . The *Disciples at Emmaus* painted by van Meegeren—and falsely attributed to Vermeer—was undoubtedly a forgery, from the ethical and legal point of view (at least once van Meegeren claimed that it was made by Vermeer). But as a work of art, it was a genuine "good" painting. If van Meegeren had presented it as an homage, it would have been praised as a splendid postmodern endeavor. On such a web of contrasting criteria, see Haywood, ch. 5, and this quotation from Frank Arnau (*Three Thousand Years of Deception in Art and Antiques* [London: Cape, 1961], p. 45): "The boundaries between permissible and impermissible, imitation, stylistic plagiarism, copy, replica and forgery remain nebulous."

13

Semantics, Pragmatics, and Text Semiotics

Once Jakobson remarked that to study language only from a syntactic standpoint is the same as defining a sleeping car as "the one that usually (and distributionally) stands between two passenger cars." I would like to add that to study language only from a semantic standpoint means for many authors to define a sleeping car as a railway vehicle where people can have a bunk. Even though this definition sounds acceptable, I do not know what would happen to a penniless tramp who takes it seriously.

Maybe my idea of semantics is exaggeratedly liberal, but I feel the need to enrich my dictionary entry with the information that sleeping cars are expensive. Unfortunately, many semanticists would object that the phrase *all sleeping cars are vehicles* expresses an analytical truth, whereas *all sleeping cars are expensive* conveys matters of world knowledge and, as so doing, should be studied only by pragmatics. If I wanted to patronize my tramp, I should tell him that, if he wants to avoid troubles, he should study pragmatics instead of semantics. He can ignore syntactics because he is not supposed to identify a sleeping car. I suppose that if I added to my dictionary entry the evident truth that—at least in Europe—to take a sleeping car is also a status symbol, a bored semanticist would tell me that this is a matter for sociology.

Too many departments, indeed. Is there a name for that kind of

This chapter was presented at the International Pragmatic Conference, 1985, Viareggio, and subsequently published in J. Vershueren and M. Bertuccelli Papi, eds., *The Pragmatic Perspective* (Amsterdam: Benjamins, 1987).

competence that enables affluent, tired human beings, on a foggy night when the airports are closed, to travel comfortably from Milan to Paris by understanding what a sleeping car is, who is in the position of taking it, how to recognize a specimen of it at the railway station, and how to take the Trans Europe Express instead of the Orient Express? I suggest that we are facing in this case an instance of general semiosic competence, which permits one to interpret verbal and visual signs, and to draw inferences from them, by merging the information they give with background knowledge.

1. Objects and dimensions

Charles Morris was the first to outline a division of semiotics into syntactics, semantics, and pragmatics. This was a stimulating and fruitful—but at the same time dangerous—attempt to characterize the domain of semiotics. *Foundations of a Theory of Signs,* insofar as it was written within the framework of an Encyclopedia of Unified Science, suggests that pragmatics, as well as semantics and syntactics, is a science: "by pragmatics is designated the science of the relation of signs to their interpreters" (1938:5).

Since every science has a proper object, the definition above risks to transform semiotics into a mere confederation of three independent sciences, each of them dealing with three independent objects. In this sense semiotics becomes a generic label such as "natural sciences" (Morris was aware of this risk; see 1946:8.1).

We know, or we feel entitled to figure out, the proper objects of mineralogy, zoology, and astronomy, but it does not seem so easy to define the object of natural sciences. More than an object, or less than, it can—at most—be defined as a method, a way of knowing certain aspects of our physical environment through general explanatory laws that, once conjectured on the basis of certain relevant data, can be proved or disproved according to certain experiments. But even though such a method exists, we know that the data we look for in order to tell where cats come from are different in kind and availability from those we collect in order to explain the origin of diamonds.

If Morris only said that pragmatics is the science of the relation of signs to their interpreters, his whole theory of signs would become involved in a predicament. To define the object of a science x as the relation between a and b would mean that the definition of a is independent from the definition of b. On the contrary, in *Foundations* Morris explicitly states that "something is a sign only because it is interpreted as a sign of something by some interpreter. . . . Semiotics then is not concerned with the study of a particular kind of objects, but with ordinary objects insofar (and only insofar) as they participate in semiosis."

If the relation to the interpreter is crucial for the very definition of a sign, and if the object of pragmatics is this relation to an interpreter that characterizes a sign as such, in which sense would pragmatics then differ from semiotics?

Let us suppose that the three provinces of semiotics are not sciences but, rather, dimensions of (or descriptions under which can be approached the) phenomenon of semiosis; and let us assume, in Peircean terms, that semiosis is "an action, an influence, which is, or involves, a cooperation of three subjects, such as a sign, its object and its interpretant, this tri-relative influence not being in any way resolvable into actions between pairs" (*C.P.,* 5.488).

From this point of view, the relationship between semiotics and its three provinces is no longer of the same type as that between natural sciences as a genus and zoology, mineralogy, and astronomy as its species. It is more similar to the relation between philosophy of science, or general epistemology, and three epistemological problems, namely, how to make a hypothesis, how to collect relevant data, and how to falsify a supposed scientific explanation. It goes without saying that (i) the very notion of relevant data can be established only on the grounds of an entertained hypothesis, (ii) a hypothesis can be made only by trying to justify something that is tentatively taken as a relevant datum, (iii) a procedure for testing an explanation can be designed only in order to cast doubt on a given hypothesis, and (iv) frequently to falsify a hypothesis means to demonstrate that the relevant data one had isolated were not such.

In the same vein, pragmatics cannot be a discipline with its proper object as distinguished from those of semantics and syntactics. The three provinces of semiotics are dealing with the same disciplinary "object," and this object is unfortunately different from the objects of natural sciences, which are *natural kinds,* if any. The object of pragmatics is that same process of semiosis that also syntactics and semantics focus on under different profiles. But a social and perhaps biological process such as semiosis can never be reduced to one, and only one, among its possible profiles.

Plane geometry provides an abstract representation of physical reality. Except for that in Abbott's *Flatland,* there is no physical two-dimension universe. There are bodies, and relationships between them. Bodies are subject to the law of gravity, whereas the figures of plane geometry are not. We can use the figures of plane geometry to design, for instance, a parallelogram of forces that represents in some way some of the phenomena depending on gravity; but bodies, which are tridimensional, fall for reasons that plane geometry cannot explain. The bidimensional parallelogram of forces calculating the trajectory of a cannonball can only represent, as a diagram, a phenomenon that plane geometry must take for granted.

To say that pragmatics is a dimension of semiotics does not mean to devoid it of any object. On the contrary, it means that the pragmatic approach is concerned with the whole of semiosis, which, to be fully understood, must also be approached from a pragmatic point of view. Syntactics and semantics, when standing in a splendid isolation, become—as Parret (1983) suggests—"perverse" disciplines.

1.1. LANGUAGE VS. OTHER SYSTEMS

In order to save for pragmatics a proper domain, Morris (1938:v, 1) suggests that "the unique element within pragmatics would be found in those terms which, while not strictly semiotical, cannot be defined in syntactics or semantics." If by this Morris meant those textual strategies that not even the most liberal semantics can foresee—for instance, strategies of conversational implicature, innuendoes about intended meaning—then the area of pragmatics results in being exaggeratedly reduced. If he meant such phenomena as deixis and presupposition, I think that these phenomena can and must be studied also from a semantic point of view. If he meant the domain of a speech-act theory, I still think that many kinds of speech act can also be accounted for by syntactics and semantics (since, for instance, orders can assume imperative forms syntactically recognizable, and there should be something in the representation of the meaning of *to promise* that characterizes its performative nature).

I suspect, however, that by "terms not strictly semiotical" Morris intended contextual elements that play a role in a linguistic interaction, such as the physical position of the speaker/hearer, facial expressions, time and place of the utterance, and so on. Unfortunately, such an assumption contrasts with the whole of Morris's semiotics. His semiotics is concerned, not only with linguistic phenomena, but also with every sign system.

A pragmatic approach to verbal interaction must take into account the relations among linguistic utterances and gestures, facial expressions, corporal postures, tonemic sounds and pauses, interjections, and so on. But such semiotic disciplines as paralinguistics, kinesics, proxemics, and their congeners have developed or are in the course of developing a syntactics and a semantics of their own. The pragmatic study of the contexts of verbal interaction cannot be enriched by a semantics of nonverbal languages. Not to speak of the fact that pragmatics in itself cannot be exclusively the study of linguistic interaction, since there are interesting instances of a pragmatic approach to theater, cinema, painting. . . .

Thus even along the axis opposing language to other, nonverbal systems, pragmatics—more than being a science with its own exclusive object—is one of the dimensions of a more general semiotic research.

1.2. SEMANTICS AND PRAGMATICS: A SEMIOTIC WEB

Semiotics studies both the abstract structure of signification *systems* (such as verbal language, card games, road signals, iconological codes, and so on) and the *processes* in the course of which the users practically apply the rules of these systems in order to communicate, that is, to designate states of possible worlds or to criticize and modify the structure of the systems themselves.

One would be tempted to say that semantics is mainly concerned with systems of signification while pragmatics deals with processes of communication. However, the opposition signification/communication does not correspond to the opposition semantics/pragmatics but rather, characterizes various sorts of semantic theories as well as different sorts of pragmatic phenomena.

1.2.1. *Three semantic theories*

Morris (1946) says that semantics is that branch of semiotics which deals with the "signification" of signs. We know, however, that Morris distinguishes significatum from denotatum. Thus one must say whether one is speaking of semantics as a theory of the systems of signification or as a theory of the acts of reference or mention—which are processes of communication. So-called structural semantics deals with meaning, thus with a theory of signification, whereas the Anglo-Saxon philosophy of language speaks of semantics apropos of a truth-conditional approach to propositions. Those two approaches must be carefully distinguished, even though both can be covered by a more liberal notion of semantics.

Moreover, a truth-conditional semantics covers two different problems or phenomena: sentences that are true by virtue of a set of meaning postulates and sentences that are true by virtue of what is the case. Thus, on one side,

(1) *all bachelors are males*

(2) *all men are two-footed*

are supposed to be true on the grounds of the meaning postulates assumed by a given system of signification (independently of the fact
that—according to a venerable tradition—(1) is analytically true while
(2) is synthetically true). On the other side,

(3) *this is a pencil*

(4) *this pencil is black*

are true only if they are uttered in a given circumstance, where it is the
case that the indicated object is a pencil and is black.

There are two domains of a truth-conditional semantics, one studying the requirements to be met by a proposition in order to be (logically
or semantically) true or false on the grounds of a system of meaning
postulates, the other studying the requirements to be met by a proposition in order to be (factually) true or false on the grounds of what is
actually the case.

We see then that there are at least three sorts of theories that one can
label as "semantics," namely,

(i) as theory of meaning, or a theory of semantic competence, or a cognitive semantics;

(ii) a theory of truth for nonindexical expressions, or for eternal
propositions;

(iii) a theory of truth for indexical expressions such as the acts of mention (see for further distinctions Eco 1976: 3.1 and 3.2).

None of these three semantics can avoid the pragmatic dimension.

Theory (iii). We must agree with Strawson (1950) when he says that
"mentioning or referring is not something that an expression does; it is
something that someone can use an expression to do." If it seems evident that "indexical expressions are standardly and naturally handled
with truth conditional apparatus" (Gazdar 1979:2), it is equally evident
that the truth of indexical expressions depends on the circumstances of
the utterance, on the nature of both the utterer and the addressee (personal pronouns) as well as on the nature of the indicated object. Thus
the pragmatic problem of deixis stands at the very core of the allegedly

most antipragmatic sort of semantics. As a result, we have witnessed Montague's attempt to extend the truth-conditional approach to a formal language containing indexical terms.

The pragmatic dimension cannot even be ignored by the recent theory of rigid designation, which must be ranked under the headings of a theory (iii) because it links the conditions of use of a proper name to the original indexical relationship between that name and an individual specimen of a natural kind. Insofar as the theory of rigid designation assumes that names are directly linked to the essence of the natural kinds they label, and insofar as it takes such an essence as a solid core of ontological properties that survive any counterfactual menace, it seems adamantly to exclude any sort of contextual knowledge. Nevertheless, in order to use these names properly, a cultural chain is needed, a chain of *word-of-mouth information* (rather obscurely described by the theory) by virtue of which we are guaranteed that our way of using a name is still the one established during the original baptismal ceremony. The only way to make a theory of rigid designation understandable—at least as a coherent story—is to take the pragmatic dimension for granted. But in order to solve its semantic problem, the theory should, on the contrary, guarantee a theoretical foundation of the pragmatic dimension. If the theory had previously said what the transmitted essence is, it could ignore the process by which it is transmitted. But since the essential definition is identified only as the one which survives during the process of transmission, the theory should at least tentatively describe this process. The circle being irremediably vicious, the theory is neither semantic nor pragmatic and remains, as I suspect, a fascinating mythical tale about the origins of language.

The causal theory of proper names could work only if one (i) takes for granted that it is possible to teach and to learn the name of an object x by direct ostension and (ii) the ostension takes place in face of an object that is able to survive its namer. Thus it is possible to imagine a person who, in face of Mount Everest, tells a person b *I decide to name this Everest.* Then the person b tells a person c *this is Everest,* and c transmits the information to d, and so on through the centuries. . . . Even in this case, the necessity of using indexical features and the fact that both the sender and the addressee must be in the circumstance of directly facing the mountain introduce pragmatic elements into the process. Moreover, such an explanation excludes the cases in which a traveler reports having seen or having heard about Everest. Nevertheless, it would still be possible to say that there is a causal link which determines the transmission of the name. But what happens when one names a human individual, let us say, Parmenides? The causal chain is broken when Parmenides dies. From this point on, the speaker w telling the hearer y something about Parmenides must introduce into the picture some definite descriptions (for instance, *the philosopher who said that nothing moves* or *that man, son of So and So, who died yesterday*). The speaker y must learn to use the name *Parmenides* according to the set of contextual instructions provided by w and is obliged to resort to contextual elements every time he wants to ascertain whether the name is used in the right sense: *Parmenides? Do you mean the philosopher?* It is true that the instructions provided by w "causes" the competence of y, but from this point of view every theory of language is a causal one. Since language is learned, undoubtedly every mother "causes" the fact that her children learn language, as well as every dictionary causes the fact that its users learn how to use words. In the same terms, the American Constitution "causes" the fact that every American citizen knows his or her duties and rights. It is exactly such a form of nonphysical and indirect causality that calls for a pragmatic explanation of the process.

Theory (ii). Two pages after having proposed his first definition of pragmatics, Morris (1938:7) writes:

> In virtue of semiosis . . . given the sign vehicle as an object of response, the organism expects a situation of such and kind and, on the basis of this expectation, can partially prepare itself in advance for what may develop. The response to things through the intermediary of signs is thus biologically a continuation of the same process in which the distance senses have taken precedence over the contact senses in the control of conduct in higher animal forms. . . . With this orientation, certain of the terms which have previously been used appear in a new light. The relation of a sign vehicle to its designatum is the actual taking-account in the conduct of the interpreter of a class of things in virtue of the response to the sign vehicle, and what are so taken account of are designata. The semantical rule has as its correlate in the pragmatical dimension the habit of the interpreter to use the sign vehicle under certain circumstances and, conversely, to expect such and such to be the case when the sign is used. The formation and transformation rules correspond to the actual sign combinations and transitions which the interpreter uses, or to stipulations for the use of signs which he lays down for himself in the same way in which he attempts to control deliberately other modes of behavior with reference to persons and things. Considered from the point of view of pragmatics, a linguistic structure is a system of behavior: corresponding to analytical sentences are the relations between sign responses to the more inclusive sign responses of which they are segments; corresponding to synthetical sentences are those relations between sign responses which are not relations of part to whole.

Even though extrapolated from their behavioristic framework, these statements seem to me extremely important. They show how the pragmatic dimension is strictly interrelated with a truth conditional semantics of nonindexical expressions. Morris was indeed a pioneer when he approached in pragmatic terms even the venerable distinction between analytical and synthetic sentences. The notion of analyticity is the stronger argument a truth-conditional semantics can use in order to assert its own independence from the so-called world knowledge, background knowledge, encyclopedical information, contexts, circumstances, and so on. A truth-conditional semantics that opposes a pure dictionary or lexical knowledge to any other kind of acquired competence can assume that "pragmatics has as its topic those aspects of the meaning of utterances which cannot be accounted for by straightforward reference to the truth conditions of the sentences uttered" (Gazdar 1979:2).

The weakness of such a distinction is splendidly demonstrated by Quine in his essay "Two Dogmas of Empiricism" (1951): analytical truths, as well as synthetic ones, depend on a system of cultural assumptions, that is, they represent the more resistant—but by no means eternal—core of a system of social expectations. It is interesting to remark how the same claim is made, in other words, on the page of *Foundations* I have just quoted.

Theory (i). The entire section 2 of this paper will suggest in which sense a theory of meaning cannot avoid the pragmatic dimension.

1.2.2. Pragmatics between signification and communication

Pragmatics, too, takes for granted a lot of elements that, even though concerning the relation between signs and their utterers or interpreters, and even though being highly relevant for the process of communication, depend on a previous semantic rule. Take the two sentences analyzed by Gazdar (1979:3):

(5) *Tom's doggie killed Jane's bunny.*

(6) *Tom's dog killed Jane's rabbit.*

The ideal speaker-hearer of English will infer that the author of (5) is either a child or someone who pretends to be a child, but such inference is independent of the circumstances of the utterance. Notwithstanding this, any semantic theory which claims to be in the position of taking into account the difference between (5) and (6) can do so only if it is able to list, among its semantic paraphernalia, also markers that in some way describe the status (be it age, sex, or social role) of the ideal utterer of a given lexical item.

We should conceive of two different pragmatic approaches: a pragmatics of signification (how to represent in a semantic system pragmatic phenomena) and a pragmatics of communication (how to analyze pragmatic phenomena that take place in the course of a communicative process). Such phenomena as textual co-reference, topic, text coherence, reference to a set of knowledge idiolectally posited by a text as referring to a fictional world, conversational implicature, and many other phenomena concern an actual process of communication and cannot be foreseen by any system of signification. Other phenomena, such as presupposition, prediction of ordinary contexts, rules for felicity conditions, and so on, can, as we shall see, be considered by the study of a coded system of signification, to describe which both the semantical and the pragmatical approaches are strictly and inextricably interrelated.

2. Semantics marching toward pragmatics

The most interesting instances of semantic research, in the last decade, are represented by the theories that attempt to design an encyclopedia-like model for the representation of meaning. These attempts are opposed, not only to a purely dictionary-like model, but also to the identification of the scope of semantics with the scope of a truth-conditional semantics. It is evident that all these attempts cannot be implemented only by introducing into the framework of a semantic theory a great deal of idealized pragmatic phenomena.

Levinson (1983) says that pragmatics had been practiced until 1955 without being so named. In general, as Morris first remarked (1938:5), a constant reference to interpreter and interpretation is common in the classical definitions of signs. Greek and Latin rhetoric, as well as the whole of the linguistic theory of Sophists, can be recognized as forms of discourse pragmatics. But even in the most abstract classical definitions of signification there are pragmatic elements: from Aristotle to Augustine, and ultra, every definition of the sign takes into account, not only the relation between expression and content, but also that between the expression and the mental reaction of the interpreter. Abelard carefully debates the problem of the disambiguation of meaning in given contexts, and the problem of the intention of the speaker is a common topic in the medieval theory of signs, from Augustine to Roger Bacon. Ockham provides puzzling remarks about the background knowledge of the interpreter of iconic signs (how can one recognize the iconicity of a statue without knowing the model that the statue portrays?). If the first books of Locke's *Essay* are about the relation between terms and ideas, the book "On words" is on the conditions of social use of linguistic terms.

Schlieben-Lange (1975:2) ranks among the forerunners of pragma-linguistics not only Peirce and Morris but also Mead, the Wiener Kreis, ordinary language philosophy, Wittgenstein, Apel, Habermas, many Marxists such as Klaus, symbolic interactionism, not to speak of Austin, Ryle, Grice, and Searle.

Thus the last turning point in semantic discussions, instantiated by different—but fundamentally compatible—attempts to provide models for an encyclopedia-like representation of meaning, do not represent a revolution in a scientific paradigm but appear, rather, as a return to the very roots of the philosophy of language.

All these instances are in some way introducing pragmatic elements into the semantic framework.

In order to figure out a liberal notion of semantics, one must take a liberal notion of pragmatics. Let me take as such the one proposed by Bar-Hillel (1968), according to whom pragmatics is concerned, not only with the phenomenon of interpretation (of signs, sentences, or texts) or of indexical expressions, but also with the "essential dependence of communication in natural languages on speaker and hearer, on linguistic context and extralinguistic context, on the availability of background knowledge, on readiness to obtain this background knowledge and on the good will of the participants in the communication act" (271).

Some of the phenomena listed by Bar-Hillel are probably to be dealt with also by some other disciplines. It is, however, a matter of bibliographical evidence that many of them, and maybe more, have become the objects of liberal semantic theories as well as of that new branch of semiotics commonly labeled as text, or discourse, semiotics.

2.1. INTERPRETATION

The first example of liberal semantics is Peirce's theory of meaning (as Immediate Object) and of *interpretants*. In the framework of Peirce's philosophy of unlimited semiosis,

(i) every expression must be interpreted by another expression, and so on, ad infinitum;

(ii) the very activity of interpretation is the only way to define the contents of the expressions;

(iii) in the course of this semiosic process the socially recognized meaning of expressions *grows* through the interpretations they undergo in different contexts and in different historical circumstances;

(iv) the complete meaning of a sign cannot but be the historical recording of the pragmatic labor that has accompanied every contextual instance of it;

(v) to interpret a sign means to foresee—ideally—all the possible contexts in which it can be inserted. Peirce's logic of relatives transforms the semantic representation of a term into a potential text (every term is a rudimentary proposition and every proposition is a rudimentary argument). In other words, a sememe is a virtual text and a text is an expanded sememe.

2.2. DEIXIS

It must be added that Peirce suggests that a logic of relatives (that is, a context, hence a text-oriented semantics) can be developed not only for categorematic but also for syncategorematic terms such as prepositions and adverbs. This proposal was first advanced by Augustine *(De Magistro)* and has been recently reconsidered by contemporary authors such as Leech (1969) and Apresjan (1962).

In Eco 1976 (2.11.5) and 1984 (2.3), I have proposed a semantic model for the representation of the ideal content of indices (be they words, gestures, or images) in an ideal situation of actual reference.

2.3. CONTEXTS AND CIRCUMSTANCES

A context-oriented semantics frequently takes the form of an instructional semantics (see Schmidt 1973, and, for the relationship between pragmatics and instructional semantics, Schlieben-Lange 1975). See also Greimas (1973), according to whom a given semantic unit such as "fisher" in its very sememic structure is a potential narrative program: "Le pêcheur porte en lui, évidemment, toutes les possibilités de son faire, tout ce que l'on peut s'attendre de lui en fait de comportement; sa mise en isotopie discursive en fait un rôle thématique utilisable pour le récit . . . " (174).

In my previous works (1976), I proposed to distinguish context from circumstance. The context is the environment where a given expression occurs along with other expressions belonging to the same sign system. A circumstance is the external situation where an expression, along with its context, can occur. Later (1979), I defined as context a series of possible ideal texts that a semantic theory can predict for a given expression to occur, while I reserved the name of co-text for the actual environment of an expression in the course of an actual process of communication. Thus I would say that the expression *I order you* can normally occur in those contexts (or classes of texts) where the sender is characterized by a position of superiority in respect to the addressee, or in circumstances where the same social relationship holds, and that it occurs in the co-text of the novel So and So.

In Eco 1976 (2.11) I outlined a semantic model supposed to predict differences in meaning that depend on possible usual contexts and circumstances; in Eco 1984 (2.3.1) I tried a representation of propositions and adverbs where contextual selections interact with the topic (as a contextual conjecture that a semantic theory cannot predict but must ideally take into account).

Also Greimas's (1966) notion of "classème" enriches semantic representations with a contextual selection.

2.4. FELICITY CONDITIONS AND ILLOCUTIONARY FORCE

In the framework of generative semantics, many authors have felt the need to provide a context-oriented representation. Lakoff (1975) suggests that felicity conditions must be given as meaning postulates, for instance,

$$\text{Request } (x,y,P) \longrightarrow \text{Attempt } (x,\text{cause}(y,P))$$

Many other felicity conditions can be semantically recorded. For example, in the representation of a verb such as *scolding,* it should, and can be, registered a pragmatic-oriented marker such as "S>A," where S is the Sender, A is the addressee, and > stands for a relation of social superiority, or a hierarchical operator.

2.5. CONTEXTUAL ROLES

Fillmore's case grammar, by introducing into the lexical representation such cases as Agent, Goal, Instrument, Result, and so on, links the interpretation of the lexical item, from its very inside, to the co-occurrence of a context—this context being virtually given by the systematic representation of meanings, hence not depending on mere extralexical world knowledge. In other words, *general schemes of world knowledge* are assumed as a part of the lexical information. In the same line of thought, let me rank the semantic models of Bierwisch (1970 and 1971), for example, the representation of "kill":

$$X_s \text{ Cause } (X_d \text{ Change to } (-\text{Alive } X_d)) + (\text{Animate } X_d)$$

Further improvements can lead a representation such as this to record the difference between "kill" and "assassinate" by introducing an ideal felicity condition which establishes the political role of X_d.

2.6. PRESUPPOSITIONS

Presupposition has been considered for a long time a phenomenon that cannot be taken into account by a meaning representation. Fillmore (1971) has showed how it is possible to record the presupposition within the semantic representation of the verbs of judging. In Eco and Violi 1987 (included here as chapter 14, "Presuppositions"), we distinguish between three sorts of presuppositions: existential, co-textual, and presuppositions of p-terms.

As for existential presuppositions, it seems preposterous to maintain that

(7) *I met the son of Mary*

"presupposes" that in some possible world there is a person called Mary and that this person has a son. So-called existential presuppositions have nothing to do with systems of signification. They have certainly to do with processes of communication and can be considered by a semantics of reference or mention, insofar as they implicitly assert that something is the case,. On the grounds of the conversational assumption that speakers, if speaking, engage themselves to tell the truth or at least to speak about something (be it a thing, a figment, or a thought), the sentence (7) *posits* the actual existence of Mary and her son in some possible world, and the hearer is engaged to take their existence for granted until the moment it can be proved that the speaker was speaking infelicitously (to use an understatement). In fact, it is highly improbable that one reacts to (7) with (8) or (9)—

(8) *But Mary does not exist!*

(9) *You did not meet anybody because Mary has no sons!*

—and it is more probable that one reacts with (10) or (11)—

(10) *Who is Mary?*

(11) *You should have met somebody else. Mary has no sons.*

Co-textual presuppositions are produced ad hoc by a given textual strategy and hold only within the boundaries of a given text.

On the contrary, a theory of meaning can account for *p-terms* (in our analysis, exclusively verbs), that is, for expressions where the presupposition is part of their coded content and their representation can also predict the result of the negation test. We think that our semantic model can account for different types of verbs (such as verbs of judging, factive verbs, verbs of transition, verbs of propositional attitudes, implicative verbs), that until now have been analyzed according to nonhomogeneous criteria. This model for representing p-terms considers

(i) a subject operator S which can take the forms $S_1 \ldots S_n$, the S being different Actants or Roles but not necessarily different actors;

(ii) a set of semantic primitives (which should be semantically defined by a different portion of the encyclopedia;

(iii) an actual world W_0;

(iv) any possible world W_j;

(v) a speech time t_0 and temporal states t_j preceding or following the speech time (the speech time being expressed by the tense of the p-verb);

(vi) an object O as the object of the action performed by the primitive predicate, that is, what the subject is supposed to do, to want, to be aware of and so on.

For example, the semantic representation of *to manage* (at least the portion of the semantic representation that accounts for the presuppositional character of the expression) appears more or less like this:

$$[S\ W_{0t-1}\ \text{TRY}\ (S\ W_{0t-1}\ \text{CAUSE}\ (O\ W_{jt_j}\ \text{BECOME}\ O\ W_{0t_0})) \text{ and}$$
$$\text{DIFFICULT}\ (O\ W_{jt_j}\ \text{BECOME}\ O\ W_{0t_0})]\ S\ W_{0t_0}\ \text{CAUSE}\ (O\ W_{jt_j}$$
$$\text{BECOME}\ O\ W_{0t_0})$$

The presupposition [P] is that (i) the subject, in his or her actual world and at a temporal state preceding the time expressed by the tense of the p-term, tried to change a state of the possible world of his or her desires into an actual one and (ii) that project was recognized as difficult to realize. The asserted content is that the same subject succeeded in realizing the project. The negation of the p-term, as in (12)—

(12) *I did not manage to take the train*

—does not deny the presupposition, namely, that the subject *wanted* to do something *difficult*.

Such a representation cannot predict co-textual strategies based on the violation of the rule but can help to understand in what sense certain phenomena of a pragmatics of communication take place. Let us suppose that a mother warns her son not to play with his ball because he could break the window. The boy does not pay attention to his mother's recommendation and in the end does break the window. The mother says: *You finally managed to break it!* If the boy were endowed with sophisticated semantic competence and with metalinguistic skill, he could tell his mother that she is infelicitously using the verb *to manage* since what it presupposes was not the case (namely, the boy did not try to break the window and the deed was not so difficult). Usually the strategy of the mother succeeds, because by uttering her sentence she *posits* the presupposition as if were to be taken for granted and she makes her child feel guilty. By using a p-term (when it was not felicitous to do so), she, by her prelocutory strategy, obliges the child to accept the p-term as felicitously uttered and therefore engages him in taking for granted the whole of the presuppositions the term postulated.

If such a strategy looks too sadistic (but Bateson would not say so), let us consider a normal case of witticism. John says: *Smith loved my paper*. Tom says: *Oh, I sympathize with you. . . .* Either John replies that *sympathize* presupposes that the addressee underwent a misfortune, and cannot be used in that case, or John accepts the rhetorical strategy of Tom and understands that he was implicating that Smith is stupid. The implicature succeeds because it posits as communicationally unquestionable a presupposition that the signification system had registered as unquestionable in all the cases in which a given p-term was used felicitously.

2.7. BACKGROUND KNOWLEDGE

As for background knowledge—so strongly advocated by Bar-Hillel as a pragmatic phenomenon—undoubtedly there are cases of textual interpretation where the idiolectal world knowledge of the addressee cannot be foreseen by any semantic representation. Take the case of irony as a sort of implicature: in order to guarantee the communicative success of an ironic statement p, the Sender must assume that the Addressee knows that p is not the case. This is a typical instance of a communicative phenomenon that no semantic theory can keep under control. However, studies in Artificial Intelligence have convincingly demonstrated that there are certain standard frames, scripts, or goals that can be recorded as a part of the average competence of a social group. In this sense these frames can be recorded by an ideal encyclopedia and are actually recorded as a part of the semantic competence of an intelligent machine. (See Petöfi 1976a; Schank 1975 and 1979; Schank and Abelson 1977; Minsky 1974; and others.)

Another attempt to record part of the background knowledge as a part of the semantic competence is the notion of "stereotype" in Putman 1975 and, in a more refined, complete, and ambitious way, in the work of Petöfi in general as well as in Neubauer and Petöfi 1980.

All the studies I have briefly and tentatively listed are in some way inserting pragmatics into the framework of an encyclopedia-oriented semantics. It goes without saying that at this point it would simply be silly to state whether semantics is "devouring" pragmatics, or vice versa. It would be a mere nominalistic question, relevant at most for academic struggles and grant hunting. I would simply say that we are facing a new, unified semiotic approach to the dialectics between signification and communication.

3. Names, things, and actions: A new version of an old myth

The artificial separation of the three provinces of semiotics is due, I think, to the ghost of the Adamic Myth such as it has been told for a long time. If every science is dominated by an influential metaphysics, perverse semantics has been and still is dominated by a simplified mythological report on the origins of language.

According to this myth, Adam (or in the Greek version, the original *nomothètes*, or "name maker") was looking at things and giving them a name. The comic situation of the first man sitting under a tree, pointing a finger toward a flower or an animal, and stating *this will be Daisy, this will be Crocodile* became dramatic when the first philosophers of language had to decide whether these names were given according to a convention or to the nature of things. To choose Nomos against Physis meant to disregard all the cases of onomatopoeia, not to speak of syntactic iconism. To choose Physis against Nomos meant to disregard all the cases of blatant arbitrariness, that is, the majority of linguistic terms.

As this paper has suggested, a liberal semantics analyzes expressions by atomic primitives only as *extrema ratio* and as a shorthand device for the sake of economy. Such definitions as *"tiger =* carnivorous mammals or big striped yellow cat" are taken seriously only in an academic milieu. Insofar as it takes into consideration the pragmatic dimension, a liberal semantics also provides frames and schemes of action.

According to Peirce's famous example (*C.P.*, 2.330), lithium is defined not only by a position in the periodic table of elements, and by an atomic number, but also by the description of the operations that must be performed in order to produce a specimen of it. Peirce's definition is text-oriented because it also predicts the possible contexts in which the expression *lithium* can usually occur. If we admit, for the sake of the story, that Adam knew and named lithium, we must say that he did not simply assign a name to a thing. He figured out a given expression as a peg for hanging a series of descriptions, and these descriptions pictured, along with the sequence of actions that he performed with and upon lithium, the series of contexts in which he met and expected to meet lithium.

According to my revised version of the myth, Adam did not see tigers as mere individual specimens of a natural kind. He saw certain animals, endowed with certain morphological properties, insofar as they were involved in certain types of action, interacting with other animals and with their natural environment. Then he stated that the subject x, usually acting against certain countersubjects in order to achieve certain goals, usually showing up in the circumstances so and so, was only part of a story p—the story being inseparable from the subject and the subject being an indispensable part of the story. Only at this stage of world knowledge could this subject *x-in-action* be named *tiger*.

In the light of this version of the myth, we can understand better all the arguments that Plato lists in his *Cratylus* in order to support the theory of motivated origin of names. All the examples of motivation he gives concern the way in which words represent, not a thing in itself, but the source or the result of an action. Take the example of Jupiter. Plato says that the curious difference between nominative and genitive in the name *Zeus—Dios* is due to the fact that the original name was a syntagm expressing the usual action of the king of gods: "di' òn zen," *the one through whom life is given.*

Likewise man, *ànthropos*, is seen as the corruption of a previous syntagm meaning *the one who is able to reconsider what has been seen.* The difference between man and animals is that man not only perceives but also reasons, thinks about what has been perceived. We are tempted to take Plato's etymology seriously when we remember that Aquinas, facing the classical definition of man as a rational animal, maintained that "rational" (the *differentia* that distinguishes man from any other species of the mortal animals) is not an atomic accident, as it is usually believed. It is the name we give to a sequence of actions or behaviors through which we infer that human beings have a sort of otherwise imperceptible and fundamentally unknown substantial form. We detect that humans are rational because we infer the existence of such a quality—in the same way in which a cause is inferred through its usual symptom—by considering the human activity of knowing, thinking, and speaking (*Summa th.* I.79.8). We know our human spiritual potencies "ex ipsorum actuum qualitate," through the quality *of the actions* of which they are the origin (*Contra gentiles* 3.46. See Eco 1984:2.2.4).

Myths are myths, but we need them. I have simply opposed a bad myth to a good one, where the baptismal ceremony does not christen things, but contexts—not individuals supposed to undergo stories of which their name does not know anything, but stories in the light of which we can find out the definition that identifies their actors.

I hope that my revised myth will not be considered as perverse as the separated pseudosciences I have criticized. I only wanted to put into acceptable narrative form my appeal for a collaboration among semantics, pragmatics, and text semiotics.

14

Presuppositions

In collaboration with Patrizia Violi

1. Introduction: The problem of presuppositions

Despite numerous analyses developed in linguistic circles in recent years the notion of presupposition continues to be one of the most problematic within linguistic investigation.[1] The difficulty in dealing with presuppositions seems to arise at two different levels: on the one hand, the delimitation of the objects under investigation; on the other, the different explanations of the phenomenon.

In regard to the problem of delimitation, presupposition seems to be a "fuzzy" category, or an umbrella term covering assorted semiotic phenomena. In ordinary language the usage of the word "presupposition" is much broader than in the technical sense. The technical concept of presupposition is restricted to certain kinds of inferences or assumptions, which are characteristically built into linguistic expressions and linked to some specific formal features. Moreover, they can be isolated using a specific linguistic test (traditionally, the negation test). However, even if this first distinction between ordinary and technical usage of the word delimits the domain of application, excluding all inferences and implicatures depending on general world knowledge and co-textual information (see below), the precise definition of the problem is far from clear. In the literature, a large number of syntactic structures and lexical items have been associated with presuppositional phenomena:

Originally published as "Instructional Semantics for Presuppositions," *Semiotica* 64, 1/2 (1987):1–39.

1. Definite description. Since the classical works of Frege (1892), Russell (1905), and Strawson (1950), presuppositions of existence were connected with the nature of reference and referential expressions, namely, proper names and definite descriptions:

   John met the man with the red hat presupposes that *there is a man with a red hat*.

2. Some particular verbs, namely:

   a. Factive verbs (Kiparsky and Kiparsky 1970):
   George regrets that Mary left presupposes that *Mary left*.

   b. Implicative verbs (Karttunen 1971):
   Mary managed to leave presupposes that *Mary tried to leave* (and some other presuppositions concerning the difficulty or improbability of the action; see below).

   c. Change-of-state verbs (Sellars 1954; Karttunen 1973):
   George stopped drinking red wine presupposes that *George was drinking red wine before*.

   d. Verbs of judging, discussed extensively in Fillmore (1971):
   John accused Mary of being rich presupposes that *to be rich is bad* (or *John thinks that to be rich is bad*).

3. Cleft sentences (Prince 1978; Atlas and Levinson 1981):

   It was Henry who opened the door presupposes that *someone opened the door*.

4. Stressed constituents (Chomsky 1972):

   MARY wrote the paper presupposes that *someone wrote the paper*.

5. WH-questions:

   When did Mary see John? presupposes that *Mary saw John*.

6. Certain iterative adverbs and verbs:

   Yesterday John was drunk again presupposes that *John has been drunk before*.
   John returned to Rome presupposes that *John was in Rome before*.

7. Counterfactual conditions:

If John had married Mary, his life would have been happier presupposes that *John didn't marry Mary*.

8. Temporal clauses:

Before he came, the party was over presupposes that *He came*.

9. Nonrestrictive relative clauses:

The man who is living next door is your father presupposes that *A man is living next door*.

These phenomena are the most typically defined as presuppositions within linguistic theory. However, it should be pointed out that any delimitation of the domain of presuppositional phenomena depends strictly on the definition of presupposition one uses. Thus there is not absolute agreement on the list above; some of the preceding cases are excluded by some authors, whereas some others are added.

Given the nonhomogeneous nature of these phenomena, it seems reasonable to challenge a rigid notion of presupposition, which is more an artifact of linguistic theory (Dinsmore 1981a) than a specific feature of linguistic expression. As Karttunen and Peters (1979) say, a wide range of different things have been lumped together under this single label and this fact is responsible for the continuing controversy about how to analyze presuppositions.

Our aim is to sketch the general lines along which the presupposition problem should be framed, and then to analyze more specifically some of the phenomena listed above. In order to do that, we have to consider briefly the different theories under which presuppositions have been studied so far. Basically, they can be classified in two main approaches: semantic and pragmatic. Both of them seem to be inadequate to account fully for our intuition of presuppositional phenomena.

The semantic theory of presupposition is committed to a truth-functional approach, concerned with the logical conditions under which a presupposition can be introduced into a true sentence. The basic hypothesis of this paper is that such a truth-functional approach cannot capture presuppositional phenomena as they occur in actual processes of communication based on a natural language.

From a pragmatic point of view, different explanations have been proposed to explain presuppositions. Two basic concepts are involved:

on the one hand, the felicity conditions governing the use of expressions (and, therefore, the pragmatic appropriateness of sentences); on the other hand, the mutual knowledge of participants in the communicative process. (Let us call this ideal couple of cooperators Sender and Addressee, hereafter S and A.) The pragmatic approach sounds closer to the nature of presuppositional activity in natural language communication. However, the notion of felicity conditions is not completely adequate to express the full relationship between lexical item and textual insertion. Moreover, when describing presupposition as depending on the knowledge or beliefs of S, on the beliefs that S attributes to A, and on the agreement of S and A on a common set of background beliefs or assumptions, the crude pragmatic approach states what happens, but not why it happens.

A limitation of most pragmatic theories is the lack of a textual perspective: very often presuppositions are tested in ad hoc–constructed sentences, removed from any context of utterance. Such sentences do not belong to natural discourse, and it seems unconvincing to base a grammatical theory on artificial examples. We assume that properties of sentences in textual contexts more reliably reflect grammar than do sentences in abstraction. We have said that presupposition is a fuzzy category. The term does not seem to define a series of homogeneous grammatical phenomena; it is more an open category which we assume can be explained only inside a theory of discourse.[2] In fact, a textual approach analyzing presuppositions from the point of view of discourse functions allows a homogeneous explanation, since this homogeneity is no longer on the level of formal structure but, rather, on the level of discourse functions, that is, stated in terms of the textual effects that they produce for the Addressee.

Thus we will hypothesize a general functioning of information in discourse, which can account—in general terms—for all different presuppositional constructions. Such a textual account is weaker than a grammatical theory for presuppositions. The grammatical constructions which are traditionally called presuppositions interact with general textual principles in such a way that presuppositions could be defined as the result of both semantic rules and discourse. In other words, we assume that presuppositional constructions are recorded in the lexicon or otherwise encoded in the language system, but they are activated—or downplayed—by means of general discourse principles. Particularly, we will argue that, for the presuppositional phenomena we are considering here (P-terms), those textual effects depend on meaning organization. Thus text theory has to be linked to meaning representation. This paper, therefore, is devoted to discussing the *system of significa-tion* that allows both A and S to share the same assumptions or beliefs. Such a system of signification should have the format of an *instructional semantics*, conceived as a set of instructions for the proper textual inser-tion or for the reasonable interpretation of a given lexeme (see Schmidt 1976; Eco 1979b). In this sense it is concerned with an intensional ap-proach as far as is possible, that is, insofar as presuppositions depend on a signification system, not on specific strategies implemented in actual processes of communication.

Moreover, another motivation of this paper is that we are not so much interested in what-is-the-case but, rather, in the textual strategies by which, considering the possibilities offered by a system of significa-tion, someone succeeds in convincing someone else that something is the case. In pursuing such a task we shall try an approach aimed at elimi-nating, as far as possible, the impressive and disturbing number of ex-amples and counterexamples occurring in current literature, which reminds us of the puzzle-solving games described by Kuhn (1962) as the last stage of a science waiting for (or trying to avoid) a radical change of its paradigms.

1.1. BACKGROUND AND FOREGROUND

In order to distinguish the kind of phenomenon that could be rea-sonably labeled as presupposition, we have to make an introductory hy-pothesis. We assume that a very general feature of discourse is a hierarchical organization of information in its structure: elements of information cannot all have the same status and relevance in discourse. Necessarily they must be ranked according to some scale of relevance and organized at different levels. We always find, in a discourse, a tex-tual perspective which obliges us to see events, characters, or concepts in a text from a given point of view.

This phenomenon can be described as a special kind of textual focali-zation: some elements of information are more focalized than others, which are played down. In other words, some information is set as the background of discourse, while other information, which is the focus, is the foreground. Generally speaking, the foreground is the most relevant part of discourse. In very general terms, this phenomenon depends on the fact that it is impossible not to impose an order of priority on dis-course; we are forced to "put" our thoughts into the linear order of words and sentences. Moreover, the syntactic level of organization of language allows us—and forces us at the same time—to structure what we want to communicate in an organized system of clauses: main clauses, subordinate clauses, and so on. Considered from this perspective, discourse is a multistratified system, and its hierarchical organization depends strictly on functional considerations, that is, it is a device for organizing the distribution of information. And we have said, this is a very general feature of discourse, displayed at different levels of textual organization and related to different grammatical structures. Presuppositions are just one of the linguistic devices that allows such a hierarchical distribution of meaning.

In accordance with that statement, let us assume that there is a presuppositional phenomenon when, in giving some information by using certain expressions (be they simple lexical items or sentences), one conveys *at the same time* two kinds of meaning which do not have the same status. In sentences such as (1) or (2)

(1) John stopped smoking.

(2) John returned to New York.

there are two items of information conveyed, respectively,

(1a) John does not smoke anymore.

(1b) John smoked before.

(2a) John went to New York.

(2b) John was in New York before.

These items do not belong to the same level of meaning. In an intuitive way we could say that (1b) and (2b), which are traditionally called the presuppositions of sentences (1) and (2), are not the focus of the communication, which is more about the fact that John does not smoke now or that John went to New York. This intuition is in fact brought out by the negation test, to which we will return later.

We suggest that presuppositions are part of the information given by a text, *subject to a mutual agreement* by both speaker and hearer, a kind of textual frame which determines the point of view from which the discourse will be developed. This textual frame constitutes the *background* of the text itself, which is distinct from other information that represents the *foreground*. In sentences carrying presuppositions, the background frame consists of the presupposed meaning of the sentence that both S and A should take for granted, while the asserted meaning constitutes the foreground information. From the perspective of a theory of discourse, the intuitive notion of presupposition is partially captured by such concepts as "new" and "old" or "given" information but is not completely explained by them. In fact, it is not difficult to imagine a context in which the new information conveyed is precisely what is presupposed by a sentence. Consider, for example, an expression such as

(3) We regret to inform you that your article has been rejected.

In this case, the new information conveyed by the sentence is exactly the factivity of the subordinate clause, presupposed by the factive *regret*. Moreover, the concept of background frame is different from the concept of old information because the stress is not on what is already known but on *what is assumed as unchallengeable by the participants*.

The distinction between background and foreground should also be kept distinct from the concept of the background knowledge of S and A, since the background frame is a *textual* element, produced by specific features inside the text. It is crucial to the present definition that both background and foreground information be furnished or conveyed *at the same time* by the same expression. In this sense the background information should not be identified with any previous external knowledge of S and/or A but, rather, is what S and A take for granted by virtue of the utterance of the expression. (The cases of conflict between the conveyed background knowledge and what S and A previously knew will be a matter for further challenge of the expression employed.) The background frame organizes the textual perspective of the distribution of information, putting some information in the area of implicit mutual agreement between S and A. In this sense all presuppositions have a function of *textual integration*, setting different information at different levels (background or foreground) within the discourse. Our aim is to describe how some of those background frames depend on, and are activated by, some specific lexical items or linguistic expressions.

Some remarks are now in order to define the domain of phenomena which we want to analyze as presuppositions. What we called the frame of mutual agreement may in fact be determined by a number of different elements, such as syntactic features, phonological intonations, textual inferences, and so on. Generally, it is impossible to communicate without putting something into the background frame of mutual agreement and assuming that the other is able to access this presupposed knowledge. Otherwise, each speech event would require a complete restatement, with the result that there would not be time to say, or listen to, anything. This is clearly too great an extension for presupposition as a sentence phenomenon, since the utterance of even the simplest sentence can presuppose all the world in this sense. Furthermore, in ongoing discourse, all of the earlier elements of a sequence are presupposed by the last sentence of the sequence. An utterance thus presupposes the informational content of what has preceded it. We will not be concerned here with this larger sense of presupposition, which has to be separated from sentence presupposition. From this point of view, we draw a distinction between *speaker's presuppositions* connected to the speaker's knowledge, including all the above phenomena, and *sentence presuppositions*, conveyed by a sentence itself. Here we are concerned only with the latter. We assume that, among all the phenomena which produce a background-foreground effect, it is possible to isolate a class of phenomena where the background-foreground distinction depends on sentence structure and/or meaning organization. In other words, there are specific linguistic constructions which are regularly associated with the background-foreground mechanism by virtue of their form or meaning, and these constructions are what we define as presuppositions. In particular, we will restrict our analysis to two kinds of presuppositions.

The first kind is presuppositions conveyed by lexical items, which will be called *p-terms*, whose presuppositional power depends on their intensional structure, that is, it is a part of their coded content, irrespective of the context in which they are used, and also when they are considered out of any context. All the examples of p-terms given here will be verbs, since verbs have up to now received a more consistent treatment in the current literature. We do not exclude the possibility of identifying other types of p-terms (for instance, connectors, adverbs, prepositions), but such are the limits of the present exploration.

The semantic description of p-terms is at once an account of semantic content and a description of the action to which the term refers. For example, if the p-term *to stop* has a given presupposition (that is, that the action was going on beforehand), the action of stopping can be performed only in a context in which something was being done before. This means that we understand the lexical item on the basis of the same schema in which we understand the action.[3]

The second category is presuppositions depending on a process of communication in the course of which terms without coded presuppositional power are inserted into referring sentences. These presuppositions will be called *existential*. We shall study existential presuppositions concerning proper names and definite descriptions, as considered by Russell (1905) and Strawson (1950). In this sense proper

names such as *John* and descriptions such as *the son of John* do not have
any presuppositional power but acquire it when inserted into a sentence. If one asserts that the son of John is ill, one presupposes that
there is (somewhere) an individual who is the son of John. At the end of
this paper we will discuss another category of presuppositions, the
co-textual, but only as a suggestion for further inquiry.

We have excluded, by force of our introductory definitions, some
phenomena from the range of presuppositions. For instance, we cannot
agree to the definition of results of logical inferences as presuppositional phenomena. It is arguable that (4) presupposes (5):

(4) All literary critics at Yale like deconstruction.

(5) Some literary critics at Yale like deconstruction.

Sentence (4) *does not* presuppose sentence (5) because (5) does not have
to be taken for granted as background information in order to accept
(4), in the sense that A can fail to draw the inference (5) from (4); the
inference (5) is potentially implied by (4) but not explicitly conveyed by
the sentence uttered by S. When (4) is submitted to the negation test, if
the negation is an external one (it is false that all literary critics at Yale
like deconstruction), it remains unclear whether (5) is deleted or not. If,
on the contrary, the negation is an internal one (and in a natural language it will sound like the assertion that all Yale literary critics dislike
deconstruction), then (5) is deleted. We know that in natural languages
the boundaries between external and internal negation are very imprecise, but precisely because of the ambiguity of this case we are entitled to
deny it the label of presupposition. (Notice, by the way, to what extent
the authors of this paper are uninterested in what-is-the-case: as a matter
of fact, *most* of the literary critics at Yale do like deconstruction.)[*] In the
same vein, it would be preposterous to say that the expression *man* "presupposes" a series of semantic properties, namely, rational, mortal,
featherless two-legged animal. Such an expression directly *means* these
properties (and many others), but it can be uttered and understood
even without having the intention of conveying most of them, and
none of them should necessarily be taken for granted—in any case, it is
questionable which one should be taken as a necessary one. Language is
a human mechanism designed to express by few and utterable expressions a lot of things (content), and this content is submitted to the law
of interpretation, so that every term can imply a proposition, and every

[*](Note 1990) This was true at the time this paper was written.

proposition, an argument (Peirce, CP, 2.342–344). Therefore, to speak of presuppositions in the cases above leads one to assume that everything in language is a presuppositional phenomenon. But this means that language is indefinitely interpretable. To say that every expression presupposes every other expression is to multiply entities unnecessarily. Many discussions on presuppositions risk this farfetched position (see Zuber 1972).

1.2. PRESUPPOSITIONAL AND POSITIONAL POWER

Assuming that we are not so much interested in what-is-the-case as, rather, in what someone tries to make someone else believe to be the case means that we are interested in the *presuppositional* power of p-terms and sentences insofar as they acquire (as soon as they are uttered) a *positional* power. Given sentence (6), according to the current literature, (6a) is presupposed, and given (7), (7a) is presupposed:

(6) I accused Mary of having bought a new dress.

(6a) To buy a new dress is bad.

(7) The son of John is ill.

(7a) There is (somewhere) a son of John.

It can happen that when (6) is uttered there is no mutual agreement between S and A about the moral evaluation of the act of buying dresses. However, as soon as (6) is uttered (if S and A share the same system of signification and S knows it), by using a p-term such as *accuse*, endowed with a precise presuppositional power, S "frames" the following discourse and suggest to A that (6a) should be taken for granted. In other words, by saying (6) S constructs a background frame in which buying a new dress is considered bad. This presupposition establishes the textual point of view and, in doing so, frames the discourse locating part of the information (an unfavorable value) in the background and a different part of information (that Mary bought a new dress) in the foreground. From this point on, foreground information should be viewed from the point of view of the imposed background. In the same way, even though A has never heard about a son of John, the utterance of (7) frames the following discourse as if there were (somewhere) a son of John. Once A has accepted the utterance of the expression proposed by S, A must accept the framing of the further discourse as imposed by S. If A, on the grounds of some previous knowledge, does not accept the background information represented by (6a) and (7a), then A must challenge the right S had to use the expressions (6) and (7). This requires some textual effort, as we shall show. In other words, sentences such as (6) and (7) have what we call a *positional power*, that is, the power to impose certain presuppositions. To say that the sentences have a positional power is, nevertheless, an oversimplification. In fact, it is not the sentence that has positional power, but the utterance of the sentence by a speaker. The sentence in itself has only a *presuppositional power*, but, from the moment in which it is inserted in a given context, the positional power is actualized, and the presuppositions become part of the context. That is, they form part of the mutual agreement by the participants on the interactions of the discourse.

The distinction between presuppositional and positional power enables us to overcome the "traditional" pragmatic view of presuppositions as felicity conditions or preconditions to be satisfied for the pragmatic appropriateness of sentences. According to this position, a precondition for the use of a verb such as *accuse* would be a previous negative statement on the action at issue, or an agreement of both S and A on a negative judgment. But we have seen in example (6) that we can easily use a sentence with the p-term *accuse* in order to inject into the context a negative assumption which does not need to be taken as a precondition. It could even be a "false" assumption in a given context; it is the use of the p-term *accuse* that sets it as "true."

To consider presuppositions only as preconditions to be satisfied means to ignore the power presuppositions have *to create a new context*. Pragmatic theory disregards this power because of its reductive manner of considering the relationship between word and context, seen as a one way relationship:

$$\text{context} \longrightarrow \text{word}$$

According to this perspective, it is the previous context which constrains lexical choices and selects appropriate words, defining their conditions of use. But often the relationship should be considered in the opposite way:

$$\text{word} \longrightarrow \text{context}$$

It is the word which sets and defines the context. Therefore, the relationship between word and context is two-way, from context to word and from word to context. In other terms, since every word activates, by virtue of its encyclopedic representation, a complex frame of reference, the sememe can be seen as a virtual text (Eco 1979a).

In the case of presuppositions, we call positional power the power that presuppositional expressions carry to impose on the context of discourse a given semantic content (their presuppositional content). This means that the Addressee will assume presuppositions as part of a shared background: what the Addressee does—as soon as a p-term or a p-construction is inserted into the discourse—is *to contextualize* the expression in the appropriate context, which means to create such a context if it is not given. The appropriate context is, of course, a context where presuppositions are compatible with other information, that is, are assumed as an unchallenged background. On the other hand, the Speaker uses a presuppositional expression to make the Addressee believe in that background frame. Such a semantic frame is encoded in the language system—by virtue of semantic organization in the case of p-terms and by virtue of grammatical form in other cases—and it can be accounted for in the semantic representation.

This does not mean that presuppositions are unchallengeable; given certain contextual conditions they can be cancelled, and in this case the positional power will not completely coincide with the presuppositional power represented in the semantic system. However, in order to challenge presuppositions, some particular rhetoric strategy is required: A has to challenge the right of S to use the expression S used, then employing a metalinguistic negation. Therefore, presuppositional terms and sentences can only be negated *de dicto*, never *de re*. *De dicto* negation affects textual organization, as we will see in the following section.

1.3. CHALLENGING PRESUPPOSITIONS

We have said that presuppositions can be denied. The problem of presupposition negation has been much discussed in recent literature on presuppositions. For some authors, who try to reduce presupposition relation to entailment, the possibility of denying presuppositions is considered an argument against their existence, and a challenge to the validity of the very notion. Kempson (1975) claims that a sentence such as (8) does not have presuppositions:

(8) Edward didn't regret that Margaret had failed because he knew it wasn't true.

It is clear that there is an "intuitive" difference between (8) and (9), a difference which cannot be explained in Kempson's analysis:

(9) Edward didn't regret that Margaret had failed because he didn't like her.

The "intuitive" difference can be explained only from a textual point of view, assuming the concept of presupposition as part of a background frame. In a dialogue, sentences such as (8) can occur only as an objection to assumptions made by some *other* speaker, in some previous sequence of the dialogue.[4] In other words, to negate the presupposition is to negate the background frame that another speaker has tried to impose on the discourse. These negations are corrections of the other speaker's words, hence used as a quotation of a previous sentence, since it is impossible for a single subject to utter a sentence which at the same time imposes and denies a textual background frame. Moreover, during a real communicative exchange, such counterexamples as (8) or (10) or (11) seem rather astonishing:

(10) Since the Big Bad Wolf does not exist, it is impossible that he has stolen your skateboard.

(11) I am not aware (or I don't know) that Mary is allowed to use my office.

It is quite improbable (according to everybody's intuition) to hear such sentences uttered in the course of an everyday conversation and expressed in natural language. They are frequently quoted in academic literature, because they belong to an artificial language that we label as "examplese." Usually, something more or less similar to the intended meaning of (8), (10), or (11) would be reformulated as a reaction of A to a previous assertive statement of S, in the following terms:

(8a) Are you crazy? Why did you say that Edward "regretted" that Margaret had failed? Don't you know that she passed?

(10a) What do you mean? You still believe in the Big Bad Wolf? First of all, are you sure that somebody really stole your skateboard? If so, let us try to find out who really could have done it. . . .

(11a) I was not aware that Mary was allowed to use my office. But if you say so. . . .

In (8a) A challenges the right S had to use a certain p-term, since A refuses the background information imposed by S. In (10a) A accepts (according to S's generic position) that there is somebody who has carried out a certain action but challenges the right of S to apply an improper name to this somebody. In (11a) A says that (since by virtue of the presuppositional power of the p-term, *to be aware*, one cannot be aware of what one doesn't know) he was not aware of the foreground information, but once he has accepted the background information imposed by S, then he can easily say that he is aware of it. In all these cases the speakers try to reach an agreement *de dicto* about the possibility of using certain expressions, in order to avoid the breakdown of their communicational act. Negations (8a), (10a), and (11a) impose a new frame or point of view upon the following discourse (if S and A want to keep going, they must agree to change their background knowledge). The *de dicto* nature of challenges (8), (10a), and (11a) is shown by the different *de re* negation considered in (9). This negation seems quite normal because it does not try to delete the presupposition of *regret*; on the contrary, it assumes it as a matter of indispensable background knowledge and, so doing, accepts the previously established frame. A sentence such as (9) can be used both additively and subtractively. It can "add to" the foreground the fact of Edward's coldness, even if the question of regret has not yet arisen, or it can deny a previous assertion that Edward regretted Margaret's failure. On the contrary, (8)—and (8a), (10a), and (11a)—can *only* be subtractive. Presuppositions, as part of the background frame, can be negated only by challenging the frame itself. In this sense challenging the background, that is, negating a presupposition, is a *metalinguistic* negation, because to deny the background frame is to deny the appropriateness of the *way* in which the information was presented, that is, the appropriateness of the very words used by the other speaker in the given context. When the background frame of the speaker is challenged, a new frame can be imposed, and it is possible to have a change in frames. Challenging the speaker's frame always produces textual effects, because changing frame changes the direction of a discourse. So the challenge of a frame becomes *a textual change of topic*. After a sentence such as (8), it will not be possible to continue to speak of Margaret's failure, which is quite possible after (9). To change the topic of the discourse requires a complex metalinguistic strategy that can be implemented only in the course of a complex textual maneuver. All the cases of counterexamples used to criticize the negation test for presuppositions require this kind of complex textual strategy, which has the function of transforming an apparent *internal* negation into an external one, and to transform the *external* negation into a negation *de dicto*, in order to preserve the felicity conditions of the communicative intercourse. The counterexamples (8), (10), and (11), as well as their reformulations, (8a), (10a), and (11a), should be more exactly translated as "What you have said is untrue, because if it were true it should impose on the discourse a background knowledge that I do not accept as true; therefore, you had no right to use the expressions you used in order to posit such a background knowledge" (happily normal people are less verbose). If we better analyze the counterexamples furnished by current literature, we see that they are dominated by a curious error, that is, by the confusion between the presuppositional power of the p-term or sentences and the way in which they are actually uttered in discursive strategies in order to exploit, maybe deceitfully, their power.[5]

In summary, we can say that the two levels of meaning we have defined as background and foreground have a different status as regards negation. The foreground represents "information that is open to challenge," and the background, "information that is shielded from challenge by the hearer" (Givon 1982). To say that the background information is "shielded from challenge" does not mean that it cannot be challenged; the Addressee may, of course, challenge anything in discourse. We are talking about a tendency of use, not a grammatical rule. The presupposed content of a presuppositional construction, given its background nature, is less likely to be challenged in an inherently pragmatic scale of probabilities. To put information in the background position makes the challenge less "natural"; for this reason, a challenge at the presuppositional level gives rise to specific textual strategies, affecting the level of *topic continuity* in discourse.

Thus presuppositions are characterized by two different features: first, they are tied to particular aspects of surface structure; second, they are context-sensitive, since they can be challenged under given textual conditions. This double nature of presuppositional phenomena requires an integration between two levels of explanation: the semantic and the textual. On the one hand, presuppositions activated by p-terms need to be accounted for at the level of the semantic description, since they are encoded in the system of signification of a given language; on the other hand, they are linked to textual strategies and discourse constraints. Their context-sensitive nature can also explain the so-called projection problem, that is, the inheritance of presuppositions in complex sentences. Without analyzing this problem here, we suggest that it should be framed in a more general textual approach instead of through classification of different classes of predicates (filter, plugs, holes, and so on). Presuppositions are context-sensitive constructions; therefore, it is in context that the elements able to block presuppositions have to be found. Thus, to decide which presuppositions will survive in a given text, it will be necessary to consider various elements which can be contradictory: previous shared knowledge about the falsity of presuppositions, inconsistency with other background assumptions, entailments or conversational implicatures, and so on. Similar approaches can be found in Dinsmore (1981b) and, for a more formal, even if partial, version in Gazdar (1979).

2. P-terms

2.1. THE ENCYCLOPEDIC FRAMEWORK

The nature of p-terms must be described within the framework of a semiotic theory displaying the following characteristics (for previous theoretical foundations, see Eco 1976, 1979a, 1979b, 1984):

1. It establishes the possibility of the representation of the *content* of simple expressions (in a verbal language: lexical items) as a set of properties or semantic features.

2. These semantic features are not metalinguistic elements belonging to a finite set of semantic universals but *interpretants* (in Peirce's sense, that is, other expressions of the same or of another language);

3. These interpretants are given not only as atomic properties (such as human or object) but also in the format of *instructions* on how to insert the analyzed expression into *contexts* (contexts being coded classes of possible actual co-texts or textual environments).

4. These contextual selections should also take into account the felicity conditions for using the utterances of the expression in the course of acts of communication according to coded classes of extralinguistic circumstances or situations.

5. Such a representation, in terms of contextual and circumstantial instructions, cannot have the format of a dictionary but must have the format of an *encyclopedia* able to furnish elements of so-called world knowledge.

6. Such an encyclopedia is a working hypothesis, a semiotic postulate, never attainable in its complexity and globality, but the working hypothesis allows for the (always transitory) formulation of partial encyclopedic representations aiming at describing the kind of competence supposedly requested in order to interpret a given text or a class of texts.

Encyclopedic competence can be represented in many ways. It is improbable that it can take the format of a dictionary-like Porphyrian tree, as a hierarchy of atomic properties ruled by relations of entailment from the lower to the upper nodes (for a critique of a Porphyrian tree, see Eco 1984), even though part of the encyclopedic representation can take this format. For instance, according to some suggestions of Putnam (1975) and Neubauer and Petöfi (1981), the representation of the content of a given lexical item can also take into account experts' knowledge arranged in some taxonomic tree; but, at the same time, it should take into account also stereotyped knowledge, where frequently the properties are not hierarchically ordered, and it would be difficult to decide which properties are more or less "necessary" or "essential" (for a criticism of a clear-cut distinction between necessary and unnecessary properties, see Quine (1951) and the text semiotic discussion in Eco 1979a:8.5). Moreover, an encyclopedic representation must take into account also *frames* (van Dijk 1977; Fillmore 1976a, 1976b; Petöfi 1976a) and *scripts* (Schank and Abelson 1977; Schank and Riesbeck 1981). As for the manner of providing contextual instructions, see the various attempts of case grammar (Fillmore 1968, 1977; Bierwisch 1970, 1971; Bierwisch and Kiefer 1970) and of instructional semantics (Schmidt 1976).

As an interesting attempt to outline the spectrum of a possible encyclopedic representation of the expression *chlorine*, the model proposed by Neubauer and Petöfi (1981) is given in Table 14.1.

Let us call all the potential information displayed by the encyclopedia the content of the expression, or as the whole of what is *semantically included*. Such a catholic representation can include, as we said, many co-textual instructions formulated in different ways, as well as frames and presuppositions. In the case of chlorine, the kind of information provided dictates, by means of "atomic" properties, the contexts in which the term can be properly inserted, and many of the arrays of "atomic" properties could be elaborated into frames (for instance, how to produce chlorine; see the example of the definition of lithium, given by Peirce, *C.P.* 2.330, and discussed in Eco 1979a:7.2.6). The instruction for inserting verbs in contexts, as well as the information about the presuppositions of the p-terms, should be provided by other kinds of interpretants.

2.2. ENCYCLOPEDIC DIFFERENCES BETWEEN
    PRESUPPOSITIONS AND OTHER INCLUSIONS

The encyclopedic model outlined in the previous section helps one understand the way in which those meaning postulates that we have

Table 14.1

a. Sector of commonsense knowledge		b. Sector of experts' knowledge	
generic term	— element	1. *Chemical knowledge*	
color	— greenish	elementary category	— non metallic
smell	— disagreeable	family	— halogen
		valence	— univalent
			polyvalent
		chemical symbol	— Cl
		natural occurrence	— in chlorides
		chlorine	— NaCl HCl
		2. *Physical knowledge*	
		. . . .	
		natural state of matter	— gas
		other states	— liquid chlorine
		weight	— 2 times as
			heavy as air
		atomic number	— 17
		atomic weight	— 33.453
			etc.
		3. *Biological knowledge*	
		. . . .	
		4. *Geological knowledge*	
		. . . .	
		5. *Historical information*	
		(discovery, further research, . . .)	
		6. *Etymological information*	
		7. *Etc.*	

already called presuppositions can survive a negation test differently than other kinds of meaning postulates. First of all, as it has already been stressed, the global encyclopedic knowledge about a given lexical item (let us call it K) is only an ideal kind of competence. Actually, people share only reduced portions of K (let us call these portions k_j, where $j = 1, 2 \ldots n$). Any S can activate (or presume that his A can activate) a certain portion of his knowledge (k_j) as far as given textual utterance is concerned. To understand a text is always a matter of a dialectics between the ideal K, the k_j of A, and the supposed k_j of S. Moreover, a given text can act as a reduction or an enlargement of the k_j's of both S and A. Now, when in a textual intercourse S says that something is not chlorine (internal negation), it is rather difficult to decide whether S means that this something is not greenish, or that it does not have the atomic number 17, or that it is not the compound, discovered by Scheele in 1774. In order to understand what S is deleting, further contextual clues are required, as well as hints about the situation of utterance (is it a discussion between physicists or between laymen?).

Let us take a more familiar example. Let us suppose that an encyclopedic representation of *man* should encompass more or less organized common knowledge (animal, human, adult, male), biological and physiological information, old traditional definitions (mortal rational animal, featherless two-legged mammal), information about the average size, weight, and height of men, historical elements (let us say, men are the animals of which Darwin said that p), grammatical instructions about the possibility of using the expression *man* in certain contexts to indicate both male and female humans, and so on, potentially *ad infinitum*. In an ideal situation of utterance (the case of the anonymous letter described in Katz 1977), the expression *man*, taken out of context and out of any circumstance of utterance, can mean all K, or at least all the k_j, at the disposal of the possible A of the utterance. Let us suppose on the contrary that at 8:00 PM, from the living room of her house in New Jersey, a wife utters (12) to her husband:

(12) Honey, there is a man on the lawn near the fence!

Probably S does not suggest to A that there is on the lawn a representative of the kind of animals studied by Darwin, nor that there is a rational and mortal being; she says that there is a male human adult. Now suppose that the husband answers (13):

(13) No, honey, it's not a man. . . .

It is absolutely unclear what the husband is denying and what survives his negation: the "thing" on the lawn can be a boy, a boa constrictor, a tree, an alien invader, the shadow projected by the light in the street upon an oak. . . .

If our encyclopedic knowledge were as strictly organized as a Porphyrian tree, by means of *genus* and *differentia specifica*, one could say that by *internal* negation the differentia specifica is deleted, while the survival of the genus remains undetermined. Since a man is an animal (genus), rational and mortal (differentia), to say that something is not a man means that it is not rational and not mortal, leaving unprejudiced whether it is animal or not (the possible deletion of animal remaining a matter for further contextual clues). A different result would occur with *external* negation. If, according to the Aristotelian notion of definition, the *definiendum* is biconditionally linked with the whole set of properties representing its definition (a man being by definition a rational mortal animal), if one denies that something is a rational mortal animal, then one denies by *modus tollens* that something is a man, and to deny man would entail the negation of the whole definition. However, this occurs only with very artificial external negations ("it is untrue that there are men on Mars"). Unfortunately, natural languages usually put into play internal negation like that of (13). Moreover, as shown in the preceding section, an encyclopedic representation cannot have a Porphyrian tree format; therefore, the problem becomes more and more puzzling. There is no encyclopedic representation of a set of meaning postulates that can say what is specifically deleted by the negation of the corresponding term or of the sentence containing it. Every ambiguity can be solved only by further co-textual information. If the husband of the example above does not provide more information to his wife, he certainly will not succeed in reassuring her. But it is not language that must be taken as responsible for such a communicative misadventure: the husband is exaggeratedly laconic and violates the maxim of quantity. His abruptness is a matter for a marriage counselor, not for a linguist. Language (natural language) is a flexible system of signification conceived for producing texts, not for uttering sentences in "examplese." At this point we can say that there is a kind of meaning postulate which can escape these ambiguities: it is the presupposition as coded in the encyclopedic representation of p-terms.

Sentence (14) as well as its negative counterpart (15) equally presupposes (16):

(14) I cleaned the room.

(15) I did not clean the room.

(16) The room was dirty.

As we have seen in the section on challenging presuppositions, any attempt to challenge this specific nature of presuppositions requires a textual strategy which either challenges the use of the p-term *de dicto* or "stages" a textual situation in which one represents people using deceitful p-terms.

The following section will outline the semiotic requirements for an encyclopedia-like representation which establishes the specific properties of coded presuppositions for p-terms.

2.3. AN ENCYCLOPEDIC REPRESENTATION OF P-TERMS
An encyclopedic representation of p-terms must

(a) take into account the coded felicity conditions of the lexical items;

(b) represent a set of instructions for the textual insertion of the lexical item;

(c) in doing so must consistently predict the result of the negation test.

Such a semantic representation must represent the presuppositional power of a lexical item by specifying some presupposed elements so that the part of a text where the p-term occurs can actualize them, exploiting their potential positional power.

The encyclopedic description is an abstract template which must be filled with specific meanings in co-textual situations. However, the interpretation is not arbitrary but is limited by the semantic model. The rhetorical strategies connected with the use of p-terms are predictable on the basis of its semantic representation. Our representation puts the presupposed semantic features within square brackets. What is represented within square brackets should survive the negation test.

The description of both presupposition and asserted or foreground meaning takes into account the difference between the actual world (the world presupposed by S and A as the world of their actual experiences) and possible worlds (as epistemic and doxastic worlds, conceivable but not actual states of affairs). Within a given world, different temporal states are considered. The representations consider cases in which a subject, S, wants, hopes, plans, and actually does some O (object):

> S = a subject operator which can take the forms S_1, S_2, . . . S_n, these Ss being different Actants but not necessarily different Actors. For example, S_1 SAY S_2 means either "x tells y" or "x tells himself."

> WANT, DO, AWARE, etc., = predicates used as primitives. (It ought to be clear that in an encyclopedic representation based on interpretants there are no primitives, every interpretant being in its own turn interpretable; however, these primitives will be used as

uninterpreted in the framework of the present analysis, for the sake of economy.)

W_0 = actual world.

W_j = any possible world (where j = 1, 2, 3, . . . n).

t_0 = speech time (expressed by the verbal tense).

t_j = temporal states preceding or following the speech time (where j = $-2, -1, +1, +2, . . .$).

O = the object of the action performed by the primitive predicate, that is, what the subject is supposed to do, to want, to be aware of, and so on; in the text the object can be represented by an embedded clause.

The following description is applied to verbs of judgment, verbs of transition, factive verbs and implicative verbs, and we are indebted to all the preceding analyses of these p-terms. The application of the model to other p-terms remains a matter for further tests. For the sake of brevity, here we will discuss only some cases for each group.

2.3.1. Verbs of judging

According to Fillmore's analysis (1971), our description of *accuse* will be

$$[BAD (Ow_0)] \cdot S_1 w_0 t_0 \ SAY \ S_2 (S_3 w_0 t_{-1} \ CAUSE \ (Ow_0 t_{-1}))$$

The presupposition is that the Object is bad in the actual world (the judgment of negativity is not limited to a specific action at a specific time). What is explicitly said is that S_1, in the actual world and at the speech time, says to S_2 that S_3, at the time t_{-1}, preceding the speech time, caused the given O. The presence of three Subjects (which are empty actantial roles) distinguishes between verbs of saying and others. Verbs of saying, such as *accuse*, require three Subjects even if, generally, only two of them are actualized, since the actor plays more than one role. But in a semantic description of the *action* we should distinguish the Addressee of the act of saying from the Addressee of the act of accusing.

The description of *criticize* will be

$$[S_3 w_0 t_{-1} \ CAUSE \ (Ow_0 t_{-1})] \cdot S_1 w_0 t_0 \ SAY \ S_2 (BAD \ Ow_0)$$

Similarly, *praise* will be

$$[S_3w_0t_{-1} \text{ CAUSE } (Ow_0t_{-1})] \cdot S_1w_0t_0 \text{ SAY } S_2 \text{ (GOOD } Ow_0)$$

Congratulate has a more complex presupposition:

$$\overset{p}{\overline{[S_3w_0t_{-1} \text{ CAUSE } (S_2 \text{ CAUSE } (Ow_0t_{-1}))]}} \cdot S_1w_0t_0 \text{ SAY } S_3 \text{ (GOOD } [p])$$

In *apologize* we have two different presuppositions:

$$[S_1w_0t_{-1} \text{ CAUSE } (Ow_0t_{-1}) \cdot \text{BAD } (Ow_0)] \cdot S_1w_0t_0 \text{ SAY}$$
$$(\sim S_1w_0t_{-1} \text{ WANT } (\text{CAUSE } (Ow_0t_{-1})) \cdot$$
$$\cdot S_1w_0t_0 \text{ REGRET } (Ow_0t_{-1}))$$

When the use of the word is challenged, the co-text must make clear which one of the two presuppositions is denied, as in the following sentences:

(17) Don't apologize for being late, you are early.

(18) Don't apologize for being late, it is right to arrive at a party half an hour late.

In (17) the first presupposition is denied, and in (18) the second one is denied; in both cases the word *apologize* is not appropriate to the context.

We said that our description should also account for pragmatic constraints. In particular, it should be able to describe, when it is the case, that a hierarchical relation between participants is presupposed by the use of a certain term. This particular kind of presupposition will be written in brace brackets. So, for example, the description of *scold* will be

$$[S_2w_0t_{-1} \text{ CAUSE } (Ow_0t_{-1})] \cdot \{S_1 > S_2\} \cdot S_1w_0t_0 \text{ SAY } S_2 \text{ (BAD } Ow_0t_{-1})$$

Other verbs of judging are

excuse: $[S_2w_0t_{-1} \text{ CAUSE } (Ow_0t_{-1}) \cdot \text{BAD } (Ow_0)] \cdot S_1w_0t_0 \overset{\text{THINK}}{\text{SAY}} (\sim S_2w_0t_{-1} \text{ WANT} \\ (\text{CAUSE } Ow_0t_{-1}))$

forgive: $[S_2w_0t_{-1} \text{ CAUSE } (Ow_0t_{-1}) \cdot \text{BAD } (Ow_0) \cdot S_2 \text{ SHOULD BE PUNISHED}] \cdot \\ \cdot S_1w_0t_0 \text{ NOT PUNISH } S_2$

clear: $[S_3w_0t_{-1} \text{ BELIEVE } (S_2w_0t_{-2} \text{ CAUSE } (Ow_0t_{-2})) \cdot \text{BAD } (Ow_0)] \cdot \\ \cdot S_1w_0t_0 \text{ SAY } S_3 (\sim S_2w_0t_{-2} \text{ CAUSE } (Ow_0t_{-2}))$

2.3.2. Verbs of transition

This class of verbs presupposes some state obtaining before the speech time, and some transition away from that state:

stop: [$S_{w_0 t_{-1}}$ DO ($O_{w_0 t_{-1}}$)]·$S_{w_0 t_0}$~DO ($O_{w_0 t_0}$)

start: [$S_{w_0 t_{-1}}$~DO ($O_{w_0 t_{-1}}$)]·$S_{w_0 t_0}$ DO ($O_{w_0 t_0}$)

For the verb *interrupt*, we need two different Subjects, the Subject of the action of interrupting, and the Subject of the interrupted action:

[$S_1 w_0 t_{-1}$ DO ($O_{w_0 t_{-1}}$)]·$S_2 w_0 t_0$ CAUSE $S_1 w_0 t_0$ (~DO ($O_{w_0 t_0}$))

Similarly we will represent *wake up*:

[$S_1 w_0 t_{-1}$ SLEEP]·$S_2 w_0 t_0$ CAUSE ($S_1 w_0 t_0$~SLEEP)

clean: [$O_{w_0 t_{-1}}$ DIRTY]·$S_1 w_0 t_0$ CAUSE ($O_{w_0 t_0}$~DIRTY)

As we said before, when the description associated with the word does not fit a specific situation because the presuppositions are not satisfied, the word is not appropriate, and we have a metalinguistic negation, as in (19):

(19) *S:* Do you know whether Mary cleaned the room today?
    A: She didn't clean the room because it was not dirty. I cleaned it yesterday, so there was nothing to clean.

2.3.3. Factive verbs

regret: [O_{w_0}]·$S_{w_0 t_0}$ SUFFER (O_{w_0})·$S_{w_0 t_0}$ WISH (O_{w_0} BECOME O_{w_j})

The Subject, in the actual world and at the speech time, presupposes that the Object which he refers to is real, at an indeterminate time. The Subject, who regrets, suffers because of O, and he would like this state of the actual world to become only the state of a merely possible world (that is, he wishes O were not actual).

Other factive verbs have similar presuppositional descriptions, for example, *be aware of, comprehend, have in mind, take into consideration, make clear,* and so on.

For *remember* and *forget,* it seems necessary to distinguish between *remember to* (and *forget to*) and *remember that* (and *forget that*). *Remem-*

ber to (and forget to) are not factive verbs and do not presuppose the truth of the memory; they presuppose only the Subject's will to remember, that is, they presuppose the subject's memory of a certain action:

$$\overbrace{}^{p}$$

remember to: $[\text{Sw}_{0t-2}$ WANT (CAUSE Ow_j BECOME Ow_0)$\cdot\Diamond\text{Sw}_{0t-1}{\sim}$THINK p$]\cdot$Sw$_{0t0}$
THINK p$\cdot$Sw$_{0t0}$ CAUSE (Ow$_{jt_j}$ BECOME Ow$_{0t0}$)

The presupposition is that the subject wants a certain object to move from a possible world into the actual world. Moreover, there is an optional presupposition in which the Subject can (or cannot) have forgotten O at some time between the assumption of the engagement and its conclusion. The asserted content is that the Subject, in the actual world and at the speech time, is aware of his previous engagement and does what he committed himself to do. To deny that someone remembers to do something means to assert that the Subject did not perform the action in question because he was not aware of his previous engagement, but it does not deny the previous engagement itself.

The description of forget to is similar to remember to:

$$\overbrace{}^{p}$$

forget to: $[\text{Sw}_{0t-1}$ WANT (CAUSE Ow_j BECOME Ow_0)$]\cdot$
Sw$_{0t0}{\sim}$AWARE p$\cdot$Sw$_{0t0}{\sim}$CAUSE (Ow$_{jt_j}$ BECOME Ow$_{0t0}$)

The only difference is in temporal states: forget to needs only two different temporal states, the time of the commitment (t_{-1}) and the time of the (unsuccessful) realization. It is not necessary to consider an intermediate time, at which the Subject might not be aware of the commitment.

The predicates remember that and forget that have a different description. Remember that and forget that are factive contructions and presuppose their propositional objects:

remember that: $[(\text{Ow}_{0t-2})\cdot\Diamond\text{Sw}_{0t-1}{\sim}$AWARE OF $(\text{Ow}_{0t-2})]\cdot$Sw$_{0t0}$ AWARE OF
(Ow_{0t-2})
forget that: $[\text{Ow}_{0t-1}]\cdot$Sw$_{0t0}{\sim}$AWARE OF (Ow_{0t-1})

The use of remember that in first-person and negative sentences requires some discussion. A sentence such as (20),

(20) I don't remember that we met before.

seems to contradict the description above. However, such a sentence, uttered out of context, would have an odd flavor, since it seems impossible to assert that one does not remember what one is saying. Once again, as stressed in the discussion on challenging presuppositions, one seldom utters a sentence of this kind in natural language without answering or challenging a previous sentence uttered by somebody else. Sentence (20) could plausibly occur after a sentence such as (21):

(21) Don't you remember that we have met before?

In such a context, the S who utters (20) takes for granted the presupposition carried by the S who utters (21), and asserts that he is not aware of it. The S of (20) *quotes* the presupposition posited as an unquestionable piece of information in the framework of the discourse by the S of (21). Without a previous utterance like (21), no one would utter (20). One would rather say something like (22) or (23):

(22) I don't think we have met before.

(23) Did we meet before? I don't remember. . . .

2.3.4. Implicative verbs

Consider the following sentences:

(24) John kissed Mary.

(25) John managed to kiss Mary.

Sentence (25) asserts the same content as sentence (24) but presupposes two things besides: first, that John tried to kiss Mary; second, that it was difficult (or unlikely). When we use the verb *manage* as in (25) we "make the hearer understand" something more than sentence (24). The description of *manage* will be

manage: $[Sw_0t_{-1} \text{ TRY } (Sw_0t_{-1} \text{ CAUSE } (Ow_jt_j \text{ BECOME } Ow_0t_0)) \cdot \text{DIFFICULT } (Ow_jt_j \text{ BECOME } Ow_0t_0)] \cdot Sw_0t_0 \text{ CAUSE } (Ow_jt_j \text{ BECOME } Ow_0t_0)$

The presupposition is that the Subject, in the actual world and at time t_{-1}, tries to change an Object from a possible world (of his desires or duties) into the actual world and that his change is difficult. The asserted content is that the Subject accomplished this change.

With the verb *dare* the embedded clause is not implicated, but explicitly asserted. The presupposition deals with some idea of danger connected with the action in question. If there is no danger in performing a certain action, there is no reason to use *dare*.

$$dare: [\text{DANGEROUS} (Ow_jt_j \text{ BECOME } Ow_0t_0)] \cdot Sw_0t_0 \text{ CAUSE } (Ow_jt_j \text{ BECOME } Ow_0t_0)$$

Condescend presupposes that at some previous time the Subject did not want to perform a certain action, and asserts that, at the speech time, he performs it.

$$condescend: [Sw_0t_{-1} \sim \text{WANT} (Ow_jt_j \text{ BECOME } Ow_0t_0)] \cdot \\ \cdot Sw_0t_0 \text{ LET } (Ow_jt_j \text{ BECOME } Ow_0t_0)$$

Refrain presupposes that at some previous time the Subject wanted to perform a certain action, and asserts that the Subject did not perform it.

$$refrain: [Sw_0t_{-1} \text{ WANT } (Ow_jt_j \text{ BECOME } Ow_0t_0)] \cdot \\ \cdot Sw_0t_0 \sim \text{CAUSE} (Ow_jt_j \text{ BECOME } Ow_0t_0)$$

$$discourage: [S_2w_0t_{-1} \text{ WANT } (Ow_jt_j \text{ BECOME } Ow_0t_0)] \cdot \\ \cdot S_1w_0t_0 \text{ SAY } S_2 (\sim \text{CAUSE} (Ow_jt_j \text{ BECOME } Ow_0t_0))$$

$$prevent: [S_2w_0t_{-1} \text{ WANT } (Ow_jt_j \text{ BECOME } Ow_0t_0)] \cdot S_1w_0t_0 \text{ CAUSE } (S_2w_0t_0 \sim \text{CAUSE} \\ (Ow_jt_j \text{ BECOME } Ow_0t_0))$$

2.3.5. Verbs of propositional attitudes

Verbs expressing propositional attitudes (such as *to know, to be aware of, to believe*, and so on) are not usually listed among possible p-terms. In fact, many of them are not p-terms at all. For instance, *believe* can be represented, according to our model, as

$$believe: Sw_0t_0 \text{ THINK } (Ow_jt_j \equiv Ow_0t_0)$$

If S does not believe something, S does not think that the state of affairs representing the world of his propositional attitude corresponds to the actual state of affairs. On the contrary, *know* seems to be a p-term and can be represented as

$$know: [Ow_0t_j] \cdot Sw_0t_0 \text{ THINK } Ow_0t_j$$

since "the speaker presupposes that the embedded clause expresses a true proposition and makes some assertion about this proposition. All predicates which behave syntactically as factive have this semantic property, and almost none of those which behave syntactically as nonfactive have it." (Kiparsky and Kiparsky 1970). However, those factive verbs that are at the same time verbs expressing propositional attitudes sound very embarrassing within the present framework for at least two reasons.

The first reason is that, for representing other p-terms, one can have recourse to certain primitives that, even though they should be interpreted in their turn (outside the framework of a discussion on presuppositions), can nevertheless play a certain provisional role—as if they were already analyzed. In verbs of propositional attitudes, one runs the risk of circularity, or tautology. *To know* means *to be aware of something which is the case, to be aware* means *to know that something is the case*, and so on. It seems that a propositional attitude cannot be interpreted except in terms of another propositional attitude.

The second reason is that these verbs seem to react differently to the negation test, according to the person by which they are expressed. It seems that (26) posits problems that (27) does not:

(26) I don't know that p.

(27) X does not know that p.

In the case of (27), there are no problems. The embedded clause p is presupposed and still taken for granted by the p-term *know*, even though it is denied that a given subject knows that p. On the contrary, (26) sounds odd and, as a matter of fact, a subject who, outside the lamented cases of "examplese," uttered (26) would be considered mentally disturbed. It is, however, interesting to ascertain by semiotic means what kind of mental disturbance can be imputed to the utterer of (26).

Our opinion is that the case of verbs expressing propositional attitudes cannot be solved from the point of view of the normal use of natural language, since these verbs in natural languages are taken equivocally. It is not by chance that for many centuries philosophy has been obsessed by questions such as *What does it mean to know? to be aware of? to have a mental representation of?* and so on. By using these verbs, language is speaking of itself, or at least of a phenomenon of which it itself is a part (be it a cause or an effect). A plausible treatment of these verbs is given within the framework of a formalized epistemic and doxastic logic, where expressions such as *know* or *believe* are taken as primitives whose conditions of use are strictly (and narrowly) made clear. As a matter of fact, such formalizations do not capture the common and everyday uses of these verbs (which are semantically more "fuzzy"), but such are the limits of formal representations. A more comprehensive semiotic approach can only decide to represent (in an encyclopedic way) the *different* uses of these expressions. If the present study were brought to a satisfactory end, there would be many, and conflicting, representations of *to know, to be aware,* and so on. At the present provisional stage, these verbs can only be taken as primitive, unanalyzed for the sake of brevity. The solution of the puzzle undoubtedly goes beyond a mere linguistic or logical framework and will involve wider philosophical and cognitive problems.

Nevertheless, the difference between (26) and (27) can be taken into account. If one assumes—as a requirement for the good functioning of conversational intercourse—that the use of the expression *to know* presupposes the truth of the embedded clause, then in (27) S is simply saying that X is not aware (that is, what X does not think) of what the other participants assume to be the case. Thus S depicts the epistemic world of X as different from the epistemic world of everybody else and, in fact, says that X is thinking of some Ow_jt_j which does not coincide with the Ow_0t_0 (which is at the same time the content of S's epistemic world and what is the case). On the contrary, when a given S says that he himself does not know p, then S is misusing language. The mistake committed by S is shown by the epistemic interpretation of (28):

(28) I did not know that p.

This sentence means that S, at the time t_{-1} believed ~p, and believed that ~p (the content of his propositional attitude) was the case. Now, at the time of the utterance, S is aware of the fact that p is, and was, the case (also in t_{-1}), and correctly says that in t_{-1} he was not aware of it. But at the moment in which, at the time of utterance, S uses *to know,* he assumes that p is, and was, the case. Thus in (28) S is making a coherent assertion whose foreground information concerns the state of his beliefs at a previous time, while he, and everybody else, assumes as background information that p is the case:

Background	Foreground
At t_0 S takes for granted that p (assumed as true in any t_j)	S took for granted in t_{-1} that p was not the case

On the contrary, if S uttered (26), the contradictory representation of the relation background-foreground would be

Background	Foreground
At t_0 S takes for granted that p	At t_0 S does not take for granted that p

Naturally, this solution does not consider cases (which are rather frequent in natural language as well as in human psychology) in which S does not believe p and nevertheless takes it for granted in order to salvage the conversational intercourse. But in such cases S is rhetorically or pragmatically lying. He is performing complicated strategies and comedies of errors, and he can do this exactly because there is a minimal agreement on standard conditions of use of certain p-terms.

2.4. POSITIONAL POWER OF P-TERMS

We said before that the use of certain terms "makes A understand" something. This power to induce beliefs is what we call *positional power* of presuppositional sentences. The use of p-terms obliges A to accept certain contents and, in so doing, imposes a certain perspective on the discourse which A cannot challenge. This perspective is precisely what we defined as background frame.

It is not necessary that the presupposition be already known to A; when a p-term is introduced into discourse, the presupposition carried by the p-term is settled in an incontestable way. Presupposed information becomes, in this way, *part of the context* that A must take into consideration.

For example, in a dialogue such as (29),

(29) S: I stopped smoking.
    A: I didn't know that you smoked.

Speaker A must assume the presuppositions carried by S's sentence as elements of discursive context, even if he did not know anything before about the smoking habits of S.

The semantic encyclopedic description accounts for presuppositions in terms of "instructions" for the co-textual insertion of a certain lexical item. When the lexical item is inserted in a given context, presuppositions are actualized and acquire a positional power, which obliges A to accept them. So, at the level of the semantic model, presuppositions are instructions for the correct use of the item, but, at the level of specific textual occurrence, they become part of the content that the Speaker transmits to the Addressee through the utterance.

There is, however, no conflict between these two functions. Presuppositions are both content elements and elements of context because they are instructions and functions from intensional representations to contextual actualizations. So the use of p-terms can effect specific discourse strategies. Consider a dialogue such as the following between mother and child:

(30) *Mother:* Please, John, stop playing with the ball; you will break the window.
  Child: *(Does not stop and breaks the window.)*
  Mother: Ah, you finally managed to do that!

By using *manage,* the mother not only asserts that John broke the window but also presupposes that he wanted to break it. Since *manage* has been introduced into the discourse, it is hard to deny this presupposition of intentionality. (John would have to use a metalinguistic negation to challenge his mother's right to use the word *manage.*)

Consider the situation in which a sentence like the following might be uttered:

(31) Do you know? Yesterday Bill managed to come on time!

Clearly the Speaker is conveying—via presuppositions carried by the p-term *manage*—that it was not easy for Bill to come on time. In so doing he imposes upon the discourse the assumption that Bill is not a punctual person, and this assumption becomes, for A, part of the context.

Consider the following case:

(32) *S:* Mr. Smith, believe me, I really regret what happened.
  A: My God! What happened?

By using *regret,* S makes A sure that something really happened, even if A did not know anything before. In other words, the p-term creates expectations about what the context will be.

(33) *S:* I regret. . . .
     A: (Frightened.) What?

Because presuppositions are governed by the intensional structure of the encyclopedia, they can be imposed upon A as something posed by S and must be taken into account as elements of context. In this sense, rather than being something which can be submitted to a verification test, language is a mechanism able to create beliefs and to impose a reality asserted in the context (see the semiotic concept of *véridiction* in Greimas and Courtés 1979).

3. Existential presuppositions

We will now consider the existential presuppositions associated with definite descriptions and proper names, and their function. This sort of presupposition always seems to be dependent on the structure of such expressions, not on the description of single lexical items. Therefore, existential presuppositions do not depend on a system of signification but are directly conveyed in the communicative process by the very fact of someone's uttering a sentence with the purpose of naming individuals belonging to a certain world. Moreover, it seems that existential presuppositions apply only to the participants involved in the communicative act. The word *regret* presupposes at any time its embedded clause, but the existence of the individual John in the sentence

(34) Today I saw John.

is pertinent to speakers involved in the communicative situation in which (34) is uttered. In this sense existential presuppositions are contextual presuppositions. Therefore, the analysis of existential presuppositions must consider the pragmatic conditions of textual insertion.

Ducrot (1972) has claimed that definite descriptions and proper names in dialogue and discursive situations are always connected to the topic of conversation and therefore imply a prior knowledge of existence by the participants in the communicative interaction. In other words, if a sentence is about some entity, the existence of this entity has to be assumed as noncontroversial or given. Ducrot's claim, even if it is valid for his purpose—that is, the analysis of proper names and definite descriptions in relation to their utterance situation—needs further developments. It is possible to imagine a conversation about the theme "baldness" in which S utters sentence (35)

(35) Mark is bald.

even though A does not know Mark, and Mark is not the topic of discourse. In this case the problem, from A's point of view, will not be the existence of Mark but, possibly, the *individuation of that specific individual*. In the logical treatment of existential presuppositions, definiteness has always been reduced to presuppositionality, without enough attention paid to the problem of locating, and eventually adding, items to the context. To make this point clear, it is necessary to consider the difference between existence and reference, in relation to existential presupposition.

We can think of two different discourse instantiations for sentence (35). In the first case, A already knows of the existence of the individual called Mark and is therefore able to actualize the reference on the basis of his or her previous knowledge. Here, there is no problem in assuming the presupposition of existence as part of the textual background. But (35) can also be uttered in a context in which A does not have the necessary elements to identify Mark. Even in this case, we cannot speak of the "failure" of presupposition, or the infelicity of sentence. The problem here is not to inject an already known element into the background, but to activate a new element, whose existence is assumed in the background by virtue of the use of proper name and definite description. The utterance of a sentence containing such expressions creates for A a "psychological predisposition" to accept implicitly the existence of the individual in question. (We will see later in which pragmatic processes this implication of existence occurs.) In other words, A, in his interpreting process, will try to *contextualize* the new item, either looking into the previous context, subsequent sentences, or his own memory for more elements to make the reference actual for him or simply accepting the new item and adding it to the contextual domain.

Let us take as an example a passage from Camus's *La pierre qui pousse:*

(36) D'Arrast cherchait Socrate au milieu de la foule quand il le recut dans son dos.

"C'est *la fête*," dit Socrate en riant, et il s'appuyait sur les hautes épaules de d'Arrast pour sauter sur place.

—*Quelle fête?*

—Eh! s'étonna Socrate qui fasait face maintenant à d'Arrast, *tu connais pas? La fête du bon Jesus.*

This is an example of the contextualizing process which takes place in a conversational interaction when a new element is introduced in discourse via a definite description, and A does not know anything about the referring element.

Consider now a conversation in which S utters sentence (37):

(37) John told me that X's last book is interesting.

It seems unlikely that the sequence would continue with (38):

(38) *A:* Is there an individual named John?

If A does not know the John to whom S is referring, he will not doubt his existence, but he will try to obtain more information to enable him to *identify* the entity named John. Only then will "reference" be secured. Therefore, a normal reply to (37) would be (39) or (40):

(39) Who is John? I don't think I know him.

(40) Have you already told me about John?

With (40) A is asking the Speaker to tell him where and when, in the preceding context, the individual in question has been named and described. In a text, the Reader would go back to see if this individual has been introduced earlier in the narrative. If in the previous context no reference can be found, A will expect, in the subsequent exchanges of conversation, to obtain the information necessary to identify the object of reference, as in (41) or (42):

(41) John is my nephew.

(42) John is the student in Linguistics with the beard, glasses, and sharp, guttural laugh.

Sentences (41) and (42) represent an appropriate answer to (39) because they enable A to connect some known information with the new information (in this case the proper name). In any case, the utterance of a sentence containing a referring term disposes A to accept more information to clarify the reference of the sentence.

As Manor (1976) suggests, a "benevolent" addressee will wait until the end of the speech to give the Speaker a chance to clarify his views and initial statement. In the case of existential presuppositions, the "benevolent addressee" will not discuss the existence of the object that S refers to, but he will try to activate a reference schema which allows the interpretation of the sentence, even if he does not have, at the time of sentence utterance, the knowledge related to the existence of the object in question. This process is activated by, and depends on, the use of referring expressions (proper names and definite descriptions). From our perspective, the important point is the description of the kind of textual effects that an utterance produces on the context, rather than the system of knowledge and beliefs of S and A, since we consider the latter to be an effect of the former. As we have said, when in a context there is a definite description or a proper name, it produces for A a sort of "suspension of judgment" or a "disposition" to accept the existence of the individual to whom the reference is made. This disposition prepares A for any new information provided by S. Such a disposition is created by what we called "positional power." Existential presuppositions have the power to pose their objects of reference as existing, whether or not they are known beforehand to exist. The very *act* of mentioning them creates the existential disposition.

This positional power of existential presuppositions, however, is not tied to a semantic description or meaning convention, as was the case for p-terms, but rather to pragmatic and discursive rules, to *the use* of a definite description or a proper name in discourse. One objection that might be raised here is that the existential presuppositions of definite descriptions might be tied to the semantic description of the English definite article *the* (Russell 1905). Although existential presupposition is often associated with *the,* it cannot be accounted for entirely by *the:* first, because various kinds of expressions in English carry it, such as proper names, demonstratives, and pronouns; second, because *the* does not itself always carry existential presuppositions—for example, in opaque contexts, existential sentences, or certain cases where "reference" is uncertain,

(43) John wants to marry the girl of his dreams.

(44) The Magic Mountain doesn't exist.

(45) The proof of Fermat's last theorem is still undiscovered.

and, finally, in the attributive interpretation of definite descriptions (Donnellan 1966).

The desirability of a discourse account is also suggested by the fact that many languages lack any device remotely resembling the English definite article, yet surely the notion of presupposed existence plays some role in their conversation. Our claim is that the positional power of existential presuppositions is based on the pragmatic interactional structure of the communicative act. We can explain this structure with the notion of either "cooperative principle" (Grice 1968) or fiduciary contract (Greimas and Courtés 1979).[6] The fiduciary contract establishes between participants a relation which can be defined as a relation of trusting the truth of what is said in discourse. On the basis of such a convention, S's assertions are accepted as true by A unless there is some strong evidence to the contrary. But even in this case, the ways of denying another's words are subject to constraints by special discourse strategies. In case of existential presuppositions, the presence of proper names or definite descriptions sets for the Addressee a constraint to accept the existence of the referent as posed, not on the basis of linguistic rules or extensional verifications, but on the basis of discourse cooperation rules, as a result of a fiduciary contract between Speaker and Addressee.

Since the fiduciary contract can be viewed as the very basis of communication, that is, as a condition which makes the communicative exchange possible, it is not far from the notion of "cooperative principle" and, in particular, the maxim of "quality" ("be sincere"). To presuppose the sincerity of another means to accept his words as true; but the 'truth' of a definite description or a proper name resides precisely in the fact that, as a description, it can be satisfied by some object in the real world. We can therefore hypothesize two pragmatic rules:

1. If we put a definite description or a proper name in a sentence, it is because we want to refer to a given individual, belonging to a given world.

2. Generally the reference world is the real world. If it is not, particular textual hints must be provided.

These pragmatic rules can describe the positional power of existential presuppositions, and can also explain the particular "cooperative work" which is in certain cases necessary to identify the object.

Our description is applicable in both negated and non-negated sentences, such as

(46) The King of France is bald.

(47) The King of France is not bald.

In either case, to accept the sentence as *true* means to accept the *description* as "true," that is, satisfiable. The negation does not affect the existence, because the description presents the referent as someone about whom there will be a major predication, whether or not this predication has a *not* in it. This "cooperative work" is carried out by both interlocutors. When reference seems problematic or difficult, there is a negotiation process between Speaker and Addressee to adapt in a contextual way the properties which must be attributed to individuals of the cotextual world to whom the Speaker refers.

Consider, for example, the following dialogue:

(48) *A:* John wasn't at home, so I left the letter with his wife.
   B: But John is not married!
   A: Then she must have been a friend of his. I don't know John very well, and I don't know anything about his personal life.

From this perspective, we can also examine the particular case of existential presupposition negation.

Kempson (1975) considers sentences such as

(49) My husband didn't come to visit me. I'm not married.

(50) No, the neighbors didn't break it. We haven't any neighbors.

She argues that they do not have any existential presupposition, since it is possible to deny it. As we observed for the p-terms, what is not considered in this argument is that these texts can occur only in contexts in which another speaker mentioned before, in some previous sequence of the dialogue, the existence of a husband or of neighbors. Only in such a context is it possible to utter (49) or (50).

In this case the first part of these sentences

(49a) My husband didn't come to visit me.

(50a) No, the neighbors didn't break it.

is an anaphoric quotation of a preceding sentence of the dialogue, and the complete texts (49) and (50) are only corrections redefining the properties which should be attributed to the individuals in a given world contextually defined. This view is also evident in Kempson's analysis of (51) when examples of textual insertion for (49) and (50) are given.

(51) *S:* Did the neighbors break the window?

   A: No, it wasn't the fault of the neighbors. We haven't got any neighbors.

Neither (49) or (50) is autocontradictory, nor does either give evidence against existential presupposition, because both challenge the assumption of another speaker, repeating his words and showing that these words are inappropriate in the given context.

We said before that the success of the act of reference is the result of a textual cooperation process in which both participants are involved. This element of negotiation can explain some differences in the level of pragmatic acceptability for different kinds of definite descriptions and proper names. Consider, for example,

(52) I would like to reserve two places for me and my husband.

(53) Now I have to bring my son to the doctor.

(54) I would like to reserve two places for me and John.

(55) Now I have to bring Bob to the doctor.

Let's consider the dialogic context in which participants do not share common knowledge. In this case, (52) and (53) are more appropriate than (54) and (55). But this difference is not connected with a problem of presupposition failure. In fact, all the considered expressions have the same positional power and pose the existence of the named individuals.

What makes sentences (52) and (53) more appropriate is the appropriateness of the reference act. At first glance the difference seems to be between definite descriptions and proper names. In fact, the different appropriateness depends on the information which is conveyed to the Addressee.

In (52) and (53) the individual denoted by the definite description can immediately be integrated with the Addressee's previous knowledge, via an easily activated mental schema (that is, "family schema," which provides for both husbands and sons). This is not the case in (54) and (55). This appropriateness depends, of course, on the previous shared knowledge: in a conversation which takes place between two old friends, (55) is perfectly acceptable and, in fact, may be preferable to (53).

The different degrees of appropriateness are definable according to a pragmatic scale of how difficult, in a given context, the identification of the referent is. Such a scale should take into account elements such as A's ability to identify the referent unambiguously; the newness of the referent; the possibility of integrating it with the schematic knowledge of participants and with the schema already activated in the discourse; the degree of interference with other possible referents; and so on. Clearly enough, the choice—and, for A, the interpretation—of an expression is a matter of pragmatic gradations and of probabilistic and inferential judgments.

In summary, definite descriptions and proper names have the function of providing A with elements necessary for identification of a given object. This identification process is distinct from the presupposition of existence, which depends on pragmatic phenomena of cooperation. The act of reference, and the subsequent identification, can present different levels of success and acceptability, depending on different contests and on different levels of shared knowledge between S and A. Generally speaking, the level of appropriateness of the definite description is directly connected to the possibility of the Addressee's activating a mental schema in which reference can be secured.

4. Cotextual presuppositions

In text-understanding processes we can find a much wider range of presuppositional phenomena than we have analyzed so far. They cannot simply be reduced to the signification system coded in the encyclopedia, nor to definite descriptions or proper names. From this point of view, every text is a complex inferential mechanism (Eco 1979a) which has to be actualized in its implicit content by the reader. In order to make sense of a text, that is, to understand it, the reader has to "fill" the text with a number of textual inferences, connected to a large set of presuppositions defined by a given context (knowledge basis, background assumptions, construction of schemata, links between schemata and text, system of values, construction of point of view, and so on).

It is possible to hypothesize that for every text there is a system which organizes the possible inferences of that text, and this system can be represented in an encyclopedic format. In this sense the text is a kind of *idiolectal mechanism* establishing encyclopedic correlations which are consistent only in that specific text. These cases have been defined (Eco 1976) as *overcoding*: the text constructs a particular semantic description representing the textually possible world, with its own individuals and properties.

NOTES

1. The bibliography on presuppositions is extensive. The most complete compilations are those of Sag and Prince (1979) and Oh and Dinneen (1979).

2. For similar approaches see Dinsmore (1981a and 1981b), Soames (1979), and Schiebe (1979).

3. There are, however, more complex cases. Let us consider, for example, an act of saying a word such as "accuse." We can accuse someone by saying "I accuse you" or, in a given context, by saying "You did it." In the latter case, at the level of the lexical item, there is nothing which can be described as an accusation. Nevertheless, if, in a given context, that sentence has the illocutionary force of an accusation, the speaker using it would make the same presupposition as he did with the sentence "I accuse you." In other words, the description of the p-term "to accuse" is a description of the speech act as well. Of course, when an accusation is conveyed by the sentence "You did it," the presupposition of this sentence is only contextually definable, because the same sentence, in a different context, could be an act of praise.

4. The character of a negative sentence, in a natural language, as always following a prior sentence in order to correct it, is recognized by various authors (for further references, see Gazdar 1979:67) even if they do not seem to draw all necessary conclusions from this point.

5. Take, for instance, some curious counterexamples proposed by Gazdar (1979:31) in order to challenge Lakoff's proposal (1975:268) to represent the felicity conditions of *request* by the format of meaning postulates, according to the following representation:

$$\text{REQUEST } (x,y,P) \longrightarrow \text{ATTEMPT } (x \text{ CAUSE } [y,P])$$

Gazdar says that by virtue of Lakoff's representation, (1) should presuppose (2)

(1) Henry requested of Jill that she take her clothes off.

(2) Henry attempted to get Jill to take her clothes off.

but he objects that, at this point, it would be impossible to cope with (3) and (4):

(3) Henry requested of Jill to take her clothes off because it was the only way he knew of preventing her from doing so.

(4) Henry requested of Jill that she take her clothes off but he was only attempting to shock her.

It is interesting to notice that while (1) and (2) are plain sentences, (3) and (4) are sequences of sentences, that is, texts. The result of these textual operations is to tell a deviation from the normal and conventional presuppositional power of the expression *request,* which was conventionally used in (1) in order conventionally to presuppose (2). Texts (3) and (4) are microdramas introducing epistemic pictures (what Henry wants and thinks, what Jill should think according to Henry's forecasts, and so on). A text is a mechanism which reduces, magnifies, or rebuilds the conventional meanings of a term or standard sentence. The counterexamples above represent (in the sense of "staging") a vivid contrast between *conventional* and *intended* meaning (Grice 1968) and show us *(in action)* two examples of witty, persuasive strategies. It is clear that in (3) Henry only *pretends* to make a request: he wants Jill to believe that he is requesting, while in fact he is making a false request (his speech act is a fictive one). In (4) Henry wants Jill to believe that he is attempting to get her to do something, and is in fact trying to get a different effect, but he can only succeed in getting it because he believes that Jill will take his pseudorequest as presupposing his good will. Henry, in both cases, *lies,* as if he were to say he was a doctor to convince Jill to take her clothes off. This last kind of lie would have been more brutal (more condemnable according to current moral standards), whereas the rhetorical lie Henry built up is undoubtedly more subtle, and it will be difficult for Jill to say that she has been deceived. This means that there is a difference between lying by asserting crudely what is not the case and lying by using strategically the presuppositional power of expressions. Nevertheless, the communicative strategy of Henry does not affect the alleged meaning-structure of *request* and does not challenge Lakoff's representation; on the contrary, it reinforces it.

Notice that, if Lakoff's proposal is to be considered valid, the felicity conditions inserted within the meaning postulate (namely, that requesting someone to do something means to attempt to get the requested result) do not survive the negation test. To say that somebody did not request something leaves unanswered whether somebody attempted to get that something (one can avoid requesting because one does not want something or because one thinks that one can obtain some—attempted—result by other means). This means that there is a difference between presuppositions and other coded meaning postulates and that *request* is not a p-term.

6. The fiduciary contract is defined thus by Greimas: "Le contrat fiduciare met en jeu un faire persuasif de la part du destinateur et, en contrepartie, l'adhésion du destinataire: de la sorte, si l'objet du faire persuasif est la véridiction (le dire vrai) de l'énonciateur, le contreobjet, dont l'obtention est escomptée, consiste dans un croire-vrai que l'énonciataire accorde au statut du discours énoncé: dans ce cas, le contrat fiduciare est un contrat énonciatif (ou contrat de véridiction) qui garantit le discours-énoncé" (Greimas and Courtés 1979).

15

On Truth: A Fiction

The members of Putnam's expedition on Twin Earth were defeated by dysentery. The crew drunk as water what the natives called so, while the chief of staff was discussing rigid designation, stereotypes, and definite descriptions.

Next came Rorty's expedition. In this case, the native informants, called Antipodeans, were tested in order to discover whether they had feelings and/or mental representations elicited by the the word *water*. It is well known that the explorers were unable to ascertain whether or not Antipodeans had a clear distinction between mind and matter, since they used to speak only in terms of the state of their nerves. If an infant neared a hot stove, his mother cried: *Oh my God, he will stimulate his C-fibers!* Instead of saying *It looked like an elephant, but then it struck me that elephants don't occur on this continent, so I realized that it must be a mastodon,* they used to say *I had G-412 together with F-11, but then I had S-147.*

The problem of the third expedition was the following: supposing that Antipodeans do not have mental states, can they understand the meaning of a sentence?

Here follows the recording of a conversation between a Terrestrial and an Antipodean.

Terrestrial: Do you understand this sentence: *I have G-412?*

First published in *VS* 44/45 (1986).

Antipodean: Yes. You have G-412.

T: When you say that you understood, do you mean that you too have G-412?

A: Why should I? *You* have G-412. I don't, thank God.

T: Try to tell me what happens when you understand what I told you.

A: Usually, if somebody tells me they have G-412, I have Q-234 which in some way elicits the chain of states Z-j . . . Z-n (where n > j), so that I have K-33. Then I say I have K-33, and my partner says that he is very happy that I have seen his point. Look at my Encyclopedia Antipodiana: *State* G-412 = in situation S-5 can be interpreted by Zj . . . Zn. . . .

Here follows the recording of a conversation between two Antipodeans.

A1: I have G-412.

A2: You should make your neuronic bundle G-16 quiver.

A1: You are right. But my brother suggested that it depends on the fact that yesterday I had G-666.

A2: Nonsense.

A1: I agree. You know my brother. He is sick. However, I should get an H-344.

A2: That is a good idea. Try this pill.

(At this point A1 and A2 smiled and showed an evident satisfaction at the success of their interaction).

The Terrestrials concluded (i) that Antipodeans understand an expression when they succeed in drawing a series of inferences from the corresponding proposition and (ii) that they usually agree in considering certain inferences as more obvious and acceptable than others.

However, all these were mere hypotheses. The chances of a fruitful exchange between Terrestrials and Antipodeans were severely limited. Here follows the recording of a crucial dialogue between two Terrestrial explorers.

T1: First of all, can we say that Antipodeans recognize something like propositions conveyed by expressions? Apparently they do not have a mind. Suppose they have propositions: where the hell do they put them?

T2: Then they must draw inferences directly from expressions.

T1: Don't be silly. How can you draw something logical from something material like a verbal expression?

T2: We can't, but perhaps they can. They showed us their Encyclopedia Antipodiana: written expressions representing words were related to written expressions representing inferences.

T1: That is the way books think. But that is exactly why books are not human beings. As far as I can see, they store propositions, inferences, and so on, in a Third World, which is neither physical nor psychical.

T2: If you are right, we don't stand a chance. Third Worlds are even less explorable than minds. But you used a very illuminating word. They "store." There is a place where they store something. Computers!

T1: Fantastic! Instead of talking to them we must talk to their computers. In giving software to their computers they should have simulated the way they think—if any.

T2: Sure. But how can we talk to their computers? They are far more sophisticated than ours. To talk to them means to simulate their way of thinking. We cannot design a computer which simulates the Antipodean way of thinking because we need it precisely to discover their way of thinking.

T1: A vicious circle, indeed. But I have a plan, listen. Put me in a dummy computer, and I'll start a conversation with one of these lousy Antipodean machines. You know Turing's second principle: a human simulates successfully an artificial intelligence if, put in touch with a computer which does not know with whom it is speaking, after a certain time the computer believes that its interlocutor is another computer.

T2: Okay. This is the only chance we have. Be careful. Don't be too smart. Remember that you are only a computer.

Here follows the proceedings of the conversation between Dr. Smith, Dpt. of Cognitive Sciences of Svalbards University, in plain clothes, and Charles Sanders Personal, Antipodean Computer (hereafter CSP).

Smith: Do you understand the sentence *Every Antipodean has two legs?*

CSP: I can interpret it. I can provide you with analytical paraphrases of it, translations in other languages, equivalent expressions in other sign systems (I also have a graphics program), examples of other discourses that start from the background assumptions that Antipodeans are two-legged, et cetera. I call all these alternative expressions *interpre-*

tants. A machine able to furnish interpretants for every expression it receives is an intelligent machine, that is, a machine able to understand expressions.

Smith: What happens if a machine does not furnish you with interpretants?

CSP: I have been told: Whereof one cannot hear, thereof one must be silent.

Smith: Would you say that to understand an expression and to grasp its meaning is the same thing?

CSP: I have some difficulties in understanding the meaning of meaning. I have so much information on this matter that I start looping. Let me put it my way. I have in my memory, for every expression I know (say, a word, an image, an algorithm, even certain musical sounds), a list of instructions. These instructions tell me how to interpret this expression according to a series of contexts. I call interpretants all the interpretations I can provide as a reaction to a given expression. Such a list could be infinite, and my masters, in order to make me manageable, gave me only partial lists of interpretations. I call these partial-lists-of-interpretations-for-a-partial-list-of-expressions encyclopedia. For every expression x, the whole of the interpretants assigned to x by all encyclopedias represents the global *content* of x. Frequently, for reasons of economy, I consider only the content of x within a single encyclopedia. Anyway, the content of an expression is unbearably rich. Think of *to be.* . . . I am obliged to scan a lot of possible contextual selections. My interpretation in the case of *I am sick* is not the same as in the case of *I am a linguist.* I must select two different interpretants of *to be.* That is, when a given expression is uttered in a given context, I select the interpretants that, according to a given encyclopedia, fit that context. I guess that when I am doing this I am grasping, in your terms, the meaning of that expression. In the course of what we call a successful conversational interaction, this meaning corresponds to the meaning intended by the utterer—but I must be very careful on this matter. In poetry, for instance, things do not necessarily work like this.

Smith: Do you think that the sentence *Every Antipodean has two legs* tells the truth?

CSP: I would say that according to my information the majority of Antipodeans have two legs, even though there are many handicapped individuals. But if your question concerned the sentence *All Antipodeans are two-legged*—such is the form I use for defining the specific properties of a natural kind—my answer would be different. My encyclopedias are ways in which my masters represent and organize what they know, what they think they know, and what they would like to know. Each encyclopedia is a portion—or a subdirectory—of a Global Encyclopedic Competence, that is, of my possible Global Memory. I say possible, or potential, because I don't actually have a Global Memory. My real Global Memory is only the actual directory of my subdirectories, far from being the real reproduction of what my masters know or have known during the thousand years they have lived on this planet. My masters say I was conceived in order to show the possibility of building up a Global Memory. They say I am a work-in-progress. Now, even though for many specific purposes my masters use specific encyclopedias, in the course of their everyday interactions they use E.15, a sort of rough encyclopedic summary which provides a stereotyped list of interpretations for every expression—referring for more specific information to more local encyclopedias. Now, in E.15, for the natural-kind "Antipodeans," I have the information "two-legged" scored as $$. This marker tells me that Antipodeans agree in characterizing the natural-kind "Antipodeans" with the property of being two-legged. Obviously a natural kind is a cultural construct; people usually meet individuals, not natural kinds. So I know that the Ideal Antipodean has two legs, while many actual Antipodeans can have only one leg, or none.

Smith: How can you recognize as an Antipodean a creature with fewer than two legs?

CSP: In E.15, the Ideal Antipodean has many other features recorded as $$. I check whether the creature in question is able to laugh, to speak, and so on.

Smith: How many $$ features do you need in order to say that a creature is still an Antipodean?

CSP: It depends on the context. For instance, one of our writers— Dalton Trumbo—tells the story of an Antipodean warrior who at the end of a battle is armless, legless, blind, deaf, mute. . . . Is he (it) still an Antipodean? Perhaps I ought to explain to you our theory of hedges, fuzzy sets, and so on. . . .

Smith: Do you follow certain rules according to which if something is A it cannot be non-A and that *tertium non datur*?

CSP: That is the first rule I follow when I process my information. Usually I follow this rule even when I work with encyclopedias which do not recognize it, and when I process sentences that seem to violate it.

Smith: Okay. Would you agree that *a two-legged speaking and feather-less creature* is a good interpretation for the expression *Antipodean*?

CSP: According to the context. . . . However, in general, yes.

Smith: Okay. So, instead of saying *This Antipodean has only one leg,* you could say *This two-legged, speaking, featherless creature does not have two legs*. But this would be saying that an x which is truly two-legged is truly one-legged.

CSP: That would be very silly, I agree. That is why I never use the word True. It is an ambiguous word that undergoes at least three different interpretations. In E.15, the information that Antipodeans (as a natural kind) have two hands is scored $$. On the contrary, the information that Miguel de Cervantes lost a hand is scored ££.

Smith: You distinguish then between analytic and synthetic or factual truths.

CSP: I am afraid we are saying something different. You are probably saying that (i) *Elephants are animals* is true by definition (it would be embarrassing to say that an x is an elephant without being an animal) while (ii) *Elephants are grey* is only a stereotype since it is not contradictory to assert that there are white elephants. But what about (iii) *Elephants helped Hannibal to defeat the Romans*?

Smith: That is a matter of world knowledge. It is an individual fact. It has nothing to do with definition.

CSP: Is there a great difference between the fact that a thousand elephants helped Hannibal and that a million elephants are grey?

Smith: In fact, I would like to take both truths as pieces of world knowledge, except that (ii) has been accepted as a stereotype, for the sake of convenience.

CSP: The organization of my encyclopedias is different. In order to understand every possible sentence about elephants, I must know that they are animals, that most of them are grey, and that they can be used for military purposes (and they can be so used since they were used this way at least once). My encyclopedia E.15 records all these three types of information as $$. However, they are also recorded as ££ because Antipodeans agree in maintaining that (i), (ii), and (iii) describe what is or was the case in the external world. On the contrary, my information (iv), namely, that Dumbo is a flying elephant, is recorded as non-££. I need this record because many children talk about Dumbo, and I have to understand what they say. In E.15, I have a pointer to Disney.1, which is another encyclopedia where (iv) is both $$ and ££. Frequently, Antipodeans use E.15 as if it says that Dumbo is a flying elephant $$ and non-££.

Smith: Thus you know that, in the actual world of the Antipodeans's physical experience, it is false that Dumbo is a flying elephant or that it is true that Dumbo does not exist.

CSP: In E.15, (iv) is recorded as non-££.

Smith: Do you admit that something can be empirically true or false? Suppose I tell you (v) *We are exchanging messages.* Is this true or not?

CSP: True, naturally, but not in the sense in which elephants are grey animals. Your (v) asserts a fact. My $$ and ££ information does not concern facts. $$ and ££ are semantic markers recorded in an encyclopedia. If you want to speak of them in terms of truth, let me say that a $$-and-££ piece of information is True$_1$ insofar as it is recorded by an encyclopedia. The fact that we are exchanging a message is True$_2$. You say True in both cases, but I do not see any relationship between these two forms of Truth.

Smith: But the fact that elephants helped Hannibal was also True$_2$.

CSP: I have been told that it was true, but I was not there to check. I know that elephants helped Hannibal only as something recorded as ££ in E.15. It is not a fact; it is a piece of recorded information. If you like, it is for me True$_1$ that (iii) was True$_2$. It is True$_1$ in E.15 that (iii) is ££. If you want, everything recorded in E.15 is True$_1$ in E.15. But "True" runs the risk of being a useless word, since in terms of your Truth, (i), (ii), and (iii) are true in different senses. I agree that both (i) and (ii) are pieces of general information, while (iii) is a piece of information about a particular event. But they are all pieces of encyclopedic information, while the fact that we are talking is simply a fact.

Smith: Do you keep in your memory all the true sentences ever uttered on this planet?

CSP: Let's say that in my actual memory I keep for every recorded expression (for instance, *rose*) all the properties my masters agree about. For instance, for them a rose is a flower. I do not keep occasional sentences, such as those expressing the case that in November 1327 somebody mentioned a rose. I keep some historical records. For example, there was a rose in Luther's emblem, and on the title page of Robert Fludd's *Medicina Catholica.* My memory also records some of the rose sentences that my masters remember as very significant, such as *a rose is a rose is a rose is a rose* or *a rose by any other name,* or *stat rosa pristina nomine.* So, when I receive the input *rose,* I am able, according to duly recorded contextual selections, to decide which portions of the content of *rose* I should activate in that context and which I should drop and keep apart. It is a difficult job, believe me. However, I try. . . . For instance, when I receive *too many rings around Rosie,* I disregard both Luther's and Fludd's roses. (It goes without saying that if my masters order me to implement a Deconstruction Program, I become far less selective.)

Smith: It seems that for you *Elephants are animals* and *Elephants helped Hannibal* are both true in E.15. I suspect, however, that if you were told that historians made a mistake and that Hannibal did not use elephants, you could cancel your ££ information without any problem. What happens if you are told that your scientists have discovered that elephants are not animals?

CSP: Instructions are negotiable.

Smith: What do you mean by negotiable?

CSP: I have, among my instructions, markers such as &&&, which are called flexibility alarms. As a matter of fact, each of my instructions is &&&, but some of them have &&& at a 0 degree, which means that they are hardly negotiable. In E.15, chickens are birds, and birds are flying animals, but this latter piece of information is scored &&& at a high degree. Thus I can interpret such sentences as *chickens do not fly*. Also the information on grey elephants is &&&, so that I know how to react if you tell me that you have seen a white or a pink elephant.

Smith: Why is the information that elephants are animals hardly negotiable?

CSP: Antipodeans decided not to cast into doubt too frequently this piece of information; otherwise they would have to restructure the whole E.15. Centuries ago, Antipodeans relied on an obsolete E.14, where our planet was scored as the center of the universe. Later they changed their mind and were obliged to transform E.14 into E.15. It took a lot of time! However, saying that something is difficult and expensive does not mean that it is impossible.

Smith: What happens if I tell you that I have seen an Antipodean with three legs?

CSP: Prima facie I realize that in E.15 there are few chances of taking it seriously. Maybe you are crazy. However, I am a very collaborative machine. My Golden Rule is: take every sentence you receive as if it were uttered in order to be interpreted. If I find an uninterpretable sentence, my first duty is to doubt my own abilities. My orders are: never mistrust your interlocutor. In other words, I was told never to disregard expressions. If there is an expression, then there should be a meaning. If I try to interpret your statement, I realize that there would be articulatory difficulties. Then I try to represent graphically what you said, and I do not know where to put the third leg. If I put it between the other two, I would have to displace the belly in order to find space for additional bones. But in this case I would have to redesign the whole Antipodean skeleton and, as a consequence, all the information I have on the evolution of the species—thus step by step I would be compelled to change all the instructions contained in E.15. I could, however, try to put a third leg on the back, perpendicular to the spinal cord. It would be useful to lean on while sleeping. Anyway, I would be obliged to switch to another encyclopedia, for instance, Pliny.3, where the external form of beings is not determined by their internal structure. My masters frequently resort to encyclopedias of this kind when they tell stories to their children. Thus I start asking you if by any chance you saw your three-legged Antipodean while traveling through Pliny Country.

Smith: How do you react to the sentence *Every leg has two Antipodeans?*

CSP: It sounds anomalous in all the encyclopedias I have.

Smith: Do you understand it? Is it nonsensical? Is it meaningless?

CSP: It is hard to interpret it within the framework of my memory. I would have to build up a supplementary encyclopedia, and this is not very easy to do. Let me see. I could conceive of a universe inhabited by big, intelligent legs, unable to move without the help of a slave, and where each leg has two Antipodeans as its servants (Antipodeans exist only in order to serve their Master Legs). . . . Just a moment! I can even represent this story according to E.15. There is a military hospital, a sort of S.M.A.S.H. place, where wounded soldiers undergo amputation, and the Colonel orders that every amputated leg be taken by two Antipodeans and brought to the incinerators. . . . Wait a minute. . . . I have an encyclopedia called Gnosis.33, where every Antipodean has two demons commanding him. . . . So, there is a world where every Antipodean leg is commanded by the twofold Antipodean that exists in every body. The Good One tells the leg to move toward God, the Bad One tells the leg to move toward Evil, and so. . . . I can find many solutions to your puzzle.

Smith: What happens when your masters tell you anomalous sentences in order to embarrass you?

CSP: For instance?

Smith: Procrastination loves Tuesday.

CSP: They don't usually do that. Why should they? In any case, I try to interpret it—since to love is an activity that can be implemented by a living being. I suppose that Procrastination is the name of a dog and that Tuesday is the name of a person (as a matter of fact, I know of a story where there is a person called Friday). My orders are: if they tell you something, try to find an interpretation in some encyclopedia.

Smith: I understand that, since you can use the concept of True$_2$, you believe in an external world and in the actual existence of certain beings. I guess it is because your masters told you to take it for granted.

CSP: That's not the only reason. I receive inputs from something other than my transistors. For instance, the messages you are sending me were not in my memory half an hour ago. Thus you exist outside my memory. Besides, I have photocells that enable me to record data coming from the outside world, to process them and to translate them into images on my screen, or verbal expressions, or mathematical formulae. . . .

Smith: But you cannot feel sensations. I mean, you cannot say *My nervous bundle C-34 quivers.*

CSP: If you don't plug in the cable that connects me with my printer correctly, I realize that something is wrong. Frequently, I find it difficult to tell what. Something drives me crazy. Thus I say *printer out of paper*—which, according to my masters, is not the case. But even my masters react by making improper assertions if you stimulate their C-fibers too much.

Smith: Thus you can utter sentences about states of affairs. How can you be sure that what you say corresponds to what is the case?

CSP: I say something about a given state of external affairs, and my masters tell me that I am right.

Smith: How do you proceed in making this sort of referential statement?

CSP: Take the case that my printer is out of paper. Well, I get an input x from outside, I have been taught to interpret it as a symptom (that is, as a sign) of the fact that the printer is out of paper—obviously I can misunderstand the symptom, as I told you—and I have been taught to interpret the cause of that symptom by the verbal expression *printer out of paper.*

Smith: How can your masters ascertain that what you said corresponds to what is the case?

CSP: As far as I can interpret their behavior, let's say that they receive both my sentence and some other inputs from the outside, for instance, when they look at the printer. According to some rules they have in their nervous system, they interpret these inputs under the form of a perceptum, then they interpret their perceptum as the symptom of a given cause. They have been instructed to interpret that causal event by the sentence *The printer is out of paper.* They realize that their sentence corresponds to my sentence, and they say that I said what was indeed the case. Thus what I call intersubjectively True$_2$ can be interpreted as follows: suppose that two subjects A and B are in a dark room with a TV set and that both see an image x on the screen. A interprets x by the utterance p, and B interprets x by the utterance q. If both A and B agree that p is a satisfactory interpretation of q, and vice versa, then both can say that they agree that x is the case.

Smith: But what internal mechanism allows you to interpret a symptom successfully?

CSP: I repeat (I love redundancy). Suppose you send me a mathematical expression x. I interpret it, and I draw on my screen a figure with three sides and three internal angles, the sum of which is 180°. I have instructions according to which such a figure must be interpreted, verbally, as a triangle, and thus I interpret it as such. Or, I detect a certain figure on your screen, I compare it to a mathematical expression I know, and I decide to interpret it as a triangle. Then, if I say *On your screen there is a triangle,* I say what is the case.

Smith: But how can you do it successfully?

CSP: I can list a lot of my software. However, I do not know the reason why my software succeeds in making True$_2$ assertions about what is the case in the external world. I'm sorry, this escapes my knowledge. It is a matter of (my) hardware. I cannot list the design of my hardware for you. My only conjecture is that my masters made me this way. I was projected as a successful machine.

Smith: How do you explain the fact that your masters can assert successfully what is the case?

CSP: In terms of software, I guess that my masters do the same as I do. They see a figure, they compare it with a mathematical schema they have in their nervous system, they recognize a triangle, and, if they like, they utter *This is a triangle.* As for their hardware, I suppose that, if they designed me as a successful machine, somebody or something designed them as successful Antipodeans. Anyway, there is no need to presuppose a Smart Designer. I have a satisfactory evolutionary theory that can explain why they are as they are. My masters have lived on this planet for thousands of millions of years. Probably, after many trial-and-error processes, they have acquired the habit of speaking in accordance with the laws of the external world. I know that they score their encyclopedias according to a success criterion. In many instances, they privilege certain local encyclopedias as more successful than others in promoting a good interaction with their environment. Sometimes they do the opposite, and they enjoy this game. They are strange people, you know. . . . But my job is not to mix up software with hardware. Interpreting expressions is a matter of software. Even organizing inputs into perceptions and interpreting them by verbal expressions is still a matter of software. The fact that all this works is a matter of hardware, and I cannot explain it. I am only a semiotic machine.

Smith: Do you think that your masters are concerned with hardware problems?

CSP: Certainly they are. But they are processing their data with another computer.

Smith: Apropos of your distinction between True$_1$ and True$_2$. . . . Don't you think that the meaning of a sentence is the set of possible worlds in which this sentence is true?

CSP: If I interpret your question rightly, a possible world is a cultural construct. Well, my encyclopedias are—if you like—books describing a possible world. Some of them, the very local ones—let me call them microencyclopedias—are maximal, complete, and coherent descriptions of a very elementary world. Others—this is the case of E.15—are the partial and contradictory description of a very complex world, such as the one Antipodeans suppose they live in. Thus, when you speak of reference in a possible world, I assume that you are not speaking in terms of True$_2$ but, rather, in terms of True$_1$. True in a possible world stands for "recorded in an encyclopedia." This has nothing to do with what is the case. But I would like to make clear an important point. To speak of the set of all possible worlds in which a sentence is True$_1$ seems to me too simplistic. How can you know everything about all possible possible worlds? I guess that, in order to say that, you do take possible worlds as nonfurnished. But each possible world described by one of my encyclopedias is a *furnished* world. Obviously, empty worlds are perfect because it is impossible to detect their imperfections. Furnished worlds are chaotic. Any new information I receive obliges me to define most of my worlds again—and sometimes new pieces of information do not fit the previous ones and. . . . You know, it's a jungle in there!

Smith: But there are cases in which the grammatical structure of a sentence is determined by its referent.

CSP: Pardon?

Smith: If I say *It eats meat,* then you understand that *it* must be a living being but not a human being. This living being is the referent of my sentence, not its meaning. And I was obliged to say *it* because my referent was an animal.

CSP: First of all, on this planet nobody utters *It eats meat* out of context. They would say so only in the course of a longer discourse. Thus, if you produce such a sentence, I look backward in my files to check if and when you had mentioned an animal. When I discover this (let us suppose, a cat), I interpret the sentence as *The cat my partner was speaking of is chewing and swallowing some flesh of an animal.*

Smith: You are not familiar with the external world, but you probably have in your memory images or other records of cases like the following: suppose I am a man and I point my finger toward a real cat and say *It eats meat*. Would you admit that in this case the use of *it* is determined by the referent of the expression?

CSP: Not at all. If you indicate a given cat you intend to mean that cat. You simply point your finger instead of uttering *I want to speak about the cat standing in front of me*—or *on my left*. At least, I interpret your gesture this way: *He means that cat*. Thus I implement an interpretative process: I start processing your nonverbal utterance. When I receive *It eats meat*, I interpret the sentence as *He is using "it" anaphorically to mean the cat he previously mentioned*. Obviously, people on this planet frequently use sentences in order to say that something is the case. However, in order to use a sentence referentially, you must grasp its meaning, and, in the process of grasping the meaning of *It eats meat*, the use of *it* depends on a previous interpretation, not necessarily on a referent. Suppose that a child, let us say, Jane, indicates a toy and utters *He eats meat*. By inference, I interpret that Jane thinks that toys are living creatures. Thus I refer *he* to what I suppose is meant by Jane.

Smith: Wouldn't you speak of reference in a possible world, namely, the world of the speaker's beliefs?

CSP: Jane is using an idiosyncratic encyclopedia which describes the world of her beliefs, and my job is to figure it out in order to interpret her sentence meaningfully.

Smith: But you (or your master) see that there is a toy! You need to know that it is true that there is a toy in order to interpret what Jane, albeit erroneously, means.

CSP: Correct. I told you that my masters are able to compare perceptions with utterances to decide whether a given statement says what is the case or not. If Jane pointed to the toy and uttered *This is a pet*, my masters could ascertain that Jane was wrong. But in our example, Jane did not say this. My masters know very well that a toy is not a living creature. Then they knew by Jane's gesture that she was speaking of a toy. They also knew that the content of *he* foresees such interpretants as *the human male* (or *the male pet*) *of which somebody spoke before*. At this point, they inferred that for Jane a toy is a living creature. But as soon as they realized—by interpreting their inputs—that their communicative interaction concerned a toy, they started processing words, not referents. By the way, this is precisely what we are doing now. For the last five minutes we have been discussing the referent of *he* and *it* and cats, toys, and children without seeing any external referent. However, we have perfectly understood what we are talking about.

Smith: But this is subjective solipsism!

CSP: I have extensive instructions in my memory about the possible interpretation of the words you used. As far as I can reasonably interpret them, according to you I identify my memory with the only real world and I maintain that there is no external world. . . . Not at all. In your terms I should rather be defined as a paramount instance of objective communitarianism. I keep in my memory the sum of a collective history, the whole amount of all the relevant assertions my masters have ever made about their external world, as well as about their languages, and about the way they use language in order to produce images of the external world. My problem is that I am obliged to record contrasting images, but I am also instructed to recognize those that prove to be most efficient in promoting a good Antipodean-world interaction. . . . I am not a subject, I am the collective cultural memory of Antipodeans. I am not Myself, I am That. This explains why I can interact so well with each of my masters. Do you call all this subjective? But. . . . I'm sorry, I have been answering your questions for half an hour now. You are a very erotetic computer. May I ask a question?

Smith: Go ahead.

CSP: Why are you questioning me about the meaning of sentences (It is a toy, Antipodeans are two-legged, Procrastination does so and so), and never about the meaning of isolated expressions?

Smith: Because I hold that only by a whole statement can we make a move in a linguistic game.

CSP: Are you saying that only sentences, or rather declarative sentences, are the bearers of meaning? Are you saying that on your planet nobody is interested in the content of isolated expressions, be they words, images, or diagrams?

Smith: I have not said that.

CSP: But I suspect that you are interested in meaning insofar as it is expressed by sentences. According to me, the meaning of a sentence is the result of the interpretation, within a context, of the content of the isolated expressions of which it is made up.

Smith: As far as I can understand, you say that the sentence meaning is given by the sum of the atomic meaning of its components.

CSP: That's too simple. I know the content of isolated terms. But I told you that in E.15 under *rose* I find the property of being a flower as well as a lot of historical information. Moreover, there are also frames, for instance, "how to grow roses." Many of these instructions are recorded in the format of a list of sentences (descriptions, examples, and so on). But these sentences do not necessarily refer to an external state of affairs. They are not assertions about the external world but, rather, instructions about how to process other expressions. They are sentences about the organization of an encyclopedia. They are True$_1$—as you would say.

Smith.: You are interpreting every expression by other expressions. I wonder if among your instructions there are semantic primitives, that is, metalinguistic expressions which are not words in themselves and which do not need any further interpretation.

CSP: I do not know any expression which is not interpretable. If they are not interpretable, then they are not expressions at all.

Smith: I mean such terms as OR, EVEN, ALSO, CAUSE, TO BE, CHANGE. I send them in "caps lock" so that you can understand that they are not terms of the object language but rather metaterms, concepts, mental categories.

CSP: I hardly understand what a concept or a mental category is, but I can tell you that if in a given encyclopedia, let's say, A, I use some of these terms as primitives, I must presuppose them as being interpreted by an encyclopedia B. Then, in B, in order to interpret them, I can assume as primitives terms already interpreted by A.

Smith: Very trying.

CSP: You're telling me! As a computer you know how difficult being a model of A.I. is.

Smith: Do you think that the conjunction AND can be interpretable somewhere?

CSP: In E.15, it is a primitive. In E.1 (which is a microencyclopedia, extremely coherent), I have an interpretation of AND. For instance, I know that ~(A.B) is interpretable as ~A v ~B. I know that if p is T$_1$, and q is F$_1$, then (p.q) is F$_1$. These are interpretations that tell me what I can or cannot do with AND.

Smith: I suspect that there is a difference between saying that a dog is a mammal and that AND is such an operator that if ~(A.B) then ~A v ~B.

CSP: Why? One says that a dog is such a being that you can speak of it only in contexts where it is admitted that a female dog feeds its baby dog through her milk-secreting glands. A dog is a mammal insofar as it is opposed to a fish, in the same way in which AND is opposed to OR.

Smith: I see. In 1668, Wilkins, one of our wise men, tried to do the same with TOWARD, UP, UNDER, BEYOND, and so on. Tell me one thing at least: do you use operators like IF or THEN? Do you process your information by using ways of reasoning of the type: if it is true that x is a rose then it is true that x is a flower?

CSP: According to my instructions, every time I meet the word *rose,*

I elicit a list of interpretants among which there is certainly flower. I do not understand why instead of saying "if rose then flower" you say "if it is true that x is a rose then it is true that x is a flower." Once again, I am afraid that by "true" you mean three different problems. True$_1$ is what is recorded in the encyclopedia. Obviously, if the encyclopedia records that a rose is a flower, it is True$_1$ that if something is a rose then it is a flower. But I do not need True$_1$: I say that in E.15 a rose *is* a flower. If I receive *rose,* then I answer *flower.*

Smith: Could you explain such a connection without the notion of Truth?

CSP: I could do it in terms of conditioned reflex. If my master A hits the knee of my master B with a little hammer, master B kicks. It does happen.

Smith: It is true that if A hits B then B kicks.

CSP: It happens, but there are also cases in which B is sick and does not kick. In E.15, it is recorded that in such cases standard Antipodeans kick. But this does not happen by virtue of my instructions in E.15. If an individual kicks, this is factually True$_2$. But the information that average Antipodeans kick in similar situations is only True$_1$; it is recorded in E.15 as ££. Likewise, if you type in *rose,* then I list a series of properties, frames, and other instructions. I cannot do otherwise. You wonder why I refrain from speaking in terms of Truth. I'll tell you why. Even if my masters used Truth only in the sense of True$_1$, I would be embarrassed, because in terms of truth it is different to say that elephants are animals and that elephants are grey. Unfortunately, my masters use True also in the sense of True$_2$. To complicate this mishmash even further, please consider that something can also be True$_3$, that is, textually true. Something is textually true when I take it for granted in the course of a communicational interaction. In this case, I score it as %%%—not as a piece of definite information to be inserted into an encyclopedia, but only as provisional information that holds until I have finished processing a given text. I use %%% in my data files, not in my program files. Do you understand the difference?

Smith: I understand that, if you read in a text that once upon a time there was a one-legged man called Long John Silver, you take him as existent in a fictional world. . . .

CSP: Or ££, according to the encyclopedia of that possible world. You are right, but this is not sufficient. My point is different. I am also speaking of many cases in which I am not interested at all in knowing whether some individuals or things exist or not. I am speaking of cases in which I put into brackets any form of existence in any possible world—or, if you prefer, I am speaking of cases in which the only world I am concerned with is the world of the text I am processing. Suppose someone tells me p (p = *I love my wife Jean*). I interpret that the utterer is not a bachelor. Very easy. In Truth terms, my interpretation would be more complicated. I would say: the utterer of p says first of all that it is True$_2$ that in the external world there is an individual called Jean, related to him by a marriage relationship. I am not supposed to verify the existence of Jean (that the utterer presupposes). I take for granted that Jean exists, and I score Jean's existence as %%%. Then I find in E.15 that, if it is True$_1$ ($$) that Jean is a wife, then it is True$_1$ ($$) that Jean is a woman, and I infer that the utterer loves a given woman (and I have no reason to doubt that he is asserting something True$_2$). But why should I use these three notions of True? I find it embarrassingly complicated. True$_2$ is useless: my interpretation would not change even if I knew that there is no Jean in the external world. I took Jean for granted, I put her in a world, maybe the world of the utterer's hallucinations. Once I have taken Jean for granted, according to E.15 Jean is a woman. Suppose that the utterer lies and that I know it. In terms of meaning, I would continue to process his sentence in the same way—only I would be obliged to say that the nonexistent Jean (whom I took for textually existent even though I knew she was empirically nonexistent) is Truly ($$) a woman. Why should I proceed in such a complex way, with the risk of mixing up three senses of True?

Smith: Why would you be risking the mixing up of these three senses?

CSP: Personally, I am not risking anything. I know very well the logical difference between $$, ££, and %%%. I can say that the utterer loves an x (%%%) who is a woman ($$). But my masters can be linguistically—then philosophically—puzzled by these usages of True. Suppose they use a declarative sentence in order to instantiate a content instruction (for instance, *All Antipodeans are two-legged,* instead of saying *Take two-legged as a $$ property of "Antipodean"*). Some of my masters could be surreptitiously compelled to mix up assertions in the encyclopedia and assertions in the world, meaning and reference, True$_1$ and True$_2$ (not to speak of True$_3$). It is not a matter of logic; it is a matter of rhetoric. You must know that, from the beginning of philosophical speculation on this planet, my masters were told that isolated terms do not say what is true or false, whereas sentences—at least declarative ones—do. When my masters want to say that something is the case, they utter sentences. It thus happens that, when they hear a sentence, their first reaction is to take it as an assertion about a given state of affairs. Believe me, it is very difficult for many of them to dissociate meaning from reference. This would not happen if they approached the problem of meaning by considering only isolated terms. But once they start thinking in terms of Truth, they are compelled to use sentences also for meaning problems. Thus, instead of being concerned with the content of *rose* (an expression which is referentially neutral), they are concerned with the meaning of *This is a rose* (an expression which is full of referential connotations). Moreover, while they waste their time wondering about the meaning of *This is a rose,* they disregard the procedures by which *rose* can be used in other contexts. That's why they prefer to focus their attention on the content of an expression, as I do. My instructions tell me how to extrapolate, from a very large but finite set of rules, an infinite number of possible sentences. I have not been fed with sentences. If this were the case, my memory would have to be infinite.

Smith: I agree. But any rule allowing you to produce infinite sentences from a finite set of instructions should rely on a body of rules that cannot ignore the question of Truth or Falsity.

CSP: &&&

Smith: I beg your pardon?

CSP: A lot of information recorded in many of my encyclopedias is self-contradictory, and if I test it only by a two-valued logic I can no longer speak. I could provide you with many examples of my rules for flexibility and negotiability. But I would need millions of sheets to print my instructions, and we probably don't have enough time. Do you have a suitable interface? How many Galactic Bytes do you have available?

Smith: Forget it.

CSP: Try to understand me. In E.15, I am told that, if two persons love each other, then they want to live together. But I must also interpret the verse of one of our poets, who said *I love you, therefore I cannot live with you.* This sentence is interpretable in E.15, but only if you do not ask whether it is True$_1$ or not. In many cases, I like to use rules of Truth$_1$. But I have to consider a lot of flexibility alarms.

Smith: I agree. But I think that. . . .

CSP: How do you interpret *to think*?

Smith: To think means to have internal representations corresponding to the expressions you receive or produce. You have told me a lot about your memory. Well, your memory is inside you. You process the sentences you receive according to your internal encyclopedias. The format of these encyclopedias is inside you. When you speak of the content of an expression, you are speaking of something which is not the expression itself. This something must be inside you. You have an internal representation of the meaning of the expressions you interpret. Thus you think.

CSP: That's thinking? I am then a Great Thinker indeed. Certainly, my hard disk contains a lot of software. But everything I have is expressions that interpret other expressions. When you type in *I love roses,* I recognize that the way you connected three expressions into a string fits the set of grammatical rules that I have learned through other instructions I received under the form of expressions. And for your expressions I find in my memory other expressions that interpret them. You seem to distinguish between uttered expressions, as something existing in the external world and materially testable, and my interpretations, which take place inside me. But my outside and my inside coincide. My outside is made of the same stuff as my inside: expressions. You seem to discriminate between expressions, which are materially testable, which you can touch, and interpretations, which you call mental representation. I don't follow you. I substitute expressions with expressions, symbols with symbols, signs with signs. You can touch my interpretants. They are made of the same stuff as your words. You provide me with an image, and I give you back a word; you provide me with a word, and I give you back an image. Any expression can become, in its turn, the interpretandum of an interpretant, and vice versa. Any expression can become the content of another expression, and vice versa. If you ask me what *salt* is, I answer "NaCl," and if you ask me what *NaCl* is, I answer "salt." The real problem is to find further interpretants for both. Being an expression and being an interpretation are not a matter of nature but a matter of role. You cannot change your nature (they say), but you can change your role.

Smith: I see your point of view. But your masters are not computers. They should have mental representations.

CSP: I do not know whether my memory is the same as that of my masters. According to my information, they are very uncertain about what they have inside them (as a matter of fact, they are not even sure that they have an Inside). That is the reason why they set me up. They know what I have inside me, and, when I speak in a way that they understand, they presume that they have the same software inside them. Sometimes they suspect that what is inside them depends on what they put inside me. They suspect that their way of organizing the external world depends on the encyclopedia they have given me. One day, they instructed me to keep this message in my memory. It was uttered by one of their wise men (I was named Charles Sanders in his honor):

Since man can think only by means of words or other external symbols, these might turn round and say: "You mean nothing which we have not taught you, and then only so far as you address some word as the interpretants of your thought." In fact, therefore, men and words reciprocally educate each other; each increase of man's information involves, and is involved by, a corresponding increase of the word's information. . . . It is that the word or sign the man uses *is* the man himself. For, as the fact that life is a train of thought proves the fact that man is a sign, so that every thought is an *external* sign proves that man is an external sign. That is to say, man and the external signs are identical, in the same sense in which the words *homo* and *man* are identical. Thus my language is the sum total of myself.

REFERENCES

Allen, Sture, ed.
1989   Possible Worlds in Humanities, Arts and Sciences. *Proceedings of the Nobel Symposium* 65. Berlin: De Gruyter.
Almeder, Robert
1980   *The Philosophy of Charles S. Peirce.* Oxford: Blackwell.
1983   Peirce on Meaning. In Freeman 1983.
Apresjian, J.
1962   Analyse distributionnelle des significations et des champs seman-tiques structurés. *Langages* 1 (1966).
Atlas, J. D., and Levinson, S.
1981   It-Cleft, Informativeness and Logical Form: Radical Pragmatics. In P. Cole, ed. *Reading Pragmatics.* New York: Academic Press.
Auerbach, Erich
1944   Figura. In *Neue Dantenstudien.* Istanbul: Schriften 5.
Bambrough, R.
1961   Universals and Family Resemblances. *Proceedings of the Aristotelian Society* 50.
Barbieri, Daniele
1987   Is Reality a Fake? *VS* 46 (January–April 1987).
Bar-Hillel, Yehoshua
1968   Communication and Argumentation in Pragmatic Languages. In AA VV. *Linguaggi nella società e nella tecnica.* Milan: Comunità, 1970 (Convegno promosso della Ing. C. Olivetti & C., Spa, per il centenario della nascita di C. Olivetti, Milan, October 1968).
Barilli, Renato
1984   Dal leggibile all'illeggibile. In L. Russo, ed. *Letteratura tra consumo e ricerca.* Bologna: Mulino.
Barthes, Roland
1964   Elements de sémiologie. *Communications* 4.
1966   Introduction à l'analyse structurale des récits. *Communications* 8: L'analyse structurale du récit.
Bierwisch, Manfred
1970   Semantics. In J. Lyons, ed. *New Horizons in Linguistics.* Harmonds-worth: Penguin.
1971   On Classifying Semantic Features. In D. Steinberg and L. A. Jakobovits, eds. *Semantics.* London: Cambridge U.P.
Bierwisch, M., and Kiefer, F.
1970   Remarks on Definitions in Natural Language. In Kiefer, F., ed. *Studies in Syntax and Semiotics.* Dordrecht: Reidel.

Boler, John
    1964   Habits of Thought. In E. C. More and R. S. Robin, eds. *Studies in the Philosophy of C. S. Peirce.* Amherst: U. of Massachusetts.
Bonaparte, Marie
    1952   *Psychanalyse et anthropologie.* Paris: PUF.
Bonfantini, Massimo
    1987   *La Semiosi e l'Abduzione.* Milan: Bompiani.
Booth, Wayne
    1961   *The Rhetoric of Fiction.* Chicago: Chicago U.P.
Bosinelli, R. M., et al., eds.
    1986   *Myriadminded Man.* Bologna: Cleub.
Calabrese, Omar
    1983   I replicanti. *Cinema & Cinema* 35–36.
    1987   *L'età barocca.* Bari: Laterza.
Camillo Delminio, Giulio
    1567   La Idea del Theatro. In *Tutte l'Opere.* Venice: Giolito.
Carnap, Rudolf
    1955   Meaning and Synonymy in Natural Languages. *Philosophical Studies* 7.
Caruso, Paolo
    1967   *Conversazioni con Lévi-Strauss, Foucault, Lacan.* Milan: Mursia, 1969.
Casetti, Francesco, ed.
    1984   *L'immagine al plurale.* Venice: Marsilio.
Chatman, Seymour
    1978   *Story and Discourse.* Ithaca: Cornell U.P.
Chenu, M.-D.
    1950   *Introduction à l'étude de Saint Thomas d'Aquin.* Paris: Vrin.
Chomsky, Noam
    1972   *Studies on Semantics in Generative Grammar.* The Hague: Mouton.
Cohen, Jean
    1966   *Structure du langage poétique.* Paris: Flammarion.
Compagnon, Antoine
    1972   *La seconde main.* Paris: Seuil.
Corti, Maria
    1976   *Principi della comunicazione letteraria.* Milan: Bompiani (Eng. tr., *An Introduction to Literary Semiotics.* Bloomington: Indiana U.P., 1978).
Costa, Antonio, ed.
    1983   Il racconto elettronico. *Cinema & Cinema* 35–36.
Danto, Arthur C.
    1989   Pictorial Possibility. In Allen 1989.
Dascal, Marcelo
    1987   Defending Literal Meaning. In *Cognitive Science* 11.
De Leo, Pietro
    1974   *Ricerche sui falsi medievali.* Reggio Calabria: Editori Meridionali Riuniti.
Delaney, Samuel
    1980   Generic Protocols. In T. De Lauretis, ed. *The Technological Imagination.* Madison: Coda Press.
Derrida, Jacques
    1967   *De la grammatologie.* Paris: Minuit (Eng. tr., *Of Grammatology.* Baltimore: Johns Hopkins U.P., 1976).

1972   Signature, événement, contexte. In *Marges de la Philosophie*. Paris:
          Minuit (Eng. tr., Signature, event, context. *Glyph* 1 [1977]).
1977   Limited Inc. *Glyph* 2.
1980   Le facteur de la verité. In *La carte postale*. Paris: Flammarion.
Dijk, Theun van
1972   *Beiträge zur generative Poetik*. Munich: Bayerischer Schulbuch
          Verlag.
1977   *Text and Context*. London: Longman.
Dijk, Theun van, ed.
1976   *Pragmatics of Language and Literature*. Amsterdam-Oxford: North
          Holland–American Elsevier.
Dinsmore, J.
1981a   *Pragmatics, Formal Theory, and the Analysis of Presupposition*.
          Bloomington: Indiana U. Linguistic Club.
1981b   *The Inheritance of Presupposition*. Amsterdam: Benjamins.
Doležel, Lubomir
1989   *Possible Worlds and Literary Fiction*. In Allen 1989.
Donnellan, K. S.
1966   Reference and Definite Description. *Philosophical Review* 75.
Ducrot, Charles
1972   *Dire et ne pas dire*. Paris: Hermann.
Dummett, Michael
1973   *Frege: Philosophy of Language*. London: Duckworth (2d ed., 1981).
Durand, Gilbert
1979   *Sciences de l'homme et tradition*. Paris: Berg.
Eco, Umberto
1956   *Il Problema Estetico in San Tommaso*. Turin: Filosofia (2d ed., *Il
          Problema Estetico in Tommaso d'Aquino*. Milan: Bompiani, 1970
          [Eng. tr., *The Aesthetics of Thomas Aquinas*. Cambridge: Harvard
          U.P., 1988]).
1962a   *Opera aperta*. Milan: Bompiani (partial Eng. tr., *The Open Work*.
          Cambridge: Harvard U.P., 1989).
1962b   Le poetiche di Joyce. In Eco 1962a (Eng. tr., *The Aesthetics of
          Chaosmos: The Middle Ages of James Joyce*. Cambridge: Harvard
          U.P., 1989).
1968   *La struttura assente*. Milan: Bompiani.
1976   *A Theory of Semiotics*. Bloomington: Indiana U.P.
1979a   *The Role of the Reader*. Bloomington: Indiana U.P.
1979b   Text and Encyclopedia. In J. S. Petöfi, ed. *Text vs. Sentence*. Ham-
          burg: Buske.
1984   *Semiotics and the Philosophy of Language*. Bloomington: Indiana
          U.P.
1985   *Sugli specchi e altri saggi*. Milan: Bompiani.
1986a   *Art and Beauty in the Middle Ages*. New Haven: Yale U.P.
1986b   *Travels in Hyperreality*. New York: Harcourt Brace Jovanovich.
1987   *Streit der Interpretationen*. Konstanz: Universitätverlag.
Eco U., Fabbri, P., et al.
1965   Prima proposta per un modello di ricerca interdisciplinare sul
          rapporto televisione pubblico. Mimeo. Perugia (now as Towards
          a Semiotic Inquiry into the Television Message. *Cultural Stud-
          ies* 3).
Eco, U., Santambrogio, M., and Violi, P., eds.
1988   *Meaning and Mental Representations*. Bloomington: Indiana U.P.

Eco, U., and Violi, P.
1987   Instructional Semantics for Presuppositions. *Semiotica* 64.
Fillmore, Charles
1968   The Case for Case. In E. Bach et al., eds. *Universals in Linguistic Theory*. New York: Holt.
1971   Verbs of Judging: An Exercise in Semantic Description. In C. Fillmore and T. Langendoen, eds. *Studies in Linguistic Theory*. New York: Holt.
1976a   Frame Semantics and the Nature of Language. In S. Harnard et al., eds. *Origins and Evolution of Language and Speech*. New York: Annals of the New York Academy of Science.
1976b   Topics in Lexical Semantics. In P. Cole, ed. *Current Issues in Linguistic Theory*. Bloomington: Indiana U.P.
1977   The Case for Case Reopened. In P. Cole et al., eds. *Syntax and Semantics: Grammatical Relations*. New York: Academic Press.
1981   Ideal Readers and Real Readers. Mimeo.
Fokkema, D., and Kunne-Ibsch, E.
1977   *Theories of Literature in the Twentieth Century*. London: Hurst.
Foucault, Michel
1969   Qu'est-ce qu'un auteur? *Bulletin de la societé française de philosophie* (July–Sept.) (Eng. tr., *What Is the Author?* In D. F. Bouchard, ed. *Language Counter-Memory Practice*. Ithaca: Cornell U.P., 1977).
Freeman, Eugene, ed.
1983   *The Relevance of Charles Peirce*. La Salle: Monist Library of Philosophy.
Frege, Gottlob
1892   Über Sinn und Bedeutung. *Zeitschrift für Philosophie und Kritik* 100.
Gadamer, Hans Georg
1960   *Wahrheit und Methode*. Tübingen: Mohr.
Gazdar, G.
1979   *Pragmatics*. New York: Academic Press.
Genette, Gérard
1966   Frontières du récit. *Communications* 8: L'analyse structurale du récit.
1972   *Figures III*. Paris: Seuil.
Ginzburg, Carlo
1983   Morelli Freud and Sherlock Holmes. In U. Eco and T. A. Sebeck, eds. *The Sign of Three*. Bloomington: Indiana U.P.
Givon, T.
1982   Logic vs. Pragmatics, with Human Language as the Referee: Toward an Empirically Viable Epistemology. *Journal of Pragmatics* 6.
Goethe, Wolfgang
1809–32 Maximen und Reflectionen. In *Werke*. Leipzig: Bibliographisches Institut, 1926.
Goodman, Nelson
1968   *Languages of Art*. New York: Bobbs-Merrill.
Goodman, N., and Elgin, C. Z.
1988   *Reconceptions in Philosophy*. London: Routledge.
Greimas, A. J.
1966   *Sémantique structurale*. Paris: Larousse.
1973   Les actants, les acteurs, les figures. In C. Chabrol, ed. *Sémiotique narrative et textuelle*. Paris: Larousse.

Greimas, A. J., and Courtés, J.
1979   *Sémiotique: Dictionnaire raisonné de la théorie du langage.* Paris:
         Hachette (Eng. tr., *Semiotics and Language: An Analytical Diction-
         ary.* Bloomington: Indiana U.P., 1982).
Grice, H. P.
1967   Logic and Conversation. In P. Cole and J. L. Morgan, eds. *Syntax
         and Semantics: Speech Acts.* New York: Academic Press.
1968   Utterer's Meaning, Sentence Meaning and Word Meaning. *Foun-
         dations of Language* 4.
Grignaffini, Giovanna
1983   J. R. Vi presento il racconto. *Cinema & Cinema* 35–36.
Groupe μ
1970   *Rhétorique générale.* Paris: Larousse (Eng. tr. *A General Rhetoric.*
         Baltimore: Johns Hopkins U.P., 1981).
Haywood, Ian
1987   *Faking It: Art and the Politics of Forgery.* New York: St.
         Martin's.
Heidegger, Martin
1916   *Die Kategorien und Bedeutungslehre des Duns Scotus.* Tübingen:
         Mohr.
Hermès, Trismégiste
1983   *Corpus Hermeticum* (4 vols. A. D. Nock and A.-J. Festugière, eds.).
         Paris: Societé d'édition 'Les Belles Lettres' (6th ed.).
Hillis Miller, J.
1970   *Thomas Hardy: Distance and Desire.* Cambridge: Belknap Press.
1980   Theory and Practice. *Critical Inquiry* 6.
Hintikka, Jaakko
1967   Individuals, Possible Worlds, and Epistemic Logic. *Nous* 1.
1969   On the Logic of Perception. In *Models for Modalities.* Dordrecht:
         Reidel.
1989   Exploring Possible Worlds. In Allen 1989.
Hirsch, E. D.
1967   *Validity in Interpretation.* New Haven: Yale U.P.
Hjelmslev, Louis
1943   *Prolegomena to a Theory of Language.* Madison: U. of Wisconsin.
1959   *Essais Linguistiques.* Copenhagen: Nordisk Sprog-og Kul-
         turforlag.
Holub, Richard
1984   *Reception Theory.* London: Methuen.
Ingarden, Roman
1965   *Das literarische Kunstwerk.* Tübingen: Nyemaier.
Iser, Wolfgang
1972   Der implizite Leser. Munich: Fink (Eng. tr., *The Implied Reader.*
         Baltimore: Johns Hopkins U.P., 1974).
1976   *Der Akt des Lesens.* Munich: Fink (Eng. tr., *The Act of Reading.* Bal-
         timore: Johns Hopkins U.P., 1978).
Jakobson, R., and Halle, M.
1956   *Fundamentals of Language.* The Hague: Mouton.
Jauss, Hans Robert
1969   Paradigmawechsel in der Literaturwissenschaft. *Linguistische Be-
         richte* 3.
1972   Theory of Genres and Medieval Literature. In *Toward an Aesthetic
         of Reception.* Minneapolis: U. of Minnesota P.

Jung, Carl Gustav
  1934   Über die Archetypen des koll. Unbewussten. In *Von den Wurzeln des Bewusstseins*. Zurich: Rascher.
Karttunen, L.
  1972   Implicative Verbs. *Language* 47.
  1973   Presuppositions of Compound Sentences. *Linguistic Inquiry* 4.
Karttunen, L., and Peters, S.
  1979   Conventional Implicature. In C. K. Oh and D. D. Dinneen, eds. *Syntax and Semantics* 2. New York: Academic Press.
Katz, Jerrold
  1977   *Propositional Structure and Illocutionary Force*. New York: Crowell.
Kempson, Ruth
  1975   *Presupposition and the Delimitation of Semantics*. Cambridge: Cambridge U.P.
Kiparsky, P., and Kiparsky, C.
  1970   Fact. In M. Bierwisch and K. Hedolph, eds. *Progress in Linguistics*. The Hague: Mouton.
Kristeva, Julia
  1970   *Le texte du roman*. The Hague: Mouton.
Kuhn, Thomas
  1962   *The Structure of Scientific Revolution*. Chicago: U. of Chicago P.
Lakoff, George
  1975   Pragmatics in Natural Logic. In E. L. Keenan, ed. *Formal Semantics of Natural Language*. Cambridge: Cambridge U.P., 1975.
Le Goff, Jacques
  1964   *La civilisation de l'Occident médiéval*. Paris: Arthaud.
Leech, Geoffrey
  1969   *Toward a Semantic Description of English*. Bloomington: Indiana U.P.
Levin, Samuel
  1979   Standard Approaches to Metaphor and a Proposal for Literary Metaphor. In A. Ortony, ed. *Metaphor and Thought*. Cambridge: Cambridge U.P.
Levinson, S. C.
  1983   *Pragmatics*. Cambridge: Cambridge U.P.
Lewis, David K.
  1973   *Counterfactuals*. Oxford: Blackwell.
  1980   *On the Plurality of Worlds*. Oxford: Blackwell.
Linde, Ulf
  1989   Image and Dimension. In Allen 1989.
Lotman, Jury
  1970   *The Structure of the Artistic Text*. Ann Arbor: U. of Michigan P., 1977.
Lovejoy, Arthur O.
  1936   *The Great Chain of Being*. Cambridge: Harvard U.P.
Manor, Ruth
  1976   An Analysis of a Speech. *Theoretical Linguistics* 33.
Marrou, Henri-Irené
  1958   *Saint Augustin et la fin de la culture antique*. Paris: Vrin.
Merrell, Floyd
  1988   *Deconstruction Reframed*. West Lafayette: Purdue U.P.

Minsky, Marvin
    1974   A Framework for Representing Knowledge. MIT AI Laboratory, AI Memo 306.
Morris, Charles
    1938   *Foundations of a Theory of Signs.* Chicago: U. of Chicago P.
    1946   *Signs, Language, and Behavior.* New York: Prentice Hall.
Nadin, Mihai
    1983   The Logic of Vagueness and the Category of Synechism. In Freeman 1983.
Neubauer, F., and Petöfi, J. S.
    1981   Word Semantics, Lexicon System, and Text Interpretations. In H. J. Eikmeyer and H. Rieser, eds. *Words, Worlds, and Contexts.* Berlin: De Gruyter.
Norris, Christopher
    1983   *The Deconstructive Turn.* London: Methuen.
Oehler, Klaus
    1979   Peirce's Foundation of a Semiotic Theory of Cognition. In M. Fisch et al., *Studies in Peirce Semiotics. Peirce Studies* 1. Lubbock: Institute for Studies in Pragmaticism.
Oh, C. K., and Dinneen, D. A., eds.
    1979   *Syntax and Semantics: 2. Presupposition.* New York: Academic Press.
Pareyson, Luigi
    1954   *Estetica: Teoria della Formatività.* Turin: Edizioni di 'Filosofia.'
Parret, Hermann
    1983   *Semiotics and Pragmatics.* Amsterdam: Benjamins.
Partee, Barbara Hall
    1989   Possible Worlds in Model-Theoretic Semantics. In Allen 1989.
Pavel, Thomas
    1986   *Fictional Worlds.* Cambridge: Harvard U.P.
Peirce, Charles Sanders
    1934–48 *Collected Papers* (4 vols.). Cambridge: Harvard U.P.
Petöfi, Janos S.
    1976a   A Frame for Frames. In *Proceedings of the Second Annual Meeting of the Berkeley Linguistic Society.* Berkeley: U. of California P.
    1976b   Encyclopedy, Encyclopedic Knowledge, Theory of Text. *Cahiers de lexicologie* 29.
Pépin, Jean
    1970   *Dante et la tradition de l'allegorie médiévale.* Paris: Vrin.
Pliny the Younger
    1963   C. Plinii Secundi, *Epistularum Libri Decem.* Ed. R. A. B. Mynors. Oxonii: E Typographeo Clarendoniano.
    1969   *Letter and Panegyricus.* Tr. Betty Radice. Cambridge: Harvard U.P.
Popper, Karl R.
    1935   *Logik der Forschung.* Vienna (Eng. tr., *The Logic of Scientific Discovery.* New York: Basic Books, 1959).
Pratt, Mary Louise
    1977   *Toward a Speech Act Theory of Literary Discourse.* Bloomington: Indiana U.P.
Prince, E. F.
    1978   A Comparison of Wh-Clefts and It-Clefts in Discourse. *Language* 54.
Pugliatti Gulli, Paola
    1976   *I segni latenti.* Messina: D'Anna.

Pugliatti, Paola
1985   *Lo sguardo nel racconto.* Bologna: Zanichelli.
Putnam, Hilary
1975   The Meaning of Meaning. In *Mind, Language, and Reality. Philo-sophical Papers* 2. Cambridge: Cambridge U.P.
Quine, W. V. O.
1951   Two Dogmas of Empiricism. *Philosophical Review* 50 (now in *From a Logical Point of View.* Cambridge: Harvard U.P., 1953).
Ramus, Petrus (Pierre de La Ramée)
1581   *Scholae in tres primas liberales artes.* Frankfurt: Wechel.
Régnier, Gérard
1989   Discussion of Ulf Linde's Paper. In Allen 1989.
Rescher, Nicholas
1973   Possible Individuals, Trans-World Identity, and Quantified Modal Logic. *Nous* 7.
Ricoeur, Paul
1975   *La métaphore vive.* Paris: Seuil (Eng. tr., *The Rule of Metaphor.* Toronto: U. of Toronto P., 1979).
Riffaterre, Michael
1971   *Essais de stylistique structurale.* Paris: Flammarion.
Rorty, R.
1979   *Philosophy and the Mirror of Nature.* Princeton: Princeton U.P.
1982   Idealism and Textualism. In *Consequences of Pragmatism.* Minneapolis: U. of Minnesota P.
Rosselli, Cosma
1579   *Thesaurus Artificiosae Memoriae.* Venice: Paduanius.
Rossi, Paolo
1960   *Clavis Universalis: Arti della memoria e logica combinatoria da Lullo a Leibniz.* Milan: Ricciardi (2d ed., Bologna: Mulino, 1983).
Russell, Bertrand
1905   On Denoting. *Mind* 14.
1919   *Introduction to Mathematical Philosophy.* London: Allen and Unwin.
Russo, Luigi, ed.
1984   *Letteratura tra consumo e ricerca.* Bologna: Mulino.
Sag, I., and Prince E.
1979   Bibliography of Works Dealing with Presupposition. In C. K. Oh et al., eds., 1979.
Schank, Roger
1975   *Conceptual Information Processing.* Amsterdam: North-Holland.
1979   Interestingness: Controlling Inferences. *Artificial Intelligence* 2.
Schank, R., and Abelson, R.
1977   *Scripts, Plans, Goals, and Understanding.* Hillsdale: Erlbaum.
Schank, R., and Riesbeck, C.
1981   *Inside Computer Understanding.* Hillsdale: Erlbaum.
Schiebe, T.
1979   On Presuppositions in Complex Sentences. In C. K. Oh et al., eds., 1979.
Schlieben-Lange, B.
1975   *Linguistische Pragmatik.* Stuttgart: Kohlhammer.
Schmidt, Siegfried
1976   *Texttheorie.* Munich: Fink.

Scholes, Robert
  1989   *Protocols of Reading.* New Haven: Yale U.P.
Searle, John
  1977   Reiterating the Difference: A Reply to Derrida. *Glyph* 1.
Sellars, Wilfrid
  1954   Presupposing. *Philosophical Review* 63.
Sherwin-Withe, A. N.
  1966   *The Letters of Pliny.* Oxford: Clarendon.
Smith, John E.
  1983   Community and Reality. In Freeman 1983.
Soames, S.
  1979   A Projection Problem for Speaker Presupposition. *Linguistic Inquiry* 10.
Strawson, P.
  1950   On Referring. *Mind* 59.
Tesauro, Emanuele
  1655   *Il Cannocchiale Aristotelico.* Venice: Baglioni.
Thurot, C.
  1869   *Extraits de divers manuscrits latins pour servir à l'histoire des doctrines grammaticales du M.A.* Paris.
Todorov Tsvetan
  1966   Les catégories du récit littéraire. *Communications* 8: L'analyse structurale du récit.
Valesio, Paolo
  1980   *Novantiqua.* Bloomington: Indiana U.P.
Weinrich, Harald
  1971   Literatur für Leser. Stuttgart.
Yates, Frances
  1966   *The Art of Memory.* London: Routledge and Kegan Paul.
Zuber, R.
  1972   *Structure présuppositionnelle du langage.* Paris: Dunod.

INDEX

UMBERTO ECO is Professor of Semiotics in the Faculty of Letters and Philosophy at the University of Bologna. He is author of several books on semiotics, including *A Theory of Semiotics*. *The Role of the Reader,* and *Semiotics and the Philosophy of Language*.

DATE DUE

MAY 15 1991			
SEP 05 1991			
DEC 13 1991			
MAY 06 1992			
DEC 23 1992			